# AMERICAN KINGPIN

NICK BILTON

# AMERICAN KINGPIN

## Catching the Billion-Dollar
## Baron of the Dark Web

*Virgin*
BOOKS

7 9 10 8

Virgin Books, an imprint of Ebury Publishing,
20 Vauxhall Bridge Road,
London SW1V 2SA

Virgin Books is part of the Penguin Random House group of
companies whose addresses can be found at
global.penguinrandomhouse.com

Penguin
Random House
UK

First published in the United Kingdom by Virgin Books in 2017
First published in the United States by Portfolio/Penguin in 2017
This edition first published in the United Kingdom by
Virgin Books in 2018

www.penguin.co.uk

A CIP catalogue record for this book is available from the British Library

ISBN 9780753547007

Printed and bound in Great Britain by Clays Ltd, Elcograf S.p.A

Penguin Random House is committed to a sustainable future for our
business, our readers and our planet. This book is made from Forest
Stewardship Council® certified paper.

*For my wife, Chrysta, and our sons, Somerset and Emerson.*
*I love all of you more than anything in this big, big world.*

No man, for any considerable period,
can wear one face to himself and another to the multitude,
without finally getting bewildered as to which may be the true.

—Nathaniel Hawthorne, *The Scarlet Letter*


I did it for me.
I liked it.
I was good at it.
And I was really . . . I was alive.

—Walter White, aka Heisenberg, *Breaking Bad*

# Contents

Author's Note                                              xiii
Cast of Characters                                         xv

PART I

1. The Pink Pill                                            3
2. Ross Ulbricht                                           13
3. Julia Vie                                               17
4. The Debate                                              21
5. Jared's Khat                                            24
6. The Bonfire                                             28
7. The Silk Road                                           33
8. Ross the Farmer                                         37
9. Opening Day of the Silk Road                            42
10. What Goes Up Must Come Down                            47
11. The *Gawker* Article                                   50
12. A Bull's-eye on My Back                                54
13. Julia Tells Erica                                      58
14. What Have You Done?!                                   62
15. Jared and the Fifty-Ton *Flamingo*                     65
16. From Austin to Australia                               69

## PART II

17. Carl Force's Tomorrow     75
18. Variety Jones and the Serpent     78
19. Jared Goes Shopping     83
20. The Dread Pirate Roberts     86
21. Carl Force Is Born Again     90
22. "O Captain, My Captain"     92
23. Ross, Hanged or Home     95
24. Carl, Eladio, and Nob     100
25. Jared's Chicago Versus Carl's Baltimore     103
26. The Mutiny     107
27. A Billion Dollars?!     112
28. The Aspiring Billionaire in Costa Rica     115
29. Variety Jones Goes to Scotland     119
30. The Armory Opens     123
31. Ross Silences Julia     127

## PART III

32. Chris Tarbell, FBI     133
33. Ross Arrives in San Francisco     137
34. Chris in the Pit     142
35. Batten Down the Hatches!     145
36. Jared's Dead Ends     150
37. A Pirate in Dominica     153
38. Carl Likes DPR     159
39. Kidney for Sale!     165
40. The White House in Utah     171
41. Curtis Is Tortured     176
42. The First Murder     180
43. The FBI Joins the Hunt     184
44. Camping and the Ball     187

PART IV

45. Gary Alford, IRS                                          195
46. Life and Death on the Road                               199
47. Gary's Big Change                                        203
48. Ross Goes Underground                                    207
49. Carl Switches Teams                                      213
50. A Parking Ticket on the Internet                         217
51. Tarbell Finds a Mistake                                  221
52. The Fake IDs, Part One                                   225
53. The Deconfliction Meeting                                231
54. Jared Becomes Cirrus                                     237
55. Julia Is Saved! Hallelujah!                              242
56. The Fake IDs, Part Two                                   245
57. Onward to Federal Plaza                                  249
58. Julia Comes to San Francisco                             254
59. I Am God                                                 258
60. The Phone Call                                           262
61. The Good-bye Party                                       269

PART V

62. The Pink Sunset                                          275
63. Carla Sophia                                             279
64. FeLiNa                                                   282
65. Arrested                                                 290
66. The Laptop                                               293
67. Ross Locked Up                                           296
68. *United States of America v. Ross William Ulbricht*      300
69. To Catch a Pirate                                        304
70. Sentencing                                               307
71. The Plural of Mongoose                                   310
72. The Museum                                               313
73. The Others                                               316

Notes on Reporting                                           323
Acknowledgments                                              327
Bibliography                                                 329

# Author's Note

My mother, who passed away in 2015 and who was a voracious reader, had a strange quirk when it came to books. She began every book by reading the last page first, then returning to the beginning. Every novel, for her, began at the end.

I tell this story because, for this book, I have decided to place the beginning—traditionally the preface, in which the author explains how the book was made—at the end.

In the "Notes on Reporting" I explain how I reported and wrote the pages you are about to read, detailing the millions of words and research, photos and videos, thousands of hours of reporting (including research from the incredible reporters Josh Bearman and Joshua Davis) that went into the creation of this book, and in doing so, I give away how the story ends. I hope reading about the reportage won't ruin this epic tale for you, but it seems unnecessary to explain how a structure was built before you've had a chance to wander through its halls.

In the book, you will see quoted conversations between the Silk Road leader and employees of the site. These are verbatim chats. With the exception of illegible typos, any spelling errors or peculiarities in the text have been left as is to preserve the authenticity of the conversations.

With that, I promise all will be revealed at the end. It always is.

# Cast of Characters

## *The Silk Road*

The Dread Pirate Roberts (Ross Ulbricht)
Variety Jones, consigliere and mentor (Roger Thomas Clark)
Nob, drug dealer and henchman (Carl Force, DEA)
ChronicPain, forum moderator (Curtis Green, Spanish Fork, Utah)
Richard Bates, friend and programmer

OTHER SILK ROAD EMPLOYEES

SameSameButDifferent, Libertas, Inigo, Smedley

## *Law Enforcement*

DHS, CHICAGO

Jared Der-Yeghiayan (undercover as "Cirrus" on the Silk Road)

MARCO POLO TASK FORCE

Carl Force, DEA, Baltimore (undercover as "Nob" on the Silk Road)
Mike McFarland, DHS, Baltimore
Shaun Bridges, Secret Service, Baltimore

FBI, NEW YORK CITY

Chris Tarbell
Thom Kiernan
Ilhwan Yum

IRS, NEW YORK CITY

Gary Alford

U.S. ATTORNEY'S OFFICE, NEW YORK CITY

Serrin Turner, assistant U.S. attorney

# AMERICAN KINGPIN

# PART I

# Chapter 1
# THE PINK PILL

**P**ink.

A tiny pink pill with an etching of a squirrel on either side. Jared Der-Yeghiayan couldn't take his eyes off it.

He stood in a windowless mail room, the Department of Homeland Security badge hanging from his neck illuminated by pulsing halogen lights above. Every thirty seconds, the sound of airplanes rumbled through the air outside. Jared looked like an adolescent with his oversize clothes, buzz cut, and guileless hazel eyes. "We've started to get a couple of them a week," his colleague Mike, a burly Customs and Border Protection officer, said as he handed Jared the envelope that the pill had arrived in.

The envelope was white and square, with a single perforated stamp affixed to the top right corner. HIER ÖFFNEN, read the inside flap. Below those two words was the English translation, OPEN HERE. The recipient's name, typed in black, read DAVID. The package was on its way to a house on West Newport Avenue in Chicago.

It was exactly what Jared had been waiting for since June.

The plane carrying the envelope, KLM flight 611, had landed at Chicago O'Hare International Airport a few hours earlier after a four-thousand-mile journey from the Netherlands. As weary passengers stood up and stretched their arms and legs, baggage handlers twenty feet below them unloaded cargo from the belly of the Boeing 747. Suitcases of all shapes and sizes were ushered in one direction; forty or so blue buckets filled with international mail were sent in another.

Those blue tubs—nicknamed "scrubs" by airport employees—were driven across the tarmac to a prodigious mail storage and sorting facility fifteen minutes away. Their contents—letters to loved ones, business documents, and that white square envelope containing the peculiar pink pill—would pass through that building, past customs, and into the vast logistical arteries of the United States Postal Service. If everything went according to plan, as it did most of the time, that small envelope of drugs, and many like it, would just slip by unnoticed.

But not today. Not on October 5, 2011.

By late afternoon, Mike Weinthaler, a Customs and Border Protection officer, had begun his daily ritual of clocking in for work, pouring an atrocious cup of coffee, and popping open the blue scrubs to look for anything out of the ordinary: a package with a small bulge; return addresses that looked fake; the sound of plastic wrap inside a paper envelope; anything fishy at all. There was nothing scientific about it. There were no high-tech scanners or swabs testing for residue. After a decade in which e-mail had largely outmoded physical mail, the postal service's budgets had been decimated. Fancy technology was a rare treat allocated to the investigation of large packages. And Chicago's mail-sniffing dogs—Shadow and Rogue—came through only a couple of times a month. Instead, whoever was hunting through the scrubs simply reached a hand inside and followed their instincts.

Thirty minutes into his rummaging routine, the white square envelope caught Mike's eye.

He held it up to the lights overhead. The address on the front had been typed, not written by hand. That was generally a telltale sign for customs agents that something was amiss. As Mike knew, addresses are usually typed only for business mail, not personal. The package also had a slight bump, which was suspicious, considering it came from the Netherlands. Mike grabbed an evidence folder and a 6051S seizure form that would allow him to legally open the envelope. Placing a knife in its belly, he gutted it like a fish, dumping out a plastic baggie with a tiny pink pill of ecstasy inside.

Mike had been working in the customs unit for two years and was fully aware that under normal circumstances no one in the federal government would give a flying fuck about one lousy pill. There was, as every government employee in Chicago knew, an unspoken rule that drug agents didn't take on cases that involved fewer than a thousand pills. The U.S. Attorney's Office would scoff at such an investigation. There were bigger busts to pursue.

But Mike had been given clear instructions by someone who was waiting for a pill just like this: Homeland Security agent Jared Der-Yeghiayan.

A few months prior, Mike had come across a similar piece of illicit mail on its way to Minneapolis. He had picked up the phone and called the U.S. Immigration and Customs Enforcement's Homeland Security Investigations office at the airport, half expecting that he would be laughed at or hung up on, as usual. But the HSI agent who answered was surprisingly receptive. At the time, Jared had been on the job for only two months and frankly didn't know any better. "I can't fly to Minneapolis to talk to a guy about one single pill," Jared said. "So call me if you get something in my area, in Chicago. Then I can go over there and do a knock-and-talk."

Four months later, when Mike found a pill destined for Chicago, Jared rushed over to see it. "Why do you want this?" Mike asked Jared. "All the other agents say no; people have been saying no to meth and heroin for years. And yet you want this one little pill?"

Jared knew very well that this could be nothing. Maybe an idiot kid in the Netherlands was sending a few friends some MDMA. But he also wondered why one single pill had been sent on such a long journey and how the people who mailed such small packages of drugs knew the recipients they were sending them to. Something about it felt peculiar. "There may be something else to this," Jared told Mike as he took the envelope. He would need it to show his "babysitter."

Every newbie agent in HSI was assigned one—a training officer—during their first year. A more seasoned officer who knew the drill, made sure you didn't get into too much trouble, and often made you feel like a total piece of shit. Every morning Jared had to call his chaperone and tell him what he was working on that day. The only thing that made it different from preschool was that you got to carry a gun.

Unsurprisingly, Jared's training officer saw no urgency to a single pill, and it was a week before he even consented to accompany his younger colleague on the "knock-and-talk"—to knock on the door of the person who was supposed to receive the pill and, hopefully, talk with them.

That day, as Jared's government-issued Crown Victoria zigzagged through the North Side of Chicago, the small Rubik's Cube that hung from his key chain swung back and forth in the opposite direction. His car radio was dialed into sports: the Cubs and White Sox had been eliminated from contention, but the Bears were preparing for an in-division contest against the Lions. Amid the crackle of the radio, he turned onto West Newport Avenue, a long row of two-story limestone buildings split into a dyad of top- and bottom-floor apartments. Jared knew this working-class neighborhood well. He'd followed the baseball games at nearby Wrigley Field when he was a kid. But now this was Hipsterville, full of fancy coffee shops, chic restaurants, and, as Jared was now learning, people who had drugs mailed to their houses from the Netherlands.

He was fully aware how ridiculous he might look in the eyes of his grizzled training officer. They were in one of the city's safest precincts to question someone about a single pill of ecstasy. But Jared didn't care what his supervisor thought; he had a hunch that this was bigger than one little pill. He just didn't know how big—yet.

He found the address and pulled over, his chaperone close behind. They wandered up the steps and Jared tapped on the glass door of apartment number 1. This was the easy part, knocking. Getting someone to talk would be a whole different challenge. The recipient of the envelope could easily deny that the package was his. Then it was game over.

After twenty seconds the door lock clicked open and a young, skinny man dressed in jeans and a T-shirt peered outside. Jared flashed his badge, introduced himself as an HSI agent, and asked if David, the man whose name was typed on the white envelope, was home.

"He's at work right now," the young man replied, opening the door further. "But I'm his roommate."

"Can we come inside?" Jared asked. "We'd just like to ask you a few questions." The roommate obliged, stepping to the side as they walked toward the kitchen. As Jared took a seat he pulled out a pen and notepad and asked, "Does your roommate get a lot of packages in the mail?"

"Yeah, from time to time."

"Well," Jared said as he glanced at his training officer, who sat silently in the corner with his arms crossed, "we found this package that was addressed to him and it had some drugs inside."

"Yeah, I know about that," the roommate replied nonchalantly. Jared was taken aback by how casually the young man admitted to receiving drugs in the mail, but he continued with the questions, asking where they got these drugs from.

"From a Web site."

"What's the Web site?"

"The Silk Road," the roommate said.

Jared stared back, confused. The Silk Road? He had never heard of it before. In fact, Jared had never heard of any Web site where you could buy drugs online, and he wondered if he was just being a clueless newbie, or if this was how you bought drugs in Hipsterville these days.

"What's the Silk Road?" Jared asked, trying not to sound too oblivious but sounding completely oblivious.

And with the velocity of those descending airliners at O'Hare, the skinny roommate began a fast-paced explanation of the Silk Road Web site. "You can buy any drug imaginable on the site," he said, some of which he had tried with his roommate—including marijuana, meth, and the little pink ecstasy pills that had been arriving, week after week, on KLM flight 611. As Jared scribbled in his notepad, the roommate continued to talk at a swift clip. You paid for the drugs with this online digital currency called Bitcoin, and you shopped using an anonymous Web browser called Tor. Anyone could go onto the Silk Road Web site, select from the hundreds of different kinds of drugs they offered and pay for them, and a few days later the United States Postal Service would drop them into your mailbox. Then you sniffed, inhaled, swallowed, drank, or injected whatever came your way. "It's like Amazon.com," the roommate said, "but for drugs."

Jared was amazed and slightly skeptical that this virtual marketplace existed in the darkest recesses of the Web. *It will be shut down within a week,* he thought. After a few more questions, he thanked the roommate for his time and left with his colleague, who hadn't said a word.

"Have you ever heard of this Silk Road?" Jared asked his training officer as they walked back to their respective cruisers.

"Oh yeah," he replied dispassionately. "Everyone's heard of Silk Road. There must be hundreds of open cases on it."

Jared, somewhat embarrassed at having admitted he knew nothing about it, wasn't deterred. "I'm going to look into it anyway and see what I can find out," he said. The older man shrugged and drove off.

An hour later Jared bounded into his windowless office, where he waited for what seemed an eternity for his archaic Dell government computer to load up. He began searching the Department of Homeland Security database for open investigations on the Silk Road. But to his surprise, there were no results. He tried other key words and variations on the spelling of the site. Nothing. What about a different input box? Still nothing. He was confused.

There were not "hundreds of open cases" on the Silk Road, as his training officer had claimed. There were none.

Jared thought for a moment and then decided to go to the next-best technology that any seasoned government official uses to search for something important: Google. The first few results were historical Web sites referencing the ancient trade route between China and the Mediterranean. But halfway down the page he saw a link to an article from early June of that year on *Gawker*, a news and gossip blog, proclaiming that the Silk Road was "the underground website where you can buy any drug imaginable." The blog post showed screenshots of a Web page with a green camel logo in the corner. It also displayed pictures of a cornucopia of drugs, 340 "items" in all, including Afghan hash, Sour 13 weed, LSD, ecstasy, eight-balls of cocaine, and black tar heroin. Sellers were located all over the world; buyers too. *You've got to be fucking kidding me,* Jared thought. *It's this easy to buy drugs online?* He then spent the entire rest of the day, and most of the evening, reading anything he could about the Silk Road.

Over the weekend, as he drove between antique fairs (his weekly ritual) near Chicago with his wife and young son, he was almost catatonically consumed with the drug Web site. Jared realized that if anyone could buy drugs on the Silk Road, anyone would: from middle-aged yuppies who lived on the North Side of Chicago to young kids growing up in the heartland. And if drugs were being sold on the site now, why not other contraband next? Maybe it would be guns, bombs, or poisons. Maybe, he imagined, terrorists could use it to create another 9/11. As he looked at his sleeping son in the rearview mirror, these thoughts petrified him.

But where do you even start on the Internet, in a world of complete anonymity?

Finally, as the weekend came to a close, Jared started to formulate an idea for how he could approach the case. He knew it would be laborious and tedious, but there was a chance that it could also eventually lead him to the creator of the Silk Road Web site.

But finding the drugs and the drug dealers, and even the founder of the Silk Road, would be easy compared with the challenge of persuading his supervisor to let him work this case based on a single tiny pink pill. Even if he could convince his boss, Jared would also have to cajole the U.S. Attorney's Office into supporting him in this pursuit. And there wasn't a U.S. attorney in all of America who would take on a case that involved one measly pill of anything. Exacerbating all of this was the fact that thirty-year-old Jared was as green as they came. And no one ever—ever!—took a newbie seriously.

He would need a way to convince them all that this was bigger than a single pink pill.

By Monday morning he had come up with a scheme that he hoped his boss would not be able to ignore. He took a deep breath, walked into his supervisor's office, and sat down. "You got a minute?" he said as he threw the white envelope on the desk. "I have something important I need to show you."

*Five Years Earlier*

# Chapter 2
# ROSS ULBRICHT

Ross, jump off a cliff."

Ross Ulbricht stood there with a slightly dumbfounded look on his face as he peered over the edge of the bluff. Below him, Austin's Pace Bend Lake curled into and around itself, leaving a forty-five-foot drop into the frigid water below.

"What?" Ross said with a goofy smile as he lifted his hands and pointed to his wide chest. "Why me?"

"Juuust do it," his sister, Cally, replied, pointing at the rocks. Twenty-four-year-old Ross was a foot taller than her, so he bent his neck downward as he considered her command. Without warning, he shrugged, yelled "Okay," and ran off the ledge and into the air, shrieking before plunging into the lake with a thundering splash.

The video camera clicked off.

It was just the beginning of a long day of filming a reality TV show audition tape that the brother-and-sister duo had been scripting for weeks, with help from their mother, Lyn. The plan was to start with the cliff scene and go from there. Ross's older sister would take the lead, introducing the Ulbricht siblings by noting that they were "willing to do anything to win *The Amazing Race,* even jump off a cliff." After blithely doing just that, the plan was to traipse around Austin putting on an over-the-top act for the camera to try to convince the producers of the show that Ross and Cally Ulbricht would be the perfect contestants.

As Ross looked up from the water to his sister and the rocks he had just leaped off, it was clear that this wasn't the way he had imagined spending this summer off from college.

There was a movie in Ross's head of an altogether different summer. In that film he had saved up for a ring and proposed to his perfect Texas girlfriend. In the script in his mind, she said yes (of course). Then the two lovebirds would graduate from the University of Texas at Dallas, him with a physics degree, and spend the next few months planning their wedding. They'd land good jobs, Ross as a researcher or theoretical physicist. They'd pop out a couple of babies, go to birthday parties and weddings. Grow old together. Live a happy life. The end.

But that version of Ross Ulbricht's life never made it past the opening credits. While Ross had saved up for the perfect ring with which to propose, when he romantically asked his girlfriend for her hand in marriage (*Say yes, please say yes*), she instead said she had to tell Ross something (*Well, this doesn't sound good*). At which point she admitted that during the past year or so she had cheated on him with several different men. (*Several? As in more than one? Yes. Several.*) To make matters worse, one of them was one of Ross's best friends.

Fade to black.

At the base of the cliff, Ross scrambled out of the water and the Ulbricht family set off to their next shooting location. When the camera clicked back on, Ross and his sister stood in front of Austin's skyline, taking turns explaining who they both were. Ross was "the brains" of their operation, his sister explained, and went on to say that he had studied physics and material science and even won a world record for creating the clearest crystal formation on earth.

As his sister spoke, Ross stared into the distance, a million thoughts climbing around in his mind like an animal lost in an elaborate maze searching for something. It was evident that there was something about this moment where Ross found himself that didn't seem right. And yet it was unclear what it was or how this had happened.

He had been born in that very city, and even before he could utter the words "Mama" or "Dada," it was instantly apparent to Lyn and her husband, Kirk, that there was something different about their son. As a toddler he was contemplative and understood things way beyond his years. He was never told, "Don't run out into traffic!"; he just somehow knew not to, as if he came into the world with an instruction manual that other people didn't have access to. At a young age he knew answers to mathematics questions his parents didn't even understand. And while, as a teen, he engaged in normal kidlike activities—sports in the park, board game marathons, and ogling pretty girls—he often preferred to read about political theory, existentialism, or quantum mechanics.

But it wasn't just that he was smart. He was genuinely kind too. As a boy he rescued animals. As an adult he opted for people. Yes, Ross was the person who would stop midsentence in a conversation and rush off to help an old lady cross the street, carrying her bags and stopping traffic as she slowly dawdled through an intersection.

Some who met him thought his overly altruistic attitude was a bit of an act. "How can anyone be that nice?" they'd say. But it was real, and it didn't take long for the people to learn just how magnanimous he was. This was evident simply from the way he spoke, often sounding painfully folksy, using words like "golly," "jeez," and "heck." If he had to curse, he would always say "fudge" in lieu of "fuck."

He had his vices too. As a teenager he had discovered a penchant for mind-altering experiences, at least mild ones. He loved heading into the nearby woods with his pals, lighting up a joint, taking his shirt off, and climbing trees. At a house party after his high school prom, he drank so much beer that his date found him floating on an inflatable raft in the home-owner's pool, still wearing his tuxedo, sneakers (he didn't own dress shoes and had worn old tennis shoes to prom), and a pair of sunglasses.

Still, the smartest guy in every room was now standing there next to his sister in a park in Austin, competing to be on a reality TV show.

But what choice did he have? It wasn't like he could go out west to Silicon Valley and get a job at a start-up. After the bubble had popped a few years earlier, companies that had been built on a wing and a prayer had siphoned people's retirements into thin air and collapsed, leaving San Francisco a meta-phorical no-fly zone. What about going east? Wasn't there opportunity on Wall Street for someone as clever as Ross? No way. The banks were collapsing from the housing market crash. And he certainly couldn't settle down and live happily ever after with his girlfriend; his dream of marriage and a white picket fence had been bulldozed by several other men.

That left graduate school, or jumping off a cliff.

He imagined reality TV fame and a pile of money as a slight detour on the way to some larger accomplishment. Ross was sure he had a grander purpose in life, though he wasn't sure exactly what it would be. Maybe one day he'd figure out what that purpose was.

Just not today.

As the daylight faded and the *Amazing Race* shoot came to an end, Ross and his sister stood in front of the camera along the streets of Austin. He had slipped on some dark sweatpants and a thick black sweater to keep the evening cold at bay.

"Ross," his sister asked, "what are you going to do with your half a million dollars when we win?"

He pretended to think for a moment and then said, "Oh, I think I'll just throw it on the ground and roll around in it for a little while."

"Well," Cally replied as she lifted her hand to give her brother a high five, "we have to win *The Amazing Race* first."

The camera clicked off again. While Ross stuffed the equipment from the shoot into the family car, he daydreamed about the opportunity that lay ahead and about the half a million dollars that he would surely win. He didn't know that chance would never arrive. Ross would not be chosen to compete on the reality TV show—the first of many failures to come. And yet, as he hopped into the car next to his sister, he also didn't know that in just five years he would be making that amount of money in a single day.

# Chapter 3
# JULIA VIE

Julia Vie's first week of college was probably the most difficult seven days of her life—at least up until that point. She had arrived at Penn State a timid eighteen-year-old with no friends and even less direction. Yet before she had the opportunity to fit in, her life was shaken to its core. She was unpacking her suitcases in her dorm room, stuffing her clothes into drawers and stacking her favorite novels onto shelves, when she got the phone call. Her mother had died of cancer.

After the funeral, still in shock, Julia returned to Penn State in search of normalcy. Maybe, she reasoned, that would come in the form of a boyfriend. She pined for someone who would take care of her. Pamper her with affection and maybe spoil her with a few lavish dinners.

Instead she met Ross Ulbricht.

It was all one big accident. Julia had been aimlessly wandering around campus, thinking about her mother, when she found herself in one of the large buildings on Shortlidge Road. As she strolled through the old halls, she could hear the sound of bongos. Loud, thudding African instruments. She followed the beats and pushed open a door to find a group of men sitting in a semicircle thumping out tunes on djembe drums. Around them, half a dozen girls bounced to and fro.

Julia crept to the back of the room, mesmerized by her discovery, and soon learned that this was the Penn State NOMMO Club, an African drumming group. As she watched them play, out of the corner of her eye she noticed a disheveled young man confidently approaching her. He reached out a hand and introduced himself as Ross. Julia looked him up and down and, noticing he wasn't wearing shoes, and that his shirt and shorts were torn and stained, thought he might be homeless. He looked like he hadn't shaved in months.

As the music thudded around them, there was no hiding from Julia that this young homeless-looking man was attracted to her. And how could he not be? This lithe, pretty thing was stunning, with light brown skin, freckles sprinkled across her checks, and big eyes with fluttering lashes. She was exotic-looking too—half African American, half something else. She politely introduced herself as Julia and then quickly brushed him off, uninterested in a conversation with someone who looked like he hadn't showered in weeks.

Julia assumed that was the end of it. But a week later she bumped into this Ross character again. Though this time something was different. Now he had shaved and was wearing pants—real pants—and shoes.

As they spoke, she was intrigued. He was funny, cute, and smart—so, so smart. He told her he was a graduate student at Penn State in the Department of Materials Science and Engineering. When she asked what that entailed, Ross explained that he was working on research to verify rare properties in crystalline materials and worked in spintronics and ferroic materials. The school even paid him a few hundred dollars a week for his research.

Within a week this freshman found herself going to dinner with Ross at a sushi restaurant off Route 35 and then, a few days later, heading back to his apartment. As he slipped off her shirt on the couch, and as she did the same in return, Julia didn't know a lot about the man she was about to fool around with, but she would soon learn. As he lay almost naked on top of her, there was a click at the front door and Ross's roommates walked in. "Let's go to my room," Ross said as they giggled and ran out of the living room.

He led her down a stairway into a basement that was dim, with slivers of light leaking inside from the tiny windows.

To Julia it smelled almost like wet cement, mildew, or both. "This is your bedroom?" she asked in disbelief as her bare feet stepped on the cold concrete floor.

"Yes," Ross replied proudly. "I live down here for *free*." Julia raised her eyebrows as she stood in the middle of the basement, surveying the bizarre setting. There was a bed next to a space heater. Cardboard boxes were strewn about like a kids' fortress. It looked like a prison cell.

She had figured Ross was relatively frugal on their first date at the sushi restaurant when he picked her up in a doddering pickup truck older than she was. On the second date she had learned that he didn't care for material things either, when he arrived looking like a bass player in a Seattle grunge band. (Ragged shorts, a dirty shirt, and shoes that had previously belonged to someone from a geriatric home.) But as she sat on his bed in the basement, looking at walls of chipped, unpainted Sheetrock, it crystallized for Julia that Ross really, really didn't have much money and really, really didn't care for the objects most people lust after in life.

"Wait, why do you live down here?" she asked as they lay on the bed, Ross trying to pick up where they had left off on the couch.

He paused to explain that he liked to live economically to prove to himself that he could. Why pay for an apartment when you could live in this mildew-ridden castle for free? Julia scowled as he spoke. It wasn't just about saving money, he explained. His lifestyle was also part of an internal experiment to see how far he could push himself to extremes without any wants or needs. For example, he had recently chosen not to shower with hot water for a month, just to test his own resilience. ("You get used to the cold after a while," he bragged.) That wasn't all. Over the summer, Ross proudly told Julia, he had survived off a can of beans and a bag of rice for an entire week.

"What about coffee?" she asked.

"I don't drink it."

"You're so cheap," she joked.

The shower and basement tests were only the beginning of Ross's peculiarities. At the foot of his bed there were two garbage bags, which he casually confessed were his "closet." One bag was for clean clothes, the other for dirty. Every item of clothing he owned—every sock, every shirt, and those geriatric shoes—was a hand-me-down from a friend.

"Oh, no, no, no," Julia said as she batted her eyelashes at him. "We're going to fix this; I'm going to take you shopping for some new clothes that actually fit you."

"Sure," Ross said as he went in to kiss her again.

But there were still things she wanted to learn about Ross. More questions about this strange yet brilliant man. "What are those books?" she asked, pointing to the pile of titles that lay near his bed.

At this query Ross paused and was attentive with his answer. He had explained to her on their first date that in addition to joining the NOMMO drumming club, he was also an avid member of a club at Penn State called the College Libertarians, a political group that met once a week to discuss libertarian philosophies and to read books on economics and theory. The books—penned by Murray Rothbard, Ludwig von Mises, and other visionaries—were what he read for fun when he wasn't devouring applied physics papers.

When Julia asked what libertarianism was, Ross, without judgment, explained: everything—from what you do with your life, to what you put in your body—should be up to each individual, *not* the government.

If it hadn't been for how smart Ross was, Julia might have walked out of the basement that day and never looked back. If it hadn't been for how handsome he was, she might never have answered the phone after their early dates. And if it hadn't been for Ross's assertiveness, which young Julia had never experienced in a man before and needed more than anything at this sad point in her life, she might not have agreed to become his girlfriend in the coming weeks.

Instead she was deeply intrigued by this peculiar and possibly perfect man. He looked back at her, smiling as he leaned in to kiss her again. It was clear to her that Ross was smitten. She, in turn, tried not to let on how besotted she was becoming with him. But what wasn't clear to either of them, as they rolled around on his dinky bed in the basement, was that the relationship they were about to embark on would be the most tumultuous romance of Ross's and Julia's adult lives.

And, for Ross, it would be his last.

# Chapter 4
# THE DEBATE

Students with backpacks and books rushed by one another as they shuffled into the Willard Building at Penn State. The lights inside the building flickered on as the fall sun set over campus. There, amid the normalcy of college life, Ross Ulbricht was pacing in one of the large lecture rooms, preparing for a school debate.

The room where he stood was wide and deep, with rows of chairs that would soon be filled by the students shuffling inside—all people who were there to hear tonight's discussion among the College Libertarians, the College Republicans, and the College Democrats on a number of U.S. election–related topics, including whether drugs should be legalized in the United States.

It had been more than a year since Ross had failed to make it onto *The Amazing Race,* but none of that mattered now. Life at Penn State was pretty spectacular, mostly because of the school clubs he had joined.

Drum group was bewitching (Ross had become so obsessed with drumming that he would play the instrument in his head while he lay in bed at night). And then there was the libertarian club, where Ross showed up for every single meeting and had, over the past year, immersed himself in every facet of libertarian political philosophy. He flew around the country to libertarian conferences to hear experts speak (the club paid his way). He also spent countless hours sitting in the Corner Room bar along College Avenue with Alex, the club's president, and other members, discussing and honing his beliefs about the government's role in society and how to reduce its unfair and often inhumane heavy-handedness.

While enthralling and stimulating, this was all coming at a price. Ross's obsession with the clubs was having a negative effect on his schoolwork.

Though that wasn't the only distraction in his life affecting his studies. There was also his now-girlfriend, Julia. The two lovebirds—it hadn't taken long for the two to say "I love you"—spent almost every moment together. As this was going to be Julia's first Christmas without her mother, he invited her to come to Austin for the holidays. Before they left, he snuck into his Penn State laboratory and created a crystal that he fashioned into a ring as a gift for her.

Ross appreciated that Julia would sit for hours and listen to him talk about his beliefs, including one of the topics of tonight's debate, which Ross knew better than anyone: the reformation of the American drug laws. "Take your seats, please," the professor managing the discussion croaked to the audience. "We're about to begin." Ross, in rare form with his tucked-in shirt, sat down at a desk next to two other College Libertarians. There were some brief introductions from the professor, and then the room fell quiet.

"It is not the government's right to tell the people what they can and cannot put in their bodies," Ross began, going on to explain that drugs—all drugs—should be legalized, as it would make society safer and people have a right to do what they want with their bodies.

There were only about forty people in the audience at the debate, and most were in attendance only because it earned them extra credit from their poli-sci professor. But Ross took the discussion as earnestly as if he were about to step in front of the U.S. Congress.

The College Republican responded to his arguments: "How can you legalize something that kills tens of thousands of people a year?" The College Democrat agreed.

Ross calmly countered, "So do you think we should outlaw Big Macs from McDonald's too, because people gain weight and have heart attacks and die as a result of them?"

As was always the case with the drug debate, Ross's opponents quickly grew flustered. They tried throwing arguments back at him, but there was nothing they could say that Ross didn't have a retort for.

"And should we outlaw cars because people get into car accidents and die?" Ross pressed his opposition. He offered arguments defending people who smoked pot, and even those who took heroin in the privacy of their own homes, noting that they were no different from someone who has a glass of wine after work to relax.

As for the violence around drug sales, he argued that this savagery existed only because the government imposed such harsh and evil laws to try to deter the sale of drugs, and dealers had to employ nefarious means to protect themselves in the wars that erupted on the streets. "There are no gang wars over the sale of alcohol or Big Macs, because those are legal," he continued. And on top of it all, he reasoned, if drugs were legalized, then they would eventually be sold in regulated form. Bad drugs, cut with rat poison or talcum powder, would disappear from the marketplace.

"It's someone's body and it belongs to them," Ross said as he looked out at the audience. "And the government has no right to tell them what they can and cannot do with it."

Ross knew in his heart that his arguments were sound and that he had thought through every aspect of the war on drugs. What wasn't clear to him still, and what he kept asking himself in the hours between school, his extra-curricular activities, and his girlfriend, was what he could do with those passionate beliefs to help change what he saw as the harmful and tyrannical drug laws in America.

# Chapter 5
# JARED'S KHAT

**N**o."

That was it. One word. A nonnegotiable syllable.

"No," Jared said again.

His supervisor looked at him in disbelief, unsure if he had really just heard a rookie Customs and Border Protection officer refuse a direct order. (Yes, he had. He definitely had.) The peon—five-foot-nothing, twenty-six-year-old Jared Der-Yeghiayan—looked even younger than normal as he sat across from his older, rotund director—like a kid sitting in a principal's office, his legs swinging back and forth in the chair, his feet never coming close to the floor.

Jared didn't feel he had much to lose with the answer. Customs and Border Protection wasn't exactly his dream job. He had ended up here only because he didn't have a choice if he was going to pursue his dream of working in law enforcement. Either he continued to work in the movie theater down in Lincolnshire, or he could come to Chicago O'Hare and stamp people's passports for a living.

Jared had tried to get into the Secret Service, his dreamiest dream job. But the examiner, an American-as-they-come questions-and-answers man, had probed Jared about his father, a sitting U.S. judge of Armenian extraction who had fled Syria during the genocide years earlier. At first Jared had answered politely, but few things could rile him up as much as doubts about his family's allegiance to America. Needless to say, after a heated debate, he didn't get the job.

Soon afterward, Jared had applied to the DEA, but he'd gotten into another overwrought debate with the polygraph tester over what constitutes a crime. He didn't get that job either.

The U.S. Marshals Service, Department of Homeland Security, and Federal Bureau of Investigation all said no to Jared because he didn't have a degree. He had dropped out of college after two weeks, with no patience for being judged by professors, and even less tolerance for the time their classes demanded. Besides, what was the point of four years of school when most of the people he knew who had gone through college still couldn't get a "real" job? He walked off campus one afternoon and never went back.

At the behest of his father, Samuel, who had once run the agency overseeing Customs and Border Protection, Jared settled for the most monotonous government job, stamping passports day after day.

His hope was that this gig would lead to something bigger and better. Which it had, but as he challenged his supervisor with that repeatedly uttered "no," it was becoming obvious that, as per usual, Jared was starting to piss everyone off.

This particular debacle had started a year earlier, in late 2007. After a few dull years on the passport line, Jared had been given the opportunity to try to find people smuggling drugs into the United States. Catching drug smugglers sounded like fun and sexy work, but not with the kind of drugs that Jared had been tasked with finding. His quest was to catch people who were sneaking a speedlike substance called khat into America. Unlike similar drugs, such as cocaine, which were processed in a lab or jungle somewhere, khat was a leafy green plant and therefore more difficult to identify than large bricks of white powder. Since it was so mild, more akin to drinking some intense coffee than snorting a line of blow, khat was also the least important drug for anyone in government to go after.

But Jared assumed the task of finding khat with the same fanatical compulsion as someone assigned to capture the world's most evil terrorists. He printed out hundreds of flight logs of people who had been caught with khat in the past, laid all the documents out on his living room floor as if he were Carrie Mathison on *Homeland,* and searched for similarities among known smugglers. He scrutinized every detail of each arrest until he found a pattern.

The first clue: all of the smugglers had booked reservations the day before a flight. Second, the couriers used only Gmail or Yahoo! e-mail accounts. And third, they had (obviously fake) phone numbers that used a shared formula. With these hints, and others, he searched through the list of incoming passengers arriving at O'Hare who fit his profile. Eventually he identified an inbound passenger who he believed would be smuggling the drug.

The following day customs officials pulled that man off an incoming flight, opened his suitcase, and discovered it was lined with khat. (*Holy shit! It worked.*) The same thing happened each subsequent time Jared ran his search on the incoming Chicago passenger database: they pulled khat out of the bag.

Jared's profiling worked so well that he started to search through the national databases, experimenting with his theory on other U.S. airports. And sure enough, it worked every time. Customs officials at JFK would be told about a target, at which point they would open the suitcases of the passenger Jared had identified and subsequently find bags of the drug hidden in socks, shirts, and other crevices of the luggage.

But there were a couple of snags, not the least of which was that JFK agents believed that khat was a pointless drug to go after in the first place. There were no nightly news briefings about officials finding a pound of khat on a flight from the United Kingdom and no awards being handed out to customs officers for these arrests. To make matters worse, Jared's success made other agents look ineffective by comparison. Not getting credit on a bust meant you couldn't climb the bureaucratic ladder to increase your pay and vacation time. And after enough unofficial complaints had come in, Jared was called into his supervisor's office.

"You have to play by the rules if you want to be successful here," Jared's supervisor said. "You're pissing off people all over the place and—"

"No," Jared interrupted.

Again? Another no? What the fuck was wrong with this guy?

"Look, I'm just doing my job," Jared tried to reason. "I'm following the trends and—"

"Yes, but you're doing your job out of your jurisdiction," the boss barked. "You're assigned to Chicago, and that's all you're supposed to do: find shit in Chicago."

Jared didn't do well when he was told what to do, and his temper was starting to flare. He had been given an assignment that he had pulled off in spades, but because of typical government bullshit, he was being told he was doing a less effective job. Shouldn't he be getting praise and applause?

"You see this?" Jared said, pointing to the gold and black Customs and Border Protection (CBP) badge clipped to his shirt. "The last time I looked, it said, 'the United States of America' on it, and I'm pretty sure that JFK airport is in the United States of America."

The supervisor looked back at Jared in shock. But the peon kept going.

"I won't talk to you about this in person anymore," Jared said as he stood up and walked toward the door. "If you want to discuss this again, please put it in writing." And in one brief moment the supervisor had just learned a lesson that everyone who met Jared eventually learned: he didn't play well with others. A trait of Jared's that would soon prove to be his biggest asset, and his most antagonistic hindrance.

# Chapter 6
# THE BONFIRE

Ross swerved his truck through the hills and away from Austin. The sun was setting over the wide Texas sky and Julia sat to his right, staring out the window at the seemingly unending rows of trees.

"Cedars," Ross said.

"Huh?" she replied, turning toward him.

"The trees; they're cedars." She looked back at the masses of green foliage that lined the edge of the curvy road. "Texans hate them," Ross added. "They can't get rid of them. They've tried all of these different approaches, but nothing works." A few moments later he finished the thought: "Nature always wins."

Julia listened and contemplated today's lesson about Texas. Ross was constantly offering new tidbits of information about her new home state. He was happy to be her on-call historian and twenty-four-hour tour guide, taking her to his favorite coffee shops, burger joints, and parks. He had shown her Pace Bend Lake, one of the best spots to cliff jump. And he'd cited innumerable facts about local buildings and sights.

Ross had introduced her to his family, and she had started to grow close to his sister, Cally (though their mother was somewhat cold to Ross's new girlfriend). Ross had even trusted Julia enough to show her his secret collection of Dungeons & Dragons miniatures, which he kept hidden in his old bedroom at his parents' house. One afternoon he had nervously laid out the dozens of intricately painted fantasy statuettes that had been wrapped safely in boxes and tucked away under his bed.

Ross appreciated that Julia was so supportive of his ideas, even if some of them didn't work out so well, like Retracement Capital Management, an investment fund that Ross had tried to start recently, which had gone bust before it had even had a chance to go boom.

"So these are all your friends from high school?" Julia asked as she turned away from the cedar trees.

"Yeah," he replied cheerfully. "These are all kids I hung out with at Westlake." Julia knew they were getting close, as she could see the orange embers of a fire spitting into the air in front of a small house. "I'm really excited to see them all," Ross said as he slowed the truck.

Ross had returned to Texas a few months earlier, settling back into life in Austin as if he had never left. He hadn't expected to end up back there, but his college obsession with the libertarian club had come at a cost. He had been so focused on the exploration of his new ideals that he had failed the candidacy exam for his Ph.D. program, where he was supposed to continue his research in the "growth of EuO thin films by molecular beam epitaxy." But there was some serendipity in his failing the exam. All those hours talking politics had made him realize that there was, at least for him, more to life than physics. So he took his master's and went south again. He had persuaded nineteen-year-old Julia to drop out of school and follow him. Yet for both of them the transition had been bittersweet.

For Julia, leaving Pennsylvania, where she had lived for so long, and going to a state that seemed—largely and without apology—racist and staunchly Republican had been jarring. But Ross's corner of the Lone Star State was (mostly) different. While a majority of Texas backed George W. Bush, and were against gays and abortion, the Austin area was more liberal and aligned with her own values, filled with Ron Paul supporters who believed that the government was too big, too powerful, and too in people's business.

For Ross the reintegration had been surprisingly hard. He had left Penn State without any idea of what to do next. He wanted desperately to do something in line with his libertarian ideals. He wanted to do something that would make him money. And, maybe most of all, he wanted to make his parents proud. Finding a career that met all of these goals was, it had become apparent, all but impossible. But that didn't stop him from talking about his new belief system to anyone who would listen.

When he bumped into childhood friends at old local bars, rather than revel in distant memories of the past, Ross wanted to talk about America's future. On a recent visit to Shakespeare's Pub in downtown Austin, he had spent most of the evening holding court with an old high school friend, describing Austrian economics and arguing that the current political system in America was designed to let the rich take advantage of the disadvantaged. He explained how wonderful it would be to build a seasteading experiment.

Seasteading, Ross had expounded, was an idea that you could create a community out at sea, away from any governments or regulations, where people could live in open waters without laws and with a free market. Some people had the idea to do this on an abandoned oil rig in the middle of the ocean, with none of the rules and laws that existed in America or elsewhere. After Penn State, Ross had tried to build a video game that would help demonstrate these theories. But it had gone nowhere. Just like all of Ross's other ideas.

Julia had been present for a number of these political discussions, and while she sometimes argued clever counterpoints, often she just let Ross have the stage. Tonight, though, as they neared the house with the bonfire outside, there would thankfully be no talk of politics or lawless countries in the middle of the ocean.

Ross steered off the road and onto a long dirt driveway toward a single-story clapboard house with warm yellow light glowing from the windows. "It's been a couple of years since I've seen some of these friends," he proclaimed as the truck wheezed off. The sun had set and darkness consumed the surrounding mountains; the smell of cinders filled the air as they walked toward a group of revelers.

"Rossman!" a friend yelled as he embraced his old high school chum.

"This is my girlfriend, Julia," Ross said proudly.

As they joined the group around the fire, people popped open beers. A joint was lit and passed around, and the friends reminisced about high school. "Remember the time Rossman talked his way out of getting in trouble with the cops for smoking that joint?" one story began. It ended with "Ross loved his weed." Laughter erupted as Julia noted, "He still does." More stories; more joints; more beers; more laughter. Ross and Julia were having a blast. That was, until the conversation turned to careers. One friend offered up that he was working for the government now; another said he was an engineer. One talked about starting his own business.

"What about you, Rossman?" A Texas drawl came from the other side of the fire. "Where are you working these days?"

Ross was silent for a moment. Tension consumed him as he peered at Julia. This was the last question on earth he wanted to deal with right now. "I don't really have a job," he said.

"That's cool," a friend sassed. "How'd you pull that off?"

The entire group around the fire grew quiet, listening.

Ross explained that he had taken on a part-time job managing a non-profit called Good Wagon Books, where he was helping out his old buddy Donny. Good Wagon went door to door through Austin collecting old books, then sold them online. Whatever couldn't be hawked on the Internet was donated to local prisons. It didn't pay much, so he subsidized his few expenses trading stocks, and had some more money saved from selling a small rental house he'd bought while he was at Penn State. (His frugal lifestyle, in which he spent most of college essentially living for free, had enabled him to save up enough money from his job as a teacher's assistant at Penn State to purchase, then sell, a tiny home in town.) Around the bonfire he told his friends that he'd been living on those winnings for the past few months.

What he didn't tell them, though, was that he had given up day-trading because it wasn't profitable, and the few times he had made some money, he had hated the inordinate regulations and taxes that Uncle Sam applied to investors. He also didn't tell them that he had failed his Ph.D. exam or that he had despised renting his house out to college students because of all the inconsequential problems that he was forced to deal with as a landlord. And he certainly didn't tell them that the gaming simulation he had been building for months, which would simulate a seasteading project, had failed, as no one wanted to purchase it. He didn't mention all those odd jobs he had done off Craigslist to make a few dollars, including editing science papers. He didn't say that everything he had done had felt like a complete failure to him. One brilliant idea after another that no one else thought was brilliant.

The subject, thankfully, changed as people told stories from a decade earlier. While Ross laughed, he appeared embarrassed by what had just happened. Sure, his friends had mundane nine-to-five jobs, but they had jobs. And what did Ross have on his résumé? Two degrees and a series of dead ends. He wanted so badly to have an impact. To do something or build something that was bigger than a nine-to-five.

It was late by the time Ross and Julia hugged everyone good-bye and slipped back into the truck for the drive back to Austin. As Ross slammed his car door closed and pulled his seat belt across his chest, Julia could sense something wasn't right. The car reversed down the driveway and onto the winding road.

"Nothing I've done has worked out," he lamented. "I really haven't accomplished anything great." The cedar trees zipped by in the darkness.

"Oh, honey," she replied, "it's okay. You're trying different things. You'll find—"

Ross spoke over Julia. "I wanted to be an entrepreneur, but I've tried to start all of these different things and nothing has worked."

"It will. You just have to—"

He continued speaking as if he were alone in the truck. "I want to see some results," he said. "I want to build something that is really successful."

"You just have to keep trying."

She was right, as Ross was about to see.

# Chapter 7
# THE SILK ROAD

S tuff, to Ross, was just that: stuff. He had no interest in any of it.

But there was one object Ross couldn't live without: his laptop. That rectangular clamshell was, in many respects, Ross's life. All of the files and folders it contained made up a map of his brilliant and, to many, enigmatic mind. And it was on that very computer that, on a late summer morning in 2010, Ross began working on a project that was going to change everything.

He had recently moved into an apartment with Julia, a live/work space in downtown Austin with shiny concrete floors. Julia had started a new business, which she called Vivian's Muse, where she photographed half-naked women for their husbands. Her pitch was simple: *What do you get the man who has everything? Sensual pictures of his wife, almost nude.* And so, several days a week Julia would set up candles throughout the main room of the apartment, play sensual techno music, and snap thousands of boudoir pictures.

In the adjacent bedroom, as Ross would get to work on his latest project, he could hear the *pop! pop! pop!* of the camera flash and Julia commanding her muse, "Stick your ass in the air," and "Now act like you're having an orgasm!"

Their bedroom, where Ross often sat to work, was its usual mess, with Julia's crumpled-up jeans, discarded dresses, and underwear littering the floor. When they weren't working, they spent hours under the covers, snuggling or watching TV shows on Ross's laptop.

The latest show they had become obsessed with was *Breaking Bad*. They would cuddle on the bed, warmed by the glow of Ross's screen, as Walter

White transformed into the terrifying and mysterious drug kingpin Heisenberg, a man who justified his evil along intellectual lines. Ross liked the drama, and it was hard not to appreciate what Heisenberg had done. Once an underachieving, largely browbeaten high school chemistry teacher, Walter White found in drugs the best way to express his technical brilliance as a chemist and businessperson. What he did may have been terrible and destructive, but he did it with such beauty and so adroitly that, to him at least, the very sin was absolved by the manner in which it was carried out.

Still, Ross thought the story line was a bit far-fetched. "That would never happen in real life," he said to Julia.

When he wasn't watching the show, Ross was now tinkering with his new idea in their Austin bedroom: an anonymous Web site where you could buy or sell anything imaginable.

The genesis of this concept had been lodged in Ross's mind for some time. Just another one of the daydreams he hoped to build in the future. The only problem was, when he had first had this particular aha moment a year earlier, the technology he needed to realize it simply hadn't existed.

At the time, he had contacted a man he'd met online who went by the nickname Arto. They had exchanged a few e-mails, with Ross asking Arto if it would be possible to build such an anonymous online store (primarily for illegal drugs, which Ross didn't think should be illegal) that the government would have no control over.

Arto, who was clearly an expert on such matters, explained that most of the technology needed to make this idea happen existed. There was a Web browser called Tor, which enabled people to slip behind a curtain online into another, separate Internet—one where the U.S. government couldn't track people because, thanks to Tor, everyone became invisible. Unlike the normal Internet, where Ross's every move was stored in databases by Facebook or Google or Comcast, on this side of the Internet, called the Dark Web, you simply couldn't be found.

But there were complicating factors to Ross's idea. Specifically, in 2009 there wasn't a good way to pay for these things anonymously online. Cash was too risky, and credit cards would leave evidence of someone buying a bag of cocaine from an illegal drug Web site.

For inspiration, Arto suggested that Ross should read a relatively unknown novel titled *A Lodging of Wayfaring Men*. The novel tells a tale of a group of libertarian freedom seekers who create an alternate online society on the Internet that operates using its own digital currency, free from government control. In the book this online world grows so quickly that the U.S. government becomes petrified by its power. FBI agents are sent out to try to stop the Web site before it destroys the very fabric of society.

Arto's advice was remarkably inspiring to Ross, but the logistical issues remained. Specifically, that there wasn't a way to pay for drugs on such a Web site.

And so, for a year, the idea sat on a shelf in Ross's mind.

That was, until now. Ross had come across a technology that had recently emerged called Bitcoin. It was being billed as a new form of digital cash that was, from the research he had done, completely untraceable. Anyone in the world could use it to buy and sell anything without leaving digital fingerprints behind.

The people (or person) who had created this new technology were anonymous, but the idea was simple: While you needed dollars to buy things in America, pounds in England, yen in Japan, or rupees in India, this new Bitcoin currency was meant to be used all around the world and specifically on the Internet. And just like cash, it was untraceable. To get some Bitcoins, you could exchange them online in the same way you could go to the airport and exchange dollars for euros. It was the missing piece Ross had been waiting for to build his experimental world with no rules.

So in the summer of 2010, while Julia was photographing naked women, Ross Ulbricht, the failed physicist who wanted so badly to make a difference in the world, sat down at his beloved laptop to realize the idea that had been lodged in his mind for so long. A Web site that would be a free and open marketplace where people from all over the planet could buy anything and everything. Things that they couldn't currently get their hands on because of the restrictions of the U.S. government—most important, drugs. As his fingers touched the keyboard and code appeared on his computer screen, he daydreamed that the site could potentially grow quickly. So quickly that the government would become petrified by its power. It could be living proof, Ross fantasized, that legalizing drugs was the best way to stop violence and oppression in the world. If it worked, it would change the very fabric of society forever.

Sure, he wanted to make money. That was the libertarian way. But he wanted to free people too. There were millions of souls crammed into jails across the country because of drugs, mostly inconsequential drugs like weed and magic mushrooms. A vile and putrid prison system kept those people locked away; lives destroyed because the government wanted to tell people what they could and could not do with their own bodies.

This new Web site he was working on could change that.

Coming up with a name for his store was a challenge, but he finally settled on the Silk Road, a title borrowed from the ancient Chinese trade route of the Han dynasty.

The biggest challenge now was finding the time to actually work on the project, given that he was still involved with Good Wagon Books and had even taken over most of the operation. Still, he had hired a couple of employees to do most of the book work, so Ross could hole up in his messy bedroom and toil away on the site, work that was difficult, even for someone as capable as Ross.

He spent innumerable hours writing front-end code, back-end code, and code that helped sew those digital dialects together. Ross was teaching himself all of these programming languages on the fly. He was technically doing the equivalent of building eBay and Amazon on his own, without any help and without any knowledge. When he got stuck, he was truly baffled as to how to fix a programming problem. It wasn't as if he could post a job listing online looking for someone to help him build a Web site that sold drugs and other illegal contraband.

For now, though, he was determined to build the site on his own, even if it was slow going. His idea, which now seemed like the obvious path to push his liberation ideals, might actually turn into something.

But there was one thing Ross hadn't figured out yet. Where was he going to get drugs for his new drug-dealing Web site?

# Chapter 8
# ROSS THE FARMER

He had to tell someone or, more important, he had to actually show someone. But he couldn't; he just couldn't—it was too dangerous. This conundrum gnawed at Ross. So after weeks of deliberation he knew exactly who it would be. "I'm going to take you somewhere," Ross said to Julia on a late-November afternoon. "But I'm going to have to blindfold you."

"Blindfold me?" she exulted as she jumped up from her chair, delighted by the possibility that something kinky was about to happen. "Great!"

He clarified very quickly that this wasn't sexual. "The blindfold is for your own protection," he said, worry spreading across his face. "It's so you can never lead anyone back to where I'm going to take you."

Still, Julia felt a thrill as Ross slipped some black fabric over her head, then pulled tightly to shut out any light from around her eyes. He wasn't his usual phlegmatic self; he seemed nervous and deep in thought. They walked in silence out of the apartment, Ross gripping Julia's arm to help her into his pickup truck. Ross could see everything, but Julia could only hear. There was the sound of keys that jingled like a dog's collar. The click of the truck's door opening. A thump as it slammed shut. An engine rumbled. Finally the vehicle edged forward into the darkness for Julia, daylight for Ross.

"Where are we going?" Julia asked again as she looked around at the shadows.

"I told you," he whispered. "It's a surprise. You'll see."

Ross didn't say another word as he drove through Austin at dusk. Julia sensed he was concerned, so she let them sit in silence.

They had been getting along so well lately. On weekends they would head over to his parents' house for dinner, which—unsurprisingly—was different from any family dinner she had encountered.

While many Texan kinfolk would spend mealtimes talking about football and F-150 trucks, the Ulbrichts talked about economics, libertarian politics, and the pitiful state of society. Ross's father, Kirk, a soft-spoken native of South Texas, always managed to one-up Ross's arguments by calmly pointing out that his son's beliefs were a tad too idealistic, and here was why. Lyn, Ross's hard-nosed Bronx-born mother, would step in and defend Ross's view, supplementing his argument with her more rigid outlook. Kirk's goal was to teach his son to think through every side of an argument; Lyn's was to push Ross's intelligence, with the hope that he would live up to his incredible potential. She had given up on her own dream of becoming a journalist, and her hope of a grand future now lay in the hands of her golden son. This fact was not lost on Ross.

Maybe this was why Ross had been working so hard of late.

Over the past few weeks Julia had seen him disappear for hours on end, not really saying what he was up to. She had imagined he was working at the Good Wagon Books warehouse or (more likely) toiling away on the Web site he was now obsessed with. He spent what seemed like days at a time on his laptop, staring intently at the screen. Maybe, she had reasoned, he was hanging out with friends in the park or volunteering at a nearby nonprofit, something Ross often did with his spare time.

But, as Julia was about to find out when the vehicle finally stopped, Ross had been up to something very different recently. She wondered where they were as the truck's engine hummed off. Maybe it was near Highland Mall or Rundberg Lane, or they had driven away from the downtown and were near Bastrop State Park, outside the city. She heard Ross get out of the truck; the keys clinked, a door slammed, and he grabbed her by the arms, helping her onto the pavement.

"Okay, hold on to me," he said as he led her forward. "We're going to walk up some stairs now."

One minute and a hundred steps later, Julia heard the sound of a door being unlocked. Ross led her forward a few feet and then slipped the blindfold off.

As the light bled into her vision, Julia looked around the room trying to survey what he had brought her to see. She looked left and right, befuddled by the emptiness of her surroundings. They were in a small and dingy space that looked like an abandoned sanatorium. The only natural light came from one small window at the other end of the room that was partially covered with some cardboard for privacy. A stained, yellowing white carpet covered the floor. There wasn't a single piece of furniture in the room, just piles of what looked like boxes and vials of chemicals. The room, she noticed, smelled like animal excrement.

"What is this?" she asked. "Where are we?"

"Come with me," Ross said as he led her into a bedroom that sat off the drab living room. As they rounded the corner, a gale of cold air from an air conditioner hit them. Then, as she entered the other room, like the conclusion to a thrilling mystery novel, it all made sense to Julia. She saw why she had been blindfolded and exactly why it wasn't safe for her to know where they were.

"I had to show you because I had to show someone," he said.

On the wall to the left, another piece of cardboard had been taped over the window. The room was empty except for a tall, lopsided shelving unit that looked like it had not been moved in a decade.

Then there was that odor. The same pungent, earthy whiff that had greeted Julia when she entered the apartment and pulled off the blindfold. Only now it was so much stronger, an aroma that smelled more like damp soil on a forest floor.

Julia examined the shelves, then looked back at Ross and smiled. He didn't need to tell her what she was looking at; this wasn't the first time she had seen him play mad scientist. He had experimented on a smaller scale in their apartment a year earlier, storing his results in a black garbage bag in the closet, stuffed in between Julia's underwear and her high-heeled shoes.

But this—this!—was grander and more impressive than anything she had ever seen. She approached the decrepit shelving unit, which spanned the width of the entire room. Everything started to make sense to her— Ross's disappearing acts. He'd been coming here, she realized.

Ross was ebullient as he bent down to one of the lower shelves and pointed at a random tray. "Look at this one," he said, his finger traversing the air as he spoke. "And this one, look at that."

Julia saw that on each shelf there sat a white tray almost two feet in diameter—more than a dozen in all—and that inside these trays were hundreds of tiny shoots sprouting into the air. From a few feet away, they looked like platters full of baby porcupines. She moved closer, now peering directly into one of the white trays, and was astonished at the sheer number of brown and white mushroom stems. These were not normal mushrooms. She knew perfectly well that they were magic.

"Look over here at this one." Ross beamed. She turned, seeing what he was pointing at; a plump hazel and milky-colored button that looked like it was ready to be picked and sprinkled on top of a salad. He was as proud as a parent.

As Julia inspected further, she started to estimate how many mushrooms he was actually growing. It was easily more than a thousand, maybe even double that. Plucked from their rectangular white plastic homes, the contents of these trays could probably fill a large black garbage bag, or even two.

"How much does this place cost?" she asked.

"It's 450 dollars a month."

"It's a total shit hole."

Ross laughed. This was fine with him. A shit hole, after all, was the perfect place to operate a secret drug laboratory.

The entire operation—his massive shroomery, the seeds of what he hoped would be his burgeoning Silk Road empire—would end up costing him more than $17,000, including rent and supplies, which were endless. There were the petri dishes, tape, and glue guns; the ingredients, including peat, gypsum, and rye; and the kitchen supplies, like the pressure cooker and kitchen timer. All of it had added up very quickly. As for the return on his investment, he estimated he could get $15 or so per gram for the mushrooms. Given that there would be several kilos of product at the end of the yield, he could easily make tens of thousands of dollars in profit. But—and this was a big "but"—this was a lot of mushrooms to offload, and it wasn't obvious that his Web site was even going to work. Would people want to buy magic mushrooms off a stranger on the Internet?

"Aren't you worried about getting caught?" Julia asked.

"Of course," he replied, as if it were the most obvious question in the world. "But I need product for my site."

He reminded her that no one else knew about this hideaway. He had taken the proper precautions to stay covert during his shroom-growing phase and even read the book *The Construction and Operation of Clandestine Drug Laboratories,* which was essentially a Dummies guide for setting up a felonious drug lab.

Though most people would have been shocked or distraught or entirely terrified to discover their boyfriend managing a secret drug farm, Julia was intrigued by the idea—she felt like someone who knew a secret no one else should know. In her mind, while she knew Ross could get into trouble if he was caught, she didn't envision the consequences being that severe; it wasn't like Ross had driven her to a secret meth lab or a heroin-making facility with a dozen half-naked workers. These were just a few trays of mushrooms.

Ross, on the other hand, was fully aware exactly what could happen if he was caught. Texas's merciless laws could result in five to ninety-nine years in prison for four hundred grams of mushrooms. Ross's secret farm was currently growing almost a hundred pounds of hallucinogens.

"We should go," he said to Julia as they walked back into the living room, and he once again placed the black rag over her eyes, tightening the slipknot to block out any light.

The door lock clicked; then she heard the jingle of keys as he bolted the lair shut behind them.

# Chapter 9

# OPENING DAY OF
# THE SILK ROAD

This was it. Holy heck! Hello, 2011 . . . the end of January had finally arrived. It was more than a year since the snowflake of the idea had first landed on Ross; several months since he had realized it could actually work; weeks since he had shown Julia his covert shroomery. Now it was only a few hours before it was time to unveil the Silk Road to the world.

To be safe, every detail had to be checked. The "product," those small, scrumptious mushrooms in the big black garbage bag, were ready to go. (Ross had tested them in the woods with a friend to make sure they were good, and they were beyond amazing.) The back-end database and front-end code sat on a hidden server that Ross had given the nickname Frosty. A green logo of a camel welcomed visitors to the Amazon of drugs. Sure, the site was missing some features, but Ross was a start-up of one—he'd fix those in due time.

And it was finally here. Opening day.

Ross almost hadn't made it to this moment—several times! First there was an absolutely, utterly, nauseatingly terrifying incident that had occurred just before the site was set to open, when Ross, by sheer fate, had almost ended up jail. Austin had been in the middle of a heat wave a few weeks earlier, and somehow there had been a water leak in the apartment housing his secret magic mushroom farm. The landlord had gone into the space to inspect the flood and instead had found Ross's drug laboratory. Irate, the landlord called Ross to tell him the next phone call was to the local police. Ross tore through the space, trying to get everything out before the cops arrived, and thankfully screeched away just in time. When he returned home that evening, smelling rank from the mushroom residue, he was so shaken up it took Julia hours to calm him. The thought of what would have happened had he been caught was enough to put Ross on the edge of a panic attack.

Still, that hadn't deterred him from realizing his vision. As his shock morphed back into confidence, he knew he had to keep going. But the near run-in with the police wasn't the only obstacle Ross had faced to get here.

Besides the reality that he still had to manage Good Wagon Books, his nonprofit book business, and his five part-time employees, he had also continued his quest to code the site alone.

The endless issues that had arisen when he tried to write the necessary code had left Ross so lost at times that he had no choice but to call an old friend, Richard Bates, whom he had met years earlier at the University of Texas, and ask for help. Ross was careful not to tell Richard what he was actually working on, but rather described his Web site as a "top secret" project. In a world where everyone has a start-up idea that they consider "top secret," Richard didn't really question his old friend and helped debug the PHP—the programming language—that Ross had tangled into a jumbled mess.

But all of that didn't matter now. What mattered was that Ross Ulbricht was ready to launch his new venture: the Silk Road.

There was, however, still one major question that gnawed at him. Would anyone use the site? Even if you could make a store that didn't have any laws or rules, would people actually want to shop there?

If this became just another line on Ross Ulbricht's résumé of failures, he would be destroyed. By himself he had essentially done the work of a twelve-person start-up, acting as the front-end programmer, back-end developer, database guy, Tor consultant, Bitcoin analyst, project manager, guerrilla marketing strategist, CEO, and lead investor. Not to mention the in-house fungiculturist. It would have cost more than a million dollars of people's time to replicate the site. Plus thousands of lines of PHP and MySQL code needed to connect to the Bitcoin blockchain—list of transactions—and a dozen widgets and whatnots in between. If it failed, Ross didn't know what he would do with himself.

But something told him this time was different, that maybe, in some strange and cosmic way, this site was why he was here, and he was going to do everything he could to see it reach its full potential. To help people, to free them, through his Web site.

He had an entire plan for how he would let the world know about his new creation, all anonymously. But first he had to tell one person—in person—about the site.

He wandered into the living room where Julia sat and announced it was time for a demonstration. *Ladies and gentlemen, boys and girls, people of all ages, and of course Julia, please take your seats. The presentation is about to begin*. Ross informed Julia that the site was finally ready and he wanted, so proudly, to show it to her. He began by asking for her silver MacBook. "So first," Ross said as he typed, "you will need to download Tor; remember, Tor is a Web browser which makes you completely anonymous online, so that the thieves"—Ross's term for the government—"can't see what you're doing and searching for."

"Good!" she declared. She was happy to download anything that protected her from the prying eyes of the thieves. *Down with the thieves!* She clapped her hands together.

"Next you go to this URL," he said as he typed one of the strangest Web site addresses Julia had ever seen into this peculiar Tor Web browser: "tydgccykixpbu6uz.onion." While it might have looked like these letters were the result of a cat walking across his keyboard, Ross explained that this was just part of the safety and anonymity of Tor.

As the site slowly loaded onto Julia's computer screen, Ross smiled, turning the laptop back in her direction. There, in all its splendid, anonymous glory, was the tiny world Ross had been working on all this time. An anonymous marketplace where, as advertised on the page now staring back at Julia, you could buy and sell anything, without fear of the government peering over your shoulder or throwing you in a cage.

"Wow," Julia said as she grabbed the laptop with both hands, "you did it, baby! So how do you buy stuff?"

Ross showed her what was for sale and how it worked. When he clicked on a green "Drugs" link, it led to a section titled "Psychedelics." And there, for sale on the Silk Road, were the magic mushrooms Ross had grown a few months earlier, listed for sale as if he were hawking a used bicycle or a box of Girl Scout cookies on Craigslist.

He then explained how to buy Bitcoins, the currency needed to buy drugs on the site. It was like buying coins at a video arcade. You exchanged your cash for tokens, and then you got to play. Just as at an arcade, at the end of the day, no one knew who had used those tokens because they all looked the same. (Bitcoin wasn't just meant for illegal purchases, either; you could use the digital cash to buy things on dozens of legitimate Web sites around the world.)

"Give me your credit card," Ross said as he navigated to an online Bitcoin exchange, where Julia could interchange her real dollars for digital gold. They typed in her credit card information and watched as the page loaded.

"How will anyone else know how to do this?" Julia said.

*Ahh, good question from the audience . . . but here at the Silk Road, we've thought of everything.*

Ross explained that he had set up a blog post that was essentially an instruction manual explaining how to go through the process he was now demonstrating to Julia.

"But how will people find that site?" she asked.

This was greeted with a proud smile from Ross.

At exactly 4:20 p.m. on Thursday, January 27, Ross had gone to a Web site called the Shroomery, which was an online haven for all things related to magic mushrooms, and registered an account under the name Altoid. He then posted a comment on the site's forum under the Altoid pseudonym, writing that he had just happened to "come across this website called Silk Road," as if he had been out for a stroll on the Dark Web and accidentally stumbled upon it. He then urged people to check it out. This, he hoped, was how people would find his new creation.

He was unsure if the anonymous posting would work, so soon afterward Ross registered the same nickname on another Web site focused on Bitcoin, under a thread discussing whether it was possible to build a "heroin store" online, and he urged people to visit the Silk Road. "What an awesome thread!" he wrote. "You guys have a ton of great ideas. Has anyone seen Silk Road yet?" Again, Ross did this incognito so it could never be traced back to him.

All he had to do now was wait. But not for long.

"It's crazy," Ross told Julia. "People have already started to come to the site from those forum posts."

"Has anyone bought anything yet?" she asked him as she clicked around on her laptop, exploring the Silk Road.

"Not yet," he said.

But he knew that they would. How could they not?

# Chapter 10

# WHAT GOES UP MUST COME DOWN

Dusk settled over Austin, and the Good Wagon Books warehouse was eerily quiet save for the sound of Ross, who stood at his desk, typing ferociously on his keyboard as he tried to finish up some coding on the Silk Road Web site so he could leave for the day.

He had never been so busy in his entire life.

Putting aside Julia (and the attention she required), he was working on his book business, managing his part-time employees, and running his drug Web site simultaneously.

He wanted so badly to give up the Good Wagon Books part of the equation, but he didn't want to upset his friend who had given him the business, and, more important, Ross didn't want to be seen by those around him as abandoning yet another unsuccessful project.

Thankfully, the daily tasks were complementary.

Each morning when Ross arrived at the Good Wagon Books storage facility, he would fire up his laptop in his tiny office, which sat off to the side of the warehouse. He checked the book orders, followed by the drug orders, before shipping both off to customers around the country.

For the books he would wander the aisles of the stacks he had built by hand over several months; dozens of rows of nine-foot-tall wooden shelves filled with old novels and nonfiction tomes that were all painstakingly organized and alphabetized. Ross stuffed titles that had sold online into puffy manila envelopes before printing the recipient's name and address on a label maker.

He would break to eat his lunch—a peanut butter and jelly sandwich on mulchlike hippie bread—before the real fun began.

It was time to package the drugs.

With a vacuum sealer normally used to keep food fresh, he encased the magic mushrooms he had grown in plastic wrap. He then dropped them into one of the same padded envelopes he used for paperbacks and hardcovers. Finally he used that same Good Wagon Books label maker to print the recipient's name and address. He took immense pride in the process.

In the weeks after the Silk Road opened for business, Ross had been shipping his shrooms off to buyers only once or twice a week. Now, a couple of months after he officially launched the site, orders were starting to come in daily. There had also been another new development on the site. An unbelievably exciting one! Ross was no longer the only person selling drugs on the Silk Road. A couple of other dealers had surfaced, hawking weed, cocaine, and small quantities of ecstasy.

When he told Julia about this development, she showed signs of worry. It was one thing to sell a few joints and little baggies of magic mushrooms on the Internet, she warned, but harder drugs could come with larger consequences. Ross argued that the system he had built was completely anonymous and safe and could never be tied back to him.

Assuring Julia that everyone was safe wasn't his only challenge; he had to convince new buyers too. To help entice potential customers to feel comfortable acquiring drugs from these mysterious new dealers on the Internet, Ross built a ratings system on the Silk Road where sellers were given "karma" points, which acted like positive or negative reviews, just as on eBay or Amazon.

While he was exhausted by all this work, he was also elated that people were finally using something he had built. And by March 2011 he had already made a few thousand dollars in revenue.

Now his biggest challenge was trying to figure out how to manage his time between his drug Web site, his book business, and Julia.

As luck would have it, one of those three things was about to vanish into a plume of dust. As he worked away on his laptop amid the empty silence of his office, he was momentarily interrupted by a ferocious *BOOM!* that erupted from inside the warehouse. It was so loud and terrifying that he stopped breathing for a moment as more bangs detonated inside the space.

His mind spun in a nanosecond with all the possibilities of what was happening. Maybe it was a raid by the police, a battering ram slamming through the door to stop the creator of the tiny Silk Road. Maybe it was a gas line explosion. Ross stood there panicked for a moment, fearing that all those hours of coding and mushroom farming had been in vain and that he was destined to be the underachieving failure that he dreaded.

Then, as soon as the thunderous claps arrived, they were gone. And in their place there was nothing but stark silence.

Ross's heartbeat started to slow slightly as he built up the courage to carefully walk around the corner into the warehouse to see what the noise had been.

There he saw that, one by one, like giant dominoes, the bookshelves of Good Wagon Books, which weighed thousands of pounds, had toppled. What he had heard was the sound of snapping wood and a mountain of books piling atop one another. It looked like a giant hand had reached in from the roof and swirled the room around.

He surveyed the damage. The mystery novels lay on top of the computer-programming books. The science fiction and romance section of Good Wagon Books was crushed beneath everything. It quickly dawned on Ross that when he had built the bookshelves, with his mind clearly preoccupied by the Silk Road, he must have forgotten to tighten several screws. The result of those actions could have killed him.

He quickly rushed back into his office to call Julia and tell her the story. But as he told her about the noises and the mess, Ross also realized that the books falling was not actually an inauspicious event that would cause him more stress and turmoil. This was serendipitous. Maybe it was a sign from God, fate, or sheer luck. But it meant that Ross now had an excuse to shut down the book business and let his part-time employees go. He could tell everyone that rebuilding the shelves and reorganizing the books would just be too laborious. He could do all of this without seeming like he was giving up.

Now, rather than split his time among the Silk Road, Good Wagon Books, and Julia, he could focus on just two of those things. Though one was about to put the other in jeopardy.

# Chapter 11

# THE *GAWKER* ARTICLE

The Café Grumpy coffee shop in Greenpoint, Brooklyn, looked like every other hipster enclave in America. Laptop screens glowed while headphones blared silently into people's ears. The men and women who sat sipping overpriced coffee wore the uniform of hipster Brooklyn: skintight jeans and bohemian tattoos that crawled up their arms and across their fingers. Outside was the industrial wasteland of McGuinness Avenue, the thoroughfare that connected Brooklyn and Queens above the sewage-laced Newtown Creek. Chop shops and gas stations lined the streets. A few trendy condos were going up—a sign that this subset of creative types, who huddled around their laptops each day, were an endangered species too. For now, though, they were the linchpins of the gentrifying neighborhood, this rump state, and Café Grumpy was its capital.

Most of the people in that coffee shop were writers trying to learn how to blog, or bloggers trying to learn how to write. A new class of creatives, living their own unique American dream, freelancing and hoping to be read by someone, somewhere.

Amid these writers sat Adrian Chen, a young Asian man, seemingly lost in his own world at his laptop as he scrolled through a long discussion on a Web forum. The chatter he was reading, with skepticism and disbelief, was about a Web site on the Dark Web that was being labeled the "Amazon for drugs."

On the forum some people complained that this Web site, called the Silk Road, was dangerous—that selling heroin on the Internet could kill people who didn't know how to use "H." Or that this new drug bazaar could give the new digital currency, Bitcoin, a bad name—while others contended that this site might make buying drugs safer and that it perfectly took advantage of online anonymity in a way that had never been done before.

But Adrian thought something entirely different: *This has to be a hoax.* After all, he knew the underbelly of the Internet better than almost any writer alive. He had been a blogger for *Gawker,* a New York–based gossip site, for almost two years. While working the weekend and graveyard shifts, he had become synonymous with finding and writing about trolls and hackers online. He trod through the dark, dangerous side of the Web and brought back stories of people doing crazy, fucked-up things.

But was anyone really crazy enough to set up a Web site like this? he wondered. Adrian knew there was only one way to find out. He downloaded Tor and navigated to the Silk Road, and sure enough, someone was.

You could buy any drug imaginable, he saw—by his count 343 different kinds of drugs, to be precise. Black tar heroin, Afghan hash, some Sour 13 weed, and ecstasy. All for street prices; in some instances less expensive than street. You simply traded some cash for Bitcoins, traded some Bitcoins for drugs, and waited for the U.S. Postal Service to deliver your drugs.

Adrian was skeptical, though, that if the Silk Road was real, anyone would actually buy drugs on the site. He registered an account on the forums under the username Adrian802 (802 was his area code from Connecticut, where he had grown up). He then posted a query asking if anyone would mind being anonymously interviewed for a story he was going to write about this defiant Web site.

He received some responses, then a man's phone number, and while pacing on the sidewalk outside Grumpy, he interviewed Mark, a software developer, about what it was like to buy drugs on the Internet.

"It kind of felt like I was in the future," Mark said over the phone, explaining that he'd ordered ten tabs of LSD from someone in Canada, and four days later the mailman dropped the acid off at his house.

Another person responded to Adrian's query too: the person who apparently ran the Silk Road.

• • •

As the Silk Road had grown, Ross's anxiety had expanded at an equal clip. When he had first posted anonymous messages on forums less than five months earlier, he had been oblivious to just how quickly it would drive people to the site. At first it was a trickle of customers, a few dozen here or there, but since he had shut down Good Wagon Books, his drug Web site had rapidly grown. Hundreds of people were now selling drugs on the site, and thousands were buying.

Ross was making money from his enterprise too. The mushrooms, most of which he had offloaded, had turned into a hefty profit of tens of thousands of dollars.

All of this came with a mixture of exhilaration and fear, and Ross had been in a constant state of worry, fretful that maybe Julia was right, that he could be tied to his creation. He constantly had to reassure himself that no one would ever be able to connect him with the Silk Road.

That was, except for two people.

Weeks earlier, Ross had been left with no choice but to tell his old college buddy Richard that he was the founder of the Amazon of drugs, as Richard had refused to help anymore without an explanation. "Tell me about this or leave me out of it," Richard wrote to Ross over chat. "I'm officially forbidding you from mentioning your secret project to me again unless you're going to reveal it." Without Richard's expertise, Ross was completely and utterly "fudged." If the site went down, Ross would be abandoned alone in a dark and complex maze. So he was left with no choice but to come clean.

At first Richard was shocked. After Ross explained his thinking behind the site, Richard agreed to continue to help. It didn't hurt that Ross gave his old pal a few baggies of his specialty magic mushrooms as a big thank-you. And that Richard started shopping on the site, buying ecstasy, weed, Vicodin, and some prescription antibiotics. (Richard was a germophobe, so he relished the ability to get medicine without a doctor's note.) And finally, Richard was confident (given that he had helped write the code) that nothing could be tied back to them.

But reassuring Julia that he wasn't in danger was a completely different challenge for Ross. Over the past two months the two had started fighting constantly about the Silk Road. There were now hundreds of people signing up for accounts every week, and Julia worried that Ross, whom she one day hoped to marry, could be caught and spend the rest of his life in prison.

"It's secure," Ross assured Julia, explaining how uncrackable Tor was and how Bitcoins were completely anonymous. "It's safe. Trust me, no one can ever figure it out it's me behind the site."

But the cautionary voice of Julia gnawed at him and, to be sure that he was covering his tracks properly and knowing full well how limited his programming skills were, Ross decided to explore hiring other experts (besides Richard) to rewrite some new security protocols on the site. He posted a job listing on the Silk Road, and some antigovernment programmers were happy to help in the battle to stop the Man, part time and for a fee.

Ross's Web site hadn't received any press yet, which was surprising given the chatter on some forums, though he wasn't entirely sure he was ready for any. Yet the time had come. Someone with the username Adrian802 had been sniffing around the site, telling Silk Road customers he was working on a story for *Gawker* about the Silk Road.

Ross knew he couldn't stop the story, so he figured it was best to message Adrian802. He was polite and grateful for the interest, voicing his belief that the Silk Road was making it safer for people to buy drugs. "Our community is amazing," Ross wrote under the guise of the anonymous administrator of the Silk Road. Then, completely oblivious to the consequences, Ross decided to go full bore with Adrian802 and took the opportunity to get his libertarian message out, explaining that the site was going to show the government that it was flat-out wrong to deny people their rights. "Stop funding the state with your tax dollars and direct your productive energies into the black market," he wrote to Adrian.

He didn't foresee that this kind of message would have vast and grim consequences.

• • •

At 4:20 p.m. on June 1, 2011, Adrian sat at Café Grumpy, sipped his black coffee, and watched as his blog post about the Silk Road went live. The title read: THE UNDERGROUND WEBSITE WHERE YOU CAN BUY ANY DRUG IMAGINABLE. The article began, "Making small talk with your pot dealer sucks. Buying cocaine can get you shot. What if you could buy and sell drugs online like books or light bulbs? Now you can: Welcome to Silk Road."

# Chapter 12
# A BULL'S-EYE ON MY BACK

What's wrong, baby?" Julia asked as she lay in bed next to Ross, admiring his jawline. Ross didn't respond to her. He was too busy reading a news article about the Silk Road.

He knew there might be a hostile response from the government after the article from Adrian Chen at *Gawker,* published a couple of days earlier. But this was a far worse response than his imagination had ever come up with.

With trepidation he clicked to play a video in the article he was reading. There, in a small rectangular window, stood Senator Chuck Schumer at a press conference podium, a vexed look on his face. To the senator's right and left, two large, oversize printouts of the Silk Road Web site rested on display stands. Below him, on the wooden rostrum, the blue, white, and gold insignia of the U.S. Senate was clear for the press corps, and Ross, to see.

"It's a certifiable one-stop shop for illegal drugs that represents the most brazen attempt to peddle drugs online that we have ever seen," Schumer said to a gaggle of press. "It's more brazen than anything else by light-years."

*Oh heck!*

This really wasn't good. Sure, Ross wanted recognition and attention. But this was more than he had ever anticipated, especially so early in the life of his drug bazaar.

The video cut to a scene of Schumer sitting in front of a computer, Ross's drug site on the screen. The senator's finger traversed the Silk Road as he listed off all of the goodies that were for sale. "Heroin, opium, cannabis, ecstasies, psychedelics, stimulants," Schumer said (briefly showing how out of touch he was with the topic at hand as he made "ecstasy" plural). The sound of camera flashes burst—*pop! pop! pop!*—as Schumer said in disbelief, "You name it, they have it!"

Ross felt sick as he read the article that accompanied the news clip, which noted that both Schumer of New York and Joe Manchin, then the junior senator from West Virginia, had asked the Department of Justice and the Drug Enforcement Administration to shut down the Amazon of drugs— immediately.

*Fudge! Friggin' fudge!* Ross had picked a fight with the biggest bully on earth, and the bully was about to punch back.

"Look," Ross said, leaning against the back of the bed as he replayed the clip for Julia. "They've painted a bull's-eye on my back."

"Ross," Julia said, petrified as she watched, "this isn't good."

The attention of the U.S. Senate was the last thing he needed at this moment. In a month, or six, maybe he could handle it. But not now.

Over the past few days, since the *Gawker* article had been published, an unremitting avalanche of press had followed in its wake. Ross's Web site had transformed from almost invisible to mainstream as it entered the national news cycle with shocking velocity. Established media brands were all over the story. The *Atlantic* picked it up; NPR talked about it on air; and TV news outlets, including ABC and NBC, produced segments devoted to it ("They call it the Amazon of drugs . . ."). Not to mention the hundreds of blog posts, discussions on drug forums and social media, and articles on libertarian Web sites.

Despite the mainstream press, most people who read about the site still didn't believe you could actually buy drugs on the Internet and have them mailed to your home. This had to be one of those Nigerian e-mail scams or a place for law enforcement to lure unsuspecting idiots who were going to be swept up in a massive online drug bust. But still, idiots or not, thousands of people downloaded Tor and signed up for the Silk Road to see. It couldn't hurt to look, right?

Ross watched with a mixture of dread and delight as his databases filled up and the site slowed down. He barely slept a wink the night after the article was published, lying awake staring at his laptop or sitting in his ergonomic chair in the bedroom, watching sign-ups from all over the world.

The day after the *Gawker* article, Ross got up, groggy and on edge, and was greeted by a total catastrophe. No, the site hadn't been shut down by law enforcement. Or knocked off-line by hackers. Nothing like that. It was much worse.

While some people had simply come to the Silk Road to window-shop, others were actually buying and selling drugs. And every time someone purchased something, some of Ross's Bitcoins vanished in the transaction. *What the hell is going on? There must be a bug in the code.* His personal profits, which were now in the double-digit thousands of dollars, were literally dwindling by hundreds of dollars every few hours. Ross had to figure out how to fix a problem he hadn't even known existed.

It was sickening.

After digging through his code for hours trying to find the error, Ross realized he had originally built the Silk Road using a standard piece of code called "bitcoind," which connected his payment system. Now he was discovering that he had created that interface improperly. He just had no idea where the mistake was in his code. All he knew was that he had essentially built a cash register where money fell out of the bottom into the ether whenever he opened it. And right now, as slews of new customers came to the site, that register was opening and closing at a staggering rate.

When he did the math, at the speed with which people were buying drugs on the site, the Silk Road was fast approaching insolvency. He would soon be the first person in history to start an underground drug Web site on the Internet and the first person in history to see it go bankrupt because he had written so much shitty code.

Ross had no choice but to start with the problems he could manage. He made the painful decision to shut off new user sign-ups to the Silk Road, which would help the servers handle the onslaught of visitors, albeit slightly. Next up was figuring out why his money was disappearing with every transaction. This would require rewriting programming language he clearly didn't know how to write in the first place.

For the next few days Ross barely slept, and ate even less. Julia tried to keep him afloat with his favorite peanut butter and jelly sandwiches, but after delivering one to his side, she would come back hours later to see the sandwich sitting untouched next to his laptop.

Through it all, anxiety pecked away at his insides.

After almost a week of these major issues, after the site had gone down and the senators had declared war on the Silk Road and its founder, the reality of what he was doing, and what the consequences were, started to settle in.

"They're looking for me," Ross said to Julia in an almost catatonic and exhausted state one evening.

"No shit they are looking for you!" she responded.

She had seen Ross like this before, when he had been caught growing mushrooms months earlier. A strange look of excitement and fear had shown in his face back then too. Almost as if there were two different people inhabiting Ross's body. One was a timid and sweet boy who truly wanted to help people and make the world a safer place; the other, a recalcitrant rebel who was ready to take on and fight the entire U.S. government. Sweet Ross and Rebel Ross.

"Ross, maybe it's time to stop doing this," Julia said to him after she, too, had realized the potential consequences. "Maybe this is growing too big and too quickly."

But Sweet Ross didn't respond. Instead, Rebel Ross was toiling away trying to figure out the problems with the code that were making his profits on the Silk Road evaporate. Not only was he not going to take Julia's advice to stop working on the site, he was instead going to batten down the hatches so those U.S. senators would never be able to find him.

# Chapter 13
# JULIA TELLS ERICA

C alm washed over Julia as she lay on the floor listening to the orchestra of sounds outside the window. New York's police sirens wailed; the trees rustled; the Bronx elevated subway trains screeched and squealed. As she waited for the weed to kick in, Julia felt relieved that she would be away from Ross for a week.

"Here you go," her friend Erica said as she leaned over and passed the joint back to Julia.

Julia pulled the embers back toward her lips, swallowing the skunklike air into her lungs. She wondered if she should tell Erica the reason for the sudden visit to New York City. Julia hadn't told anyone—not a solitary soul—about the Silk Road, the mushrooms, the senators, and the hackers Ross now employed to help him with his Web site. None of this had ever passed her lips. But lately she had become scared, not only for Ross but also for herself. She didn't know if she was an accomplice in all this. She hadn't written a line of code or profited a penny, but it still terrified her. For some perplexing reason, Ross had continued to share each new secret with her and expected her to keep them—and to be perfectly okay from a moral standpoint.

In the beginning, eight months earlier when Ross had started the Silk Road, she had been fine with these random unknowns, as the site was so small and unimportant. But things had changed since then.

Selling weed, she was fine with. She had never heard of a single recorded instance of someone overdosing from a bong hit. And mushrooms, well, they grew in the ground and they made you happy. But in recent months new products had become available on the site. Crack, cocaine, heroin, variations of highly addictive drugs she had never even heard of that were made in secret labs in Asia. Her doubts grew.

"What if someone overdoses?" she said when crack and heroin surfaced on the Silk Road.

"We have a rating system," he replied resolutely. "So if someone sells bad drugs, they get a bad rating and no one will buy from them again."

"And if they're dead? How are they supposed to give someone a bad rating if they're dead?"

These conversations would go on for hours, just spinning, spinning, spinning, and finding no end. No matter what Julia said, Ross always had an answer, often baked in intellectual analysis or libertarian theory. When the tête-à-tête went round in circles too many times, he would simply end the conversation by saying, "Well, we will just have to disagree on this."

Those disagreements, combined with the attention the site was now getting from the media and government, had turned the lovebirds' once-in-a-while wrangles into a once-a-day war. "You have to quit," Julia would yell. "You're going to end up in jail for the rest of your life, and how am I supposed to get married and have a family with someone who is in jail?" To which Ross would calmly reply, "I can't get caught because I'm protected by Tor and Bitcoin." He would then begin a rehearsed diatribe about his legacy. The site, he proclaimed, would be his greatest contribution to society. He was helping people, keeping them safe from the streets, where drug deals could get one thrown in jail or, worse, hurt or killed. Didn't Julia see that? Didn't she want to be a part of it?

As if they were repeatedly reading from the same script, a verbal brawl would ensue, and then one of them would storm out of the apartment or into another room. A few hours later, love would magnetically draw them back together. They would make up and fall asleep in each other's arms, Julia dreaming of a white picket fence and a couple of giggling children running around in the yard, Ross's reveries of the Silk Road growing so large that one day he would overturn the drug laws and be lauded for the positive impact he had had on society.

The next morning the pugnacious lovers would start all over again.

The site had also started to affect other areas of their relationship. Julia wanted to go out dancing or be taken to a nice restaurant with all the money he was now making from his commissions. And yet Ross was perfectly happy eating peanut butter and jelly sandwiches while tapping out code on his laptop. Days would go by where he wouldn't shower, would barely talk to her, and would just sit in his chair in their bedroom (often naked) on his computer.

Julia had begun worrying so much about the state of their relationship, and Ross's well-being in general, that she had started to have panic attacks on a regular basis. She peered at men in the grocery store and wondered if they were undercover cops who knew that she lived with the man who had started the Silk Road. She cried in the shower. She loved Ross so much, but he appeared to love his Web site more.

Life went on like this for weeks, each day echoing the last, until one evening Ross came home with fervent excitement in his eyes. Enraptured, he told Julia he had to show her something. He opened his laptop, fiddled around for a few seconds, and then spun the computer around for her to see. Over time he had made every effort possible to convince Julia that the hard drugs should be listed on the Silk Road, using his salient argument that the government should have no right to tell you what you could and could not put in your own body and that crime and violence would fall if there were no drug wars. While she didn't necessarily agree with his viewpoints, she understood his reasoning, and it made sense in theory. But there would be no convincing Julia of the merits of what he was about to show her.

"Look," Ross said proudly as he pointed at his laptop screen. "There are guns that just got listed on the site."

Julia stared in disbelief, a feeling of nausea enveloping her. "Ross," she said pleadingly. "This isn't normal."

"Why isn't it normal? It's our constitutional right to have guns, we should be able to have—"

She interrupted him: "Tell me why would someone need to buy guns anonymously."

"That's not my responsibility to ask; it's not up to me to decide why someone does something," he remarked, annoyed that Julia didn't share his excitement. "It's the people's choice."

"Yes, but—" she began, but he cut her off.

"So the government can have guns, but the people can't?" Ross said. (He would echo this on the Silk Road, privately telling his new employees, "I've always been pro gun. It is a power equalizer against tyrannical governments.")

Julia intuitively knew her conscience was right. But even when she offered clever, cogent retorts, Ross would shut the conversation down by simply saying, "Well, we will just have to disagree on this."

For Julia, the guns were an enough-is-enough moment. Light drugs? Absolutely. Hard drugs? Fine. Maybe Ross was right; maybe we all did have the right to put whatever we wanted in our own bodies. How could the government say that we could drink alcohol, which killed ninety thousand Americans a year; or that people could smoke cigarettes, which killed forty thousand people a month in the United States; or even red meat, which caused hundreds of heart attacks a day; and it wasn't okay to smoke weed, which killed no one? But buying illegal guns anonymously? This Julia couldn't agree with. A few weeks later she boarded a plane to New York City.

She figured that fall in the Northeast would help clear her head. Erica greeted her with a big hug. Then they sprawled out on the living room floor and talked. In the distance, through the window, she could see the soft white and blue lights of Yankee Stadium radiating into the night sky. The setting couldn't have been more different from the chaos of the past few months, and as the sounds of the Bronx hummed outside, Julia made a decision. She sat up from the floor and turned to Erica. "I have to tell you something," Julia said.

"What?" Erica replied.

"You have to promise me you will *never* tell anyone," Julia pleaded. "Never! Ross would kill me."

"I swear!" Erica said, now curious about the secret that loomed between them. "I promise."

Julia took one more deep drag of the joint and held the smoke in her lungs for a few seconds. She blew out, watching the cloudy whiteness dissipate into the air, and then she told Erica everything.

# Chapter 14

# WHAT HAVE YOU DONE?!

Tears welled up in Ross's eyes as he frantically ran up the stairs toward Julia's apartment. He was overtaken by fear, mixed with anger, as he swung the door open, barged inside, and started yelling at her. "I can't believe what you've done!" he shrieked, jolting the door closed behind him. "I'm done!"

"What are you talking about?" Julia stammered, looking up from her laptop, shocked by the abrupt intrusion and then even more astonished by the very visible look of terror on Ross's face.

"You betrayed my trust!" Ross screamed as he wiped tears from his eyes. "I can't believe you told someone." Panic grabbed and shook him as he tried to figure out what to do. In his entire life he had never been this angry. Never this afraid.

In that moment Julia knew exactly what had happened, though it would be another few minutes before she knew exactly how it had happened. It dawned on her very quickly that this had to have something to do with Erica. But how did Ross know about it now? And why was he so frightened? Julia played the events of the past few weeks over in her mind as Ross stood in front of her seething.

After Julia had returned from New York City in the early fall, she had decided to break up with Ross, telling him that if he wanted to continue running his site, he would have to do it elsewhere; she wouldn't allow it in her apartment any longer. He had chosen to do just that and rented his own place across town in Austin.

Though resentment had driven them apart, love (and sex) kept them in each other's lives and they continued to date sporadically.

Soon after Ross moved out, Julia had convinced her friend Erica to move from New York City to Austin, renting the spare bedroom in Julia's studio. Everything was moving along just fine until one evening, while partying, Erica had a bad acid trip from drugs purchased on the Silk Road and ended up in the hospital. When she returned, a fight erupted between her and Julia. Ross, who just happened to be there, tried to break up the brawl. This only exacerbated Erica's and Julia's tempers, and the fight grew so raucous that the police were called. Ross, who at first was trying to be helpful, soon lost his patience and pushed Erica out of the apartment. As Erica left in a taxi to the airport to return to New York City, Ross and Julia assumed that was the end of it. *Good riddance, Erica; thanks for the story we'll get to tell our friends tomorrow.*

But the next morning, when Ross went back to his apartment, he opened his beloved laptop, and checked the stats on the Silk Road before navigating to his social media accounts. There, in all its terrifying glory, was a new message from Erica posted on his Facebook wall, publicly, for all to see. "I'm sure the authorities would like to know about Ross Ulbricht's drug website," she had written, like a giant neon billboard on the Internet.

The earth could have swallowed Ross whole. He began crying. He quickly deleted the message. Hands quivering, heart thumping, he picked up the phone and called Erica.

"Please, I am so sorry," Ross stammered on the phone, tears streaming down his face. "Please promise me you will never tell anyone about the site." Hearing Ross cry, sounding like he was going to kill himself, Erica assured him that she wouldn't say anything to anyone and hung up.

But Ross's mind swirled in a hurricane of thoughts. Who else knew? *Fudge!*

There was only one person who could answer these questions. Ross got into his truck, floored it to Julia's house, and then stormed up the stairs.

"You betrayed my trust!" he yelled. "Who else did you tell?"

"No one, I swear," Julia pleaded as rivulets of tears rolled down her cheeks. "I can't believe I told her. I'm so, so sorry. It was so stupid. It just came out of my mouth, I didn't mean to—"

Ross grew angry. "You're a liar. I can't trust you."

Hearing his accusations, Julia became defiant. "You left me alone in all of this. You told me all of this stuff and didn't think about the risk to me."

"This is a huge breach to my security," Ross replied, "because someone actually knows me and knows my face and knows I made the site."

Ross was remorseless and stern. Julia had broken his trust, and to Ross, that was much worse than any situation he had ever placed her in. Having simply uttered his name to someone else, having shared his most guarded secret in the world, she was done. Julia looked into his eyes, sensing that her explanation had only pissed him off more.

"Maybe this is a sign that you shouldn't even be doing this site anyway," Julia whimpered as she fell to the floor in tears, pleading for his forgiveness.

"No, it's . . . not," Ross stammered as he tried to calculate what he was going to do. "It means I'm going to have to hide. I'm going to have to leave Austin. All because of you."

"I'm sorry, I'm—" Julia said, sobbing. But it was too late.

"This is over," Ross said. He turned and walked out of the studio, the door slamming shut behind him.

# Chapter 15

# JARED AND THE FIFTY-TON *FLAMINGO*

Chicago's Federal Plaza appeared dark and morose against the late-November sky—except for two specks of color that punctured the gloominess. There was the red-white-and-blue American flag, rattling voraciously in the wind. And the massive bright red sculpture, called the *Flamingo,* that stood motionless in the center of the plaza's black pavement.

That fifty-ton *Flamingo,* with its abstract steel arches, was the first thing many people saw as they exited the L train onto the plaza, with most wandering past or below it as they headed into one of the adjacent federal buildings, including the post office, the courthouse, or the most intimidating of all, the thirty-story black tower at 219 South Dearborn Street known as the Dirksen Federal Building.

On a late-November morning in 2011, two men with the last name Der-Yeghiayan were inside the Dirksen Federal Building. On the nineteenth floor, fifty-nine-year-old Samuel Der-Yeghiayan adjusted his robes and court documents as he prepared for the cases he would hear later that day as a U.S. federal judge. Sixteen floors below Samuel's chambers his thirty-one-year-old son, Jared, was walking through the halls of the U.S. Attorney's Office, his giant backpack over his shoulder, which was bulging with laptops, a Rubik's Cube, and folders with pictures of evidence inside. In his hands he carried a large white mail-room tub filled with thirty or so envelopes of all shapes and sizes.

Young Jared Der-Yeghiayan's nerves were frayed as he made his way toward what would be the most important meeting of his career. It wasn't lost on him that if he screwed this up, the story of his fuckup would make its way up all those flights of stairs to his father's office.

Jared had traded the baggy street clothes he wore at O'Hare for an oversize black suit and a crisp white shirt. His group supervisor from HSI followed behind at a leisurely pace. The two men arrived at the office of the assistant U.S. attorney for narcotics, who oversaw all prosecutions of drug-related cases in the state of Illinois.

After a few introductions Jared dropped the mail tub in his hands onto the office floor with a thud. The attorney looked down at the container, then back at Jared, noticeably confused. This wasn't exactly what the attorney had expected to see when he agreed to this meeting about drug smuggling through the Internet. A picture of a couple of big bricks of heroin? Sure. Some salty white kilos of cocaine? Yeah. Pounds of marijuana? You betcha. But a box of empty envelopes in a mail carton? Not so much. Still, the attorney sat back to see what this was all about.

Jared began explaining what the Silk Road was and how it worked, and as he did, he placed envelopes from the mail tub on the table one by one, as if he were dealing a deck of cards at a casino. "This one," Jared said as he pointed to one of the envelopes, "had LSD inside." He reached down and grabbed another package. "This one had amphetamines." And then another. "This one had cocaine." "Ketamine." "Heroin." He then pulled a white square envelope with a Chicago address from the tub. "And this," he said as he rummaged in his backpack for the Silk Road case file, laying a picture on the desk of what appeared to be a tiny pink pill, "had this hit of MDMA inside."

Since June, when Jared had discovered that first pill of ecstasy in the envelope from the Netherlands, he had been trying to figure out how to persuade his supervisor, and now the U.S. Attorney's Office, to let him build a case against the Silk Road Web site.

Everything over the past few months had been leading up to this very moment.

After his supervisor at HSI had given him the go-ahead to start investigating the site as a side project, Jared had obsessively started collecting every smidgen of evidence coming through Chicago O'Hare. Each night he would drive his ancient government-issued car (which other agents had nicknamed the Pervert Car because it looked like it belonged to a child molester) to the mail center at the airport where he would collect envelopes of drugs that had been plucked from the scrubs earlier that day.

"I need you to seize and store every single envelope," Jared had said to Mike, the customs officer who found the first pink pill.

"What do you want it for?" Mike had asked, perplexed by the request. "No one ever wants these small packages of drugs."

"I'm working on something," Jared told Mike. "Just keep collecting them, bagging them as evidence, and I'll keep getting them from you."

After the *Gawker* article had published, the number of seizures had risen exponentially. In turn, Jared collected more envelopes, and his office at HSI had started to resemble a mail facility itself. There were now more than a hundred envelopes sitting neatly in three mail buckets on the floor behind his desk, a selection of which he was now presenting to the assistant U.S. attorney.

"It can't be that easy," the attorney said, dubious of the words coming out of Jared's mouth and the images on his laptop. Even if it was "that easy," these were such small amounts of drugs, the attorney wasn't sure that this was the biggest drug-related issue his office should be dealing with.

"This isn't about the drugs," Jared said ardently. "This isn't about that one little pill." He had been practicing this speech for weeks, and he took a deep breath and continued. "This is about the site overall and what it stands for. It's about how the people on this site are using our Internet—built by the United States government—to run an anonymous Web browser—also built by the United States government—and the United States postal system—to circumvent the laws of our country. And there is nothing we can do to stop them."

The office was silent as the words sank in.

"This is just the beginning," Jared continued. "It's drugs now, but this could be used for terrorism next; imagine a worst-case scenario, where a group like al Qaeda uses the site, or the exact same setup, to coordinate attacks against America—all with tools built by the United States." His point was simple. The Silk Road wasn't just a digital drug cartel. It was a highly lucrative start-up with a lot of optionality. Amazon had begun as a virtual bookstore before becoming our everything supermarket. And Google, which had started as a search engine, was trying to build cars that could drive themselves. The issue, Jared reiterated, was not what the Silk Road was, but what it could be. The site was clearly run by some sort of genius who seemed to understand technology and politics as much as he understood his audience. And whoever that prodigy was, he or she had to be stopped before this site became a movement and ultimately unstoppable.

As Jared spoke, the totality of what he was saying hit the attorney with utmost fear. Jared was there warning that, in the same way the hijackers who flew planes into the World Trade Center did so using American-owned jets, the people behind the Silk Road could destroy the very fabric of the United States using tools built by America. The implications were terrifying.

The attorney interrupted Jared midsentence. "Yes," he said as he looked at the envelopes on his table and then up at Jared. "Yes, we'll assign someone to your case."

# Chapter 16

# FROM AUSTIN
# TO AUSTRALIA

I'm selling my truck," Ross told all his friends on Facebook. "Make me an offer!"

Fall had blanketed over Austin, with 2011 nearing its end, and Ross had only two weeks to get his life packed into boxes and sell everything else before he left town.

*Fudging Erica.* If she hadn't posted that tormenting message on Facebook about Ross being a drug lord or kingpin or whatever, he wouldn't be in such a rush to leave the country. Weeks before the chaos erupted he had been thinking of going to see his sister, Cally, in Australia for a while, to get some space from Julia and his Texan friends and family, but now the trip was a must, and it was on fast-forward.

Ross was pretty sure he had deleted Erica's terrifying post in time, but if he had not, and someone had actually seen it, he would find himself in more trouble than he was capable of dealing with. He also had no way of knowing if Erica's Facebook outburst was the last he would hear from her. If she truly wanted to be vindictive, she could easily go one step further and tell the FBI or DEA, or even those senators who had painted a bull's-eye on the Silk Road months earlier.

One thing was certain: Ross didn't want to take any chances. He scrambled, getting his life in order to make a quick and easy break from Austin to Australia.

The truck sold quickly. His personal belongings were handed down or given away. He stuffed other things in boxes and hid them under his bed at his parents' house, next to the box of Dungeons & Dragons miniatures he had painted as a child. He packed the few belongings he needed day to day, including his gray V-neck T-shirt, his single pair of jeans, and, most important of all, his laptop.

Paranoia had started consuming his thoughts, leaving Ross on edge about those around him. Was the DEA or the FBI hunting for him? Was he a cop? Was she? What did everyone know? But the most stressful thoughts centered around those whom he had told about the Silk Road.

It wasn't that Ross had been stupid or naive in telling them about the site. Rather, back then, when he first shared his secret, Ross could never have predicted that the Silk Road would grow as big as it had. In his mind on opening day, he had imagined a few dozen people shopping in his online marketplace. That had quickly turned into thousands. Now, with the media, the senators, and who knew how many people in law enforcement looking for him, he needed to backtrack.

A few days before he left for Australia, his bags packed, his passport and laptop ready to go, Ross went over to his friend Richard Bates's house and knocked on his door. Richard had all but stopped helping Ross with the programming problems on the Silk Road, fearing the site was growing too big and terrified by the attention it was receiving in the press. But he was still the only person besides Julia who knew the true identity of the site's creator. Ross had to fix that before anyone else found out.

It was early evening on November 11, 2011, and for weeks nerdy Richard had been planning a party to celebrate the mathematical anomaly of 11/11/11, when the day, the month, and the year all lined up to create a string of elevens. Ross showed up before the festivities began, knocking on Richard's door with a somewhat panicked rattle.

"I need to talk to you about something," Ross declared. They both wandered inside Richard's stark white, almost medically clean apartment, marred only by a few decorations for that night's festivities. "Have you told anybody about—you know—about my involvement in the Silk Road?"

Richard spoke in his usual timid whisper, explaining nervously that he had almost told someone but then hadn't, so in short, no. No one else knew.

Ross expanded on his question, telling Richard that someone had posted a message on Facebook about Ross running a drug Web site that the authorities would surely like to know about.

Hearing this, Richard felt that familiar wave of fear shroud him. Surely he was an accomplice to Ross, having helped him build the site and knowing who ran it. Frail Richard could go to jail for the rest of his life, as could Ross.

And if there was one thing Richard was definitely not built for, it was life behind bars. "You've got to shut the site down," Richard pleaded. "This is not worth going to prison over."

Ross had anticipated this response. "I can't shut the site down," he replied.

"Why?"

"Because," Ross solemnly said to his friend, "I gave the site to someone else."

# PART II

# Chapter 17

# CARL FORCE'S TOMORROW

Most people go through life thinking that tomorrow they're going to do something great. Tomorrow will be the day that they wake up and discover what they were put on this earth to do. But then tomorrow comes—and goes. As does the next day. Before long, they realize that there aren't that many tomorrows left.

Carl Force knew this feeling well. He never thought he'd end up this way, sitting in a mauve-colored cubicle in a nondescript skyscraper in downtown Baltimore, staring at his computer until the moment he could collect his things and leave.

Another day, another tomorrow.

Carl was what's known in law enforcement as a "solar agent," a guy who works only when it's light outside. (He often referred to himself this way, half joking and half proud of the title.) When the clock struck three, Carl would slip out of the office and drive back across Baltimore to his wife and kids in his government-issued Chevy Impala.

To anyone who walked by his cubicle, Carl looked like the kind of person he was trying to scrub off the streets: a drug dealer. He almost always wore a black beanie over his bald head. His sunken dark eyes and a peppery beard of stubble hid the wrinkles in his stout face. And then there were the tattoos covering his body, including the black Celtic tribal pattern that swerved across his back and down his arms.

Like most of the old-timers at the Drug Enforcement Administration, Carl was in his midforties and jaded. Sure, he was a narcotics cop, but his job was as mundane as any other corporate office worker's. He spent most of his days staring at his desktop computer, sipping stale coffee from one of the promotional mugs he had picked up at DEA conventions over the years. Sometimes he listened to Hope 89.1, a local Christian radio station that would whisper the Lord's Prayer into his ear, promising that if Carl followed the ways of the Bible and did the right thing, he would be granted the life he had always wanted.

Life hadn't always been this way. Thirteen years earlier, in late 1999, when he joined the administration, he ate, slept, and shit the DEA. In those early days he absolutely loved the thrill of a bust. Waking at 4:00 a.m., slipping on his bulletproof vest, checking the chamber of his gun, and kicking in a door or two, yelling at some big-time dealers or low-level meth heads to "freeze!" and "get the fuck on the floor!"

It was as exciting a job as anyone could wish for. But over time the early mornings started to strain. The door kicks were less exciting. When one dealer went to jail, another filled his seat on the street.

The metamorphosis from rash young newbie to jaded old-timer had happened slowly. At first Carl couldn't find good cases on his own. Then he had trouble making busts. There was also the high pressure of undercover work, where you have to catch someone or they'll catch you. His downward trajectory was compounded by the fact that he'd secretly developed his own substance abuse problem. Finally, all the strain had been too much, and Carl was eventually arrested for a DUI while he was an agent, which led to a mental breakdown four years later. He almost lost it all—the family, the job, the cat. But the Lord had stepped in, and Carl had been offered amnesty with this desk job as a solar agent. Since then there hadn't been many opportunities arriving at his cubicle.

But on a late-January day in 2012, that was about to change.

He was sitting at his desk waiting for another day to pass when his supervisor, Nick, yelled for Carl to come into his office. These moments came often: a shriek from Nick and some sort of order to take on cases that most agents thought were ridiculous. This included the regular request to go and do "jump-outs," the name given to the act of driving around Baltimore, pulling up to a street corner, jumping out of the car, and grabbing low-level dealers. Most agents thought this was a pathetic way of trying to beat the drug problem, as opposed to going after the big bosses, where they believed they could actually have an impact.

Still, when Nick called, you went. Nick's office was dark, as usual. While Carl's supervisor was lucky enough to have a window with a paltry view of frozen and barren Baltimore, he always kept the blinds drawn, blocking out even the tiniest pinprick of light. Adding to the darkness, Nick had pinned posters of Iron Maiden and Metallica all over his office walls.

"So," Nick said to Carl, "I just got a call about the Silk Road Web site."

Carl perked up. He had heard about this strange Web site a month earlier at a law enforcement meeting when an investigator with the U.S. Postal Service had given a brief presentation on it. There was a new phenomenon, the postal inspector had said, that was starting to infect mail ports all across the United States, and lots of people were sending small amounts of drugs through the system. The inspector had explained that the connection point for these dealers and buyers was called "the Silk Road."

Later, intrigued by what the postal inspector had said, Carl searched online and read a few articles, including Adrian Chen's piece on *Gawker*. He then thought about the implications, which were momentous. You couldn't do jump-outs online, he reasoned. But given that Carl had no knowledge of computer forensics, it wasn't a case he would have even thought of being assigned to. That was, until Nick called Carl into his office and asked if he wanted to assist a group of HSI agents in Baltimore. "They've picked up an informant who says he can lead them to the owner of the site," Nick told Carl.

When Carl asked why he was being asked to join the case, Nick explained: The HSI group in Baltimore was not a drug team and usually tracked counterfeit stuff or, as Nick put it, "fake Louis Vuitton bags and shit like that." So if the Baltimore group wanted to go after drugs, they needed a DEA agent on the team. "You want in?" Nick asked.

Carl thought about it for a moment. He was at the point in his career where he could have easily said, "No, not interested," walked out of Nick's dark office, and continued living life as a solar agent, coaching his son's football games, going to church with his wife and kids on weekends, and hopefully realizing one day that *his* tomorrow was his family. Or he could get involved in this investigation and maybe—just maybe—make a name for himself at the DEA.

"Sure," Carl said to Nick. He would take on the case.

Carl walked out of his supervisor's office unaware that with the single word—"sure"—he was about to enter an underground world so dark and full of avarice that it would drag him in headfirst, and that as a result of the temptations of the Silk Road, Carl Force was going to lose everything that mattered to him.

# Chapter 18

# VARIETY JONES AND THE SERPENT

Ross had been in Australia for only a few weeks when he woke up from a strange dream. In his sleep he found himself face-to-face with a giant hundred-foot-long centipede with dark eyes and massive, twiddling legs. Hovering in the background was a looming snake, larger and more sinister than the centipede, slithering around in the darkness.

When he awoke the next morning, Ross didn't know what the dream meant or why he wasn't afraid of these sinister creatures. To him they didn't seem evil at all. Or maybe they were, and he simply wasn't able to see their true nature. But as he set about his day, he couldn't get those slithering creatures out of his mind, eventually sharing a story on Facebook about the dream, curious what it might mean.

Maybe it was just the daunting reality of the past few months breaking through his subconscious. Back in Texas, the twin pressures of maintaining the Silk Road and keeping his involvement a secret had worn him thin. At particularly fraught moments he even wondered if he should forfeit his business, just give it up. But ever since he had moved to Sydney to be closer to his sister, life had gotten so much better. His mounting anxiety in Texas was giving way to a laconic calmness Down Under. Now Ross spent his days surfing at the golden beaches, drinking beer with his new pals at tiki bars, successfully flirting with girls, and, in between these social gatherings, working on the Silk Road.

But even the pleasures of Bondi Beach, where he was staying, couldn't entirely eradicate the fears that came with running a start-up that trafficked in the multinational drug trade. In particular Ross still could not entirely shake the fact that, other than Erica, whose words he could always deny as hearsay, two real people—Julia and his old friend Richard—definitively knew that he had created the Silk Road.

Sure, he had cobbled together a story for Richard, explaining that he had given the site away to someone else. But the Julia problem remained. And no matter what fabrication he could possibly come up with, both would always know he had fathered the site. Ross, though a genius at many things, was clueless when it came to untangling this particular mess.

Luckily, someone was about to become a staple in his life who knew exactly how to fix these issues, and many other formidable challenges that impeded the Silk Road's progress.

Ross interacted with dozens of different people on the Silk Road each day, including vendors, customers, and a couple of new libertarian part-time employees who helped with the site's various programming problems. They all went by pseudonyms to hide who they really were, names like SameSameButDifferent, NomadBloodbath, and SumYunGai. (Ross's own nickname was simply Silk Road or Admin.) But one of the people Ross had recently started talking to on the site, a man who operated under the nom de plume Variety Jones, seemed almost immediately to be different from everyone else.

He sold weed seeds, but he wasn't just any weed seed dealer. Variety Jones was a sommelier, someone capable of telling you a seed's variety—its viticulture—along with the strain, just by looking at a picture of it. And unlike the hordes of impatient and pushy drug dealers on the Silk Road, Variety Jones, or "VJ" as he was known in the forums, was guileful and intelligent. He (assuming he really was a "he") knew everything about everyone, on the site and off—even the creator of the site.

Just two days after the menacing serpent-and-centipede dream, Ross and VJ started chatting on TorChat, a messaging platform that promised privacy for those using it. "I want to talk to you about security stuff," Variety Jones wrote in one of their earliest correspondences. "Lots of security stuff."

Ross was eager to hear, now fully aware that he was no longer just being targeted by the U.S. government but was very likely being hunted by authorities in dozens of countries. Given that real money was now flowing into the site too, with Ross pulling in tens of thousands of dollars a week in revenue for the sale of drugs and guns, there would surely be more authorities hunting him soon. The only way to hide from the cops was to build better security into the site. Ross was a gifted coder, sure, with a quixotic vision of the future, but he knew better than anyone that he was out of his depth when it came to fixing the site's vulnerabilities.

Yet the more he chatted with Variety Jones, the more Ross realized he was interacting with a very able complement—someone whose strength seemed to be the very area in which Ross was weakest. Perhaps most important, Jones quickly indicated that he could be the perfect lieutenant—a proverbial bad cop to a kinder boss. "There isn't anyone who knows me even a little bit that would ever dream of crossing me," VJ warned Ross. "If they did dream of it, [they] would wake up and call to apologize."

Variety Jones said that he was forty-five years old and from Canada but now lived in England, and it was apparent by his answers to Ross's programming questions that he knew what he was doing. He told Ross that a few months earlier, shortly after the *Gawker* article had been published, VJ and an associate had found a secret back door into the Silk Road servers. Late one night, like a couple of burglars breaking into someone's home just to look around, VJ had rummaged through the site's files to make sure it wasn't being run by law enforcement. (Hearing this obviously scared the shit out of Ross. Who else might have been sniffing around in there?)

When VJ believed that the mastermind behind the Silk Road was legitimately trying to end the war on drugs and wasn't an undercover DEA agent trying to arrest poor unsuspecting citizens, Variety Jones wanted to help the cause (after all, if the site grew, VJ could make more money by selling more drugs). And here he was. Advice at the ready.

But first VJ wanted to ensure that the creator of the site knew what was at stake here. "Not to be a downer or anything," he wrote to Ross, but "understand that what we are doing falls under U.S. Drug Kingpin laws, which provides a maximum penalty of death upon conviction . . . the mandatory minimum is life."

Ross knew this better than anyone. But he felt like what he was doing was truly going to change the world and free people. Given that, life in prison, or taking his last breath in an electric chair, was not enough to deter him. "Balls to the wall and all in my friend," Ross replied, vociferating how unafraid he was of those consequences.

After this was clear, their collaboration moved to the next phase. VJ started to give Ross pep talks.

"Just always remember Life magazine," VJ proffered. "So successful, they had to shut it down." According to VJ, the cost to print the luscious postwar photo magazine exceeded the newsstand price, so the more people who purchased *Life*, the less money it made. Until one day it had grown so much that it "went bankrupt with success." This, he warned, could happen to the Silk Road if its founder wasn't careful about the server costs and hiring the right employees as it grew.

Ross was rapt as he read the words on his screen. Until this moment he had felt so alone running the site, with no one to talk to about the questions rattling around in his head. Now here was a man who seemed to have answers to questions Ross had never uttered aloud to anyone. "Tell me more," he replied to VJ.

Before long he started seeking out all kinds of advice from VJ. Ross would write questions for his new friend while he sat in his apartment in Sydney or in a nearby coffee shop, slurping up everything Variety Jones had to offer. They went from speaking every few days to every few hours to— eventually—every few minutes. Each tête-à-tête was an instructive lesson for Ross, whether he was learning how to set up a Bitcoin config file on the server, managing warring factions of dealers on the site, or understanding how he was perceived by the proletariat who used the Silk Road.

At its core, though, the relationship was personal. VJ's greatest value was as an executive coach of sorts—someone who could mentor the young founder through problems germane to any start-up, like Bill Campbell, who had helped the creators of Twitter and Google, or Marc Andreessen, who offered advice to Mark Zuckerberg at Facebook.

"What are my strengths?" Ross asked VJ one afternoon, hoping that his new confidant could hold up a mirror for Ross to see himself, a view that Ross, in his secret solitude, was incapable of discerning on his own.

"You play your cards close," VJ replied. "You really do get that it's gone from fun and games to a very serious life or death lifestyle you've created." He then listed a handful of attributes of the leader of the Silk Road, including that he was obviously well educated and that many on the site saw him as "the Steve Jobs" of the online drug world.

"Awesome," Ross replied. Then he followed with a more vulnerable question: "What are my weaknesses?"

Variety Jones didn't skip a beat. "Your inability to discern between a garter snake and a copperhead," he wrote, "and the gaping holes in your knowledge of security."

"Wait," Ross interrupted, "what's the snake metaphor?"

"Recognizing something as dangerous, when you think it's harmless."

It was a pointed comment, one that left Ross searching for more answers. In that pregnant moment, as Ross heard the waves on Bondi Beach and felt the soft air of Australia, a pressing question was left unspoken. Could Variety Jones, this unlimited dispenser of wisdom, this ostensible genius in the realm of cybersecurity, be offering Ross a hint that maybe this new friend wasn't here just to help but had a larger plan in the works? If VJ was trying to offer a warning, Ross was too caught up in the conversation to see it, and he didn't stop to question which of these two snakes Variety Jones might be. The harmless garter or a hundred-foot venomous demon.

"Tell me more," Ross wrote instead. "Tell me more."

# Chapter 19

# JARED GOES SHOPPING

It was still dark outside when Jared opened his eyes and looked through the open window in the living room. It took him a few groggy seconds to realize that he had fallen asleep on the couch, once again, still fully clothed with the television flickering. He'd come home from work at midnight and probably dozed off around 2:00 a.m. watching his favorite program, *Antiques Roadshow*. Given that it was now almost 6:00 a.m., he had maybe—3:00, 4:00, 5:00 . . .—pulled off four whole hours of sleep. For Jared that seemed like something of a record.

Most nights he was kept up by his idée fixe: the Silk Road, a case that Jared was trying to solve alone, but that was mired in soupy bureaucratic minutiae and nonstarters. Every direction he had been turning to was tangled in red tape. Bosses, bosses of bosses, and people he didn't even know existed in government were starting to ask what this young newbie agent was doing and why he was doing it. Should an HSI agent really be going after a Web site that appeared to be selling a few bags of drugs? Weren't there more important things that kid should be working on? Who the fuck did he think he was?

The case had been such a burden, with all the work adding a heavy strain to Jared's marriage, and his wife, Kim, growing understandably frustrated that Jared spent less time in the house than he spent out of it. On top of that, all the hours were not amounting to much. He had no leads and no idea how to tackle a Web site that was a den of anonymity.

Thankfully for Jared, that was about to change.

For weeks he had been working on his plan of attack. He knew he couldn't find the leader of the site—or leaders, perhaps, he acknowledged—as they were securely cloaked by the Tor browser online. But he also knew how any crime network worked, and that if you start at the bottom, you will eventually make your way to the top. The bottom for Jared meant buying drugs. Lots of drugs.

He hadn't anticipated how difficult it would be to buy narcotics online. Not because it was hard to procure heroin or crack from the Silk Road (it was actually shockingly easy) but rather because no one in the Department of Homeland Security had ever before embarked upon an online drug-shopping spree. Unlike seizing some contraband at a port or orchestrating a controlled delivery in the street to arrest someone, online drugs were a true Wild West with no existing protocols. It took several layers of approval, numerous meetings, and copious paperwork before Jared was finally allowed to commence his binge-shopping on the Amazon of drugs.

Then there was the challenge of buying the Bitcoins. He was allocated $1,001 for his shopping excursion. So he took the cash, deposited it in a bank, then went to a Bitcoin exchange Web site where he could swap the dollars for Bitcoins. It wasn't as easy as picking up drugs with cash on the street or finding a used bicycle on Craigslist, but it was still surprisingly painless considering what he was buying.

During his first expedition to the Silk Road, Jared had three goals. The first was to trace drugs back to their dealers. The second was to match listings on the Web site to actual physical drugs and packaging, enabling him to build a profile of what mail from the Silk Road looked like, as he had done with the khat back at Customs and Border Protection. And finally, Jared wanted to perform a small but important test.

He knew that the postal workers at ports across the United States were finding drugs in the mail system, but—and this was a big "but"—no one had any idea what percentage of drugs were not being found; how many pills and bags of powder were just swimming past officials. As far as Jared knew, the Silk Road could be a site peddling a few thousand dollars a year of narcotics, or it could be vending tens of millions of dollars in illegal contraband a month. Nobody knew which it was. But Jared had a hunch he could figure it out.

First Jared filled his shopping cart on the Silk Road, picking up a few pills of ecstasy, some opium "tea," some synthetic weed, and a miscellany of stimulants from more than half a dozen countries around the world. In all he purchased from eighteen different dealers on the site and directed them to send his narcotics to a secret PO box at O'Hare.

Besides Mike, who had discovered that first luminous pink pill, and a few higher-ups at HSI, no one knew anything about his orders—or that they would be arriving today, on a mid-January morning in 2012.

As Jared sat up from the couch and rubbed his weary eyes, a plane was flying through the air 35,000 feet above him, getting ready to touch down at Chicago O'Hare International Airport with a few envelopes on board, destined for that secret PO box. Despite his exhaustion, Jared was invigorated. This was exactly the meaningful work he craved. For years, indeed, he had felt like that pink pill: a tiny droplet in a giant ocean. Now he was afforded the chance to have an impact. Maybe even make a name for himself.

He rolled off the couch and sluggishly wandered upstairs to help his wife get their son, Tyrus, ready for day care. There were kisses good-bye, a couple of giggles from Tyrus. Then it was out to the Pervert Car to work.

His day began like any other, at HSI as he worked on other cases, then by nightfall it was back to the airport to look for drugs. As evening came, so did the cold. Jared felt it as he walked up to the colossal mail center at the edge of the airport, trudging across the frozen ground toward the back door of the mail unit and stepping inside the land of halogen lights.

Mike was waiting for him in the seizure room, gleeful. He had a surprise for Jared: a couple of four-by-eight white envelopes from the same dealer with Jared's PO box address on the front. "I found your drugs!" Mike said proudly.

But that would be the only package Mike would find that day, or any other. Of the eighteen orders that Jared had placed on the Silk Road, one was lost en route, and the other sixteen arrived in his PO box unnoticed by anyone in the federal government. It didn't bode well for the new war on drugs.

That evening Jared, Mike, and another mail-room worker grabbed all of the drugs, slipped on protective blue rubber gloves, and splayed everything out on the conference room table at the mail center, taking pictures, tagging what they had found, and marking every mundane detail as evidence.

By midnight Jared would begin his hour-long drive home, and as he made it back to the couch and *Antiques Roadshow,* his mind was filled with a single thought: who were the leaders of the Silk Road, and what could Jared do to capture them?

# Chapter 20

# THE DREAD
# PIRATE ROBERTS

F ireworks exploded in front of Ross from every direction, and with
them came the ferocious sounds from above. *Boom! Boom! Boom!*
Reds and greens and pinks reflected across the lake. He watched in
awe as he brushed up against his new friend Laura and her sister to stay
warm. He had landed in Vietnam a couple of days earlier, after spending the
night on a bench in Singapore's airport—an accommodation more befitting
the old *Amazing Race* Ross than the millionaire he was now on his way to
becoming. The Silk Road, which he had started only a year earlier, had just
crossed a line of $500,000 a month in drug sales, which would subsequently
turn into hundreds of thousands of dollars in commissions that flowed right
into Ross's pocket. Still, to Ross money wasn't something that was meant to
be spent on ostentatious things, so when he landed in Hanoi, the American
kingpin settled into his hostel and was elated to find he made it just in time
to celebrate the Lunar New Year and see the divine fireworks show.

The Lunar New Year was the perfect revelatory moment for Ross. It was
a signal of a new beginning. A time, as Ross had read, when it was okay to
forget about the troubles of the past year and to hope for a better year to
come. More important, this cultural celebration was a reinvention of sorts,
which was exactly what Ross had been through over the past week.

A few days earlier he had been working on the Silk Road when his new
confidant and friend, Variety Jones, had messaged him with a bizarre question. "Have you even seen The Princess Bride?" VJ asked.

It was a completely random query, even for Variety Jones. And even
more bizarre given that a few minutes earlier Ross had been talking to
VJ about coding problems and drug sales. The movie he had asked about,

*The Princess Bride,* was a cult dark comedy from the mideighties about a farmhand who becomes a pirate and has to save Princess Buttercup from a fire swamp.

A very random question from VJ, indeed. But often the conversations between the two men would veer in any number of directions.

Over the past few weeks they had chatted for several hours a day about a medley of different topics. Since they had become friends, there was barely an hour that went by without Ross and Variety Jones checking in with each other.

They had become so close that most evenings ended with some digital pillow talk. ("Alright, off to sleep. See you in a few," Ross would write. "You make sure you get some sleep," VJ would reply.) Most mornings began with another aloha to see how the other was doing. ("Hey, good morning," one would say. "Howdy, rowdy," the other would reply.) During the rest of their waking hours, they would banter about politics, the war on drugs, porn, and books, and laugh at each other's jokes. VJ was always able to make Ross chortle. "My mailman is a drug dealer," VJ wrote when a package arrived. "He just doesn't know it."

The bond between Variety Jones and Ross had blossomed so much that in recent weeks the longest period of time that had passed without them chatting was a two-and-a-half-day period over New Year's Eve. As Ross rang in January 1 watching a fireworks show in Australia and fixing someone's elbow after a drunken incident, Variety Jones was in London, fast asleep after dropping a couple of tabs of ecstasy, drinking two bottles of champagne, and passing out thirty minutes before the ball dropped. Their bond had grown so strong that Ross had even greeted VJ when he returned to work after the holiday by saying, "I missed you :)."

VJ was likable and funny and witty, but more important, he was someone whom Ross could really trust in a world where you couldn't trust anyone. For the first time since he'd started the Silk Road, Ross Ulbricht had a best friend. Variety Jones, of course, was also making money from the friendship. Ross paid him for his services, sometimes as much as $60,000 at a time, which covered travel expenses and subordinate programmers who worked for VJ.

It was the perfect time for such a connection to blossom, as the stresses of running the site were only growing more intense. When it had begun, the site offered a few magic mushrooms and some weed. Now it was home to almost every narcotic imaginable, some of which were being sold in very large quantities. People were also hawking lots of different guns; you could buy Uzis, Beretta handguns, AR-15 assault rifles, endless rounds of ammunition, and silencers. All of this brought more press, with the media taunting the government, noting that it still hadn't shut down the site. EIGHT MONTHS AFTER SEN. CHUCK SCHUMER BLASTED BITCOIN, SILK ROAD IS STILL BOOMING, read one headline.

The pressure this put on Ross was monumental. But his new best friend had a plan. A plan that was somehow rooted in a discussion about the movie *The Princess Bride*.

Ross replied to VJ's query about the film with a sort-of yes: like many kids of his generation, his parents owned a copy of the movie on VHS.

"So," Variety Jones wrote, "you know the history of the Dread Pirate Roberts?"

Ross couldn't quite recall, but he began typing what he remembered about the movie and the name of the main character. When he was lost, Variety Jones finished the summary for him: something about a guy called Westley, who took on the name of the Dread Pirate Roberts from someone else . . . and over the years, a new person would take on that name, and the old one would retire. So no one knew who the original Dread Pirate Roberts really was.

"Yep," Ross replied. That was it. That was the movie.

And then here it was. "You need to change your name from Admin, to Dread Pirate Roberts," VJ wrote.

The words "Dread Pirate Roberts" hung on the screen as if they were suspended in some sort of alternate reality.

Dread. Pirate. Roberts.

What a brilliant idea. Ross loved it. *Ooooh, that's good. That's really good.* The moniker "the Dread Pirate Roberts," who was technically a pirate, also went along perfectly with Ross's "captain" analogy, which he had used on the site's forums before.

VJ noted that, most important, changing his name to Dread Pirate Roberts would allow Ross to erase his old trail from the past, to maintain that he really had given up the Silk Road. It was the perfect alibi: saying he had retired and passed ownership, and the name of the site's leader, along to someone else. "Start the legend now," Variety Jones pressed.

Variety Jones had no idea how seriously Ross would take his suggestion, though he assumed Ross would be enthusiastic. Ross had already told VJ that two people knew about his connection to the Silk Road after Jones had wondered who, if anyone, might know. "IRL," VJ had asked back in December (Web slang for "in real life"), "is there anyone with a clue at all" that you—whoever you are—started the Silk Road? "Girlfriend, boyfriend, bunny you talk to, online buddys who you've known for years? Gramma, priest, rabbi, stripper?"

"Unfortunately yes," Ross had replied. "There are two [people], but they think I sold the site and got out." Ross paused before going on to explain that he had told these two people a couple of months earlier that he had sold the site and given it away to someone else. "One [person] I'll prob never speak to again, and the other I'll drift away from." He added: "Never making the mistake of telling someone again."

Now, as the Lunar New Year approached, it was the perfect time for Ross to reinvent who he was. To forget about the troubles of the past year and to hope for a better year to come. And his new best friend, Variety Jones, had come up with a brilliant, astounding, amazing idea to solve not only the Julia Problem but also the Richard Problem, the Erica Problem, and any other problem that could arise from people who found out he had created the site.

Sure, if he was ever caught, Ross could hypothetically admit that sadly, yes, he had been involved in the early days of the Silk Road, but the site had just become too stressful. And if someone asked, "What did you do with the site after you stopped working on it?" Ross could respond that he "gave it away to someone else." And if they asked, "To who?" he could simply say, "I don't know who it was. All I know is that he called himself the Dread Pirate Roberts."

# Chapter 21

# CARL FORCE IS BORN AGAIN

The two-story white Colonial home on the outskirts of Baltimore looked idyllic. In the front, a blissful stone walkway swerved past two giant oak trees. The back of the home overlooked a serpentine brook, where foxes and deer ran through the bramble and past the fragrant crab apple trees.

This scene, a utopia, had been enough to make Carl Force and his wife fall in love with the home—the perfect place to raise their kids and maybe one day retire.

Yet from the day Carl had signed the paperwork with the bank, the home had been nothing short of a nightmare, plagued with every problem imaginable, including electrical issues, leaks, and the painful discovery that most of the walls had no insulation. A house built of paper that had sapped the family's savings account of almost all its worth. "The Lemon," as Carl called it, was just one more box of stress to pile on top of all the other stresses. Carl often found himself lying awake at night, staring up into the dark, the silence of suburbia screaming in the background, as he thought about his past, his future, and how he was going to recoup his losses from the home.

Unlike most people who would ease their tension after a long day at the office by plopping on the couch, turning on the TV, and cracking open a beer, sober Carl had done the polar opposite. He would come home, a bald grown man with tattoos all over his body, and fluff pillows. He couldn't help himself; the stress of work, the stress of the decaying house, the stress of where he was in life all led to a one-hour cleaning session before he could settle down for dinner. Sometimes he blamed this quirk on his self-diagnosed obsessive-compulsive disorder, but really he didn't care what it was. Shaking a pillow in the air until all the feathers inside were evenly spaced was more calming than any beer could ever be.

But in recent weeks, a change in the wind had made his stresses flit away. In fact, Carl—for the first time in as long as he could remember—was invigorated by life. He was born again. Baptized by the Silk Road.

At first when he was assigned to the HSI Baltimore team to help with the case, Carl had been intrigued but nonchalant about the operation. It was an opportunity to work a different kind of case from the normal jump-out, but it wouldn't change his solar-agent lifestyle. Then one of the agents from Baltimore had shown him how to download Tor and how to navigate the Silk Road forums, and Carl had become obsessed.

He soon realized that this site could change everything. The DEA might become a cybercrimes operation. Other agencies, like the FBI or NSA, which never led drug cases, might create new divisions to go after these online targets. It was a new frontier, he saw, the Wild West. And he wanted to be one of the sheriffs in the O.K. Corral.

He started inhaling anything he could find about the Silk Road. He scrolled through the endless discussions on the Silk Road, from how to inject heroin into your eyeballs to how to secure packages of drugs to ensure they weren't discovered by the U.S. Postal Service. He read the writings of the site's leader, a character who used to call himself Admin but had recently renamed himself the Dread Pirate Roberts.

Carl had been warned, sternly, by the HSI Baltimore agents not to sign up for an account on the Silk Road yet. "Don't do anything stupid on the site," he was told by his supervisors. "We don't want anyone knowing that law enforcement is on there."

But Carl had someone to hunt, and the feelings he had experienced in his early days as an agent were returning. His body buzzed with the thrill. It was like someone had pulled back a Carl Force curtain and a younger, sprightlier Carl Force was there waiting to prove himself to his boss, to his coworkers, to his wife—to himself.

Soon his solar-agent days started to grow longer too. Now when the sun went down, Carl would pull into his driveway, run upstairs to the spare room in the back of the house, and flip open his DEA laptop to scour the Silk Road and read the new postings by its leader. For now the pillows in the Colonial house would have to wait. There was work to do. He needed to burrow deeper into the Silk Road and figure out a strategy to take down the site.

# Chapter 22

# "O CAPTAIN, MY CAPTAIN"

The Silk Road tribe didn't just like their leader's new name; they fucking loved it. It was a rallying cry for everyone involved. A masked face for the leader of a revolution. If Cuba had Che Guevara and Ireland had Michael Collins, then the war on drugs would have the Dread Pirate Roberts.

The site's forums, where people could discuss anything about the Silk Road, were bubbling with chatter about its leader's nom de plume. The dealers and buyers were galvanized with a feeling that they weren't simply buying or selling drugs but were on the fringes of an insurrection that was going to change the entire legal system forever.

Ross's employees also immediately took to the new moniker, as it gave an identity to someone who, until now, had had no selfhood. One minute their boss was an anonymous elusive figure behind a keyboard; the next he was a feared pirate who was going to lead them into battle with the U.S. government. And by fucking God was he going to win that battle.

Everyone started respectfully referring to Ross as either the Dread Pirate Roberts or DPR for short. And those closest to him (mostly his employees) chose an even more important title: "Captain." Dozens of times a day they addressed their commander this way.

"Mornin', captain."

"Ready when you are, cap'n."

"My thoughts exactly, Captain."

"Sweet dreams, captain."

"Night, captain."

Ross loved it—all of it. For the first time in months he felt invigorated by the site and the direction he could steer the ship. And it was his ship. No one else's.

"O captain, my captain."

Before meeting Variety Jones, Ross had questioned what he was doing. *Was all of this worth it?* At first he had lived with the constant fear that running the site could land him in jail for the rest of his life, or even force him to walk the green mile to an electric chair. He had come to terms with this by reminding himself that he was fighting for something he believed in, and because he was helping people, the risk was worth the reward. But after overcoming that obstacle, he couldn't quite come to terms with the reality that he had to constantly lie to those around him.

His few employees had helped pull him out of this depression, reiterating to their leader how proud they were to be a part of something so grand and revolutionary. Sure, they were being paid, with most making a few hundred dollars a week for their programming services, but it wasn't just about the money; they were grateful to be involved.

One employee told Ross he had walked away from his other jobs and responsibilities in life "to pursue all of this." The prospect of legalizing drugs and ensuring that future generations would not spend their lives in prisons for selling, or even doing, drugs was more important than anything else, the employee said. Another proclaimed proudly: "We really can change the world. . . . We are really lucky. . . . This opportunity is on the scale of a few times in a millennia."

The tide had turned so much, and with so many prospects for the Silk Road, Ross had decided to start writing a diary. In one of his first journal entries, realizing the profundity of his vision, he wrote, "I imagine that some day I may have a story written about my life, and it would be good to have a detailed account of it." There were plenty of reminders to illustrate his rising importance. From a financial standpoint the site was so successful and was processing so many orders that he had now become a millionaire. Though being frugal Ross, he didn't buy anything showy with the money, beyond a few nice meals. All of his possessions still fit snugly in a small bag.

But while the Silk Road side of his life was perfect, he still was troubled that he had to lie to people. When his family and friends asked what he was doing for work, Ross told a different story to each of them. "I'm a day trader." "I'm working on a video game." "I buy and sell digital currencies." Each time he told one of those stories, Ross was filled with guilt. He had always been obsessed with being "true to his word," as he put it, and this constant deceit gnawed at his conscience.

It wasn't like he could go to the Silk Road and be honest there, either. He had no choice but to lie to everyone there too—for obvious reasons. Though on several occasions he had slipped, sometimes by accident, more often because he needed to tell someone something. Ross had told Variety Jones one recent afternoon that he used to be an "experimental physicist." He had blundered with Smedley, his new chief programmer, and told him about his travels through Australia and Asia. He had told his other employee, Inigo, about camping trips he used to take with his father, Kirk. On more than one occasion he had talked about how much he loved fishing.

Now Ross had a better system for separating fact from fiction. By becoming the Dread Pirate Roberts, he could wear a mask that made him into two different people. In the real world he would be Ross Ulbricht; online he would be the Dread Pirate Roberts.

"Yes, cap'n!"

As Ross, he could still talk about his ideals about legalizing drugs, libertarianism, and his work with Bitcoin, all without going anywhere near the Silk Road in his mind and, more important, never feeling like he was fibbing to those he loved. And once the Dread Pirate Roberts mask was slipped on, a different person could steer the ship into uncharted and potentially unethical waters. DPR could cross lines that Ross would never have come up against, all of which he had to negotiate to take the site to the next level.

"O captain, my captain."

As the Dread Pirate Roberts, Ross didn't have to constantly lie anymore. Except to himself.

# Chapter 23

# ROSS, HANGED OR HOME

Ross's fingers throbbed as he typed. The red edges along the rims of his nails were nearly bleeding from his constant, savage biting. The problem was, he didn't know how to stop himself. Anxiety would course through his body and the chewing would begin.

It was a pattern that was developing and Ross had no idea how to end it. One minute the site would be expeditiously moving along, as smooth as water to a stone, and then out of nowhere—*BOOM!*—some sort of cataclysmic event would occur. Server crashes, hackers trying to break into the Bitcoin bank, bad code that needed replacing, good code that needed updating, conflicts between drug buyers and drug dealers, lost packages, scam artists, and stolen Bitcoins. While these issues were understandable given the nature of his work, they would come out of nowhere and Ross was forced to fix them immediately, no matter where he was.

Sometimes these problems were easily resolvable (like plugging holes in the ship when hackers attacked). Other problems had been plaguing the site since it began (like finding where those holes were before the hackers found them). And yet occasionally, a problem arose that would cost Ross tens of thousands of dollars in a matter of minutes. For example, in a single day recently, he had found out, someone had managed to steal $75,000 in Bitcoins because of some second-rate programming Ross had written. Those were the days that he would begin incessantly biting his nails.

Luckily for Ross, losing $75,000 wasn't going to bankrupt him. He was now making so much money from the site that he was having trouble laundering it into physical cash. Back in December the Silk Road had been processing $500,000 in drug sales each month. Now, in late March, the site was doing $500,000 in sales a week. When Variety Jones looked at the growth charts, his response to the Dread Pirate Roberts was apropos: "Fuck me," he wrote. "I mean, in my mind I knew it, but seeing the graph, well . . . fuck me!" The graph he was referring to was of a yellow line that illustrated growth and profits on the site and pointed straight upward to the right and all the way off the page.

Variety Jones took a few minutes to do some math. His calculations predicted that, at the current growth rate, sales would be up to $1 million a week by April, just a month from now, and double that by midsummer. He told Ross that in the worst-case scenario 2012 would end up being a $100 million year for the site. And if things stayed on the current trajectory, by the end of 2013 the Silk Road would be processing nearly $1 billion a year in drug sales.

Ross's cut from the commission fees was now averaging $10,000 a day and growing higher—quite literally—by the hour. In reality Ross's wealth was doubling and tripling every few weeks as the exchange rate for Bitcoins rose. If Ross had $100,000 in one of his Bitcoin accounts on Monday, it could be worth as much as $200,000 by Friday without his doing a thing. If VJ's predictions were correct, in a bear case Ross could personally be making $100 million a year by 2014. In a bull case, if the current value of Bitcoins continued to grow as it had been doing, he could be making ten times that in no time at all.

But the pile of digital money introduced a whole new set of problems. Besides the issue of turning it into cash—and doing so without the tax man finding out—more money meant more customers, and that brought a slew of issues. There were the rampant conflicts on the site between dealers and buyers, slowing servers overloaded with new visitors, and a lot more attention from law enforcement.

"All that money won't be worth much if we're behind bars," Ross wrote to VJ as they discussed the site's vertiginous growth and the anxiety that came with it—anxiety that Ross knew he had to take ahold of, or it would take ahold of him, inevitably leading to a mistake. A mistake was the surest way to be caught. And being caught was the absolute last thing Ross, VJ, or the tens of thousands of people now buying and selling on the site wanted.

"We need . . . contingencies," VJ argued, "and a plan."

So with Variety Jones's guidance, Ross came up with just that: a plan.

First and foremost, Ross would leave Australia and go home. Traveling had given him some much-needed perspective, but months on the road had also given him a whole new set of worries. At first he had found solace and comfort staying with his sister in Australia. He fell in love with the idyllic climate and the fun that came with that, including being battered around by the Bondi Beach waves. With no day job to tie him down, Ross had soon set out for a month jaunting around Asia. Looking just like every other backpacker trekking through the islands around the Pacific Ocean, he stayed in youth hostels and ate noodles from roadside vendors. The only difference between him and the throwaway friends he met along the way was that they were mostly broke college students exploring the world before they moved back to America or Europe to get a job and settle down. Whereas Ross was surreptitiously running the biggest drug-dealing Web site in the world and was personally worth millions of dollars.

Blending in had been easy, with his scarce belongings and scraggly hair. That was, until something went wrong on the site.

Ross had been left with no choice but to try running the Silk Road from Internet cafés and glacially slow Wi-Fi hot spots across Asia, which meant every single time he had to check the site there were dozens of prying eyes to peer over his shoulder. This meant that in the middle of conversations he would tell his employees he had to relocate.

"I'm going to move location," he wrote, "brb."

"Moving location."

"I don't like this spot anymore."

"Gotta move, I'll be right back."

"Changing location."

Sometimes he would just slam his laptop shut if someone caught a glimpse of his computer screen. Then he would scurry away (hopefully) unnoticed. But often he didn't have any choice but to be stuck near the Internet, hovering like a fly waiting for a dog to take a shit. Under the guise of the Dread Pirate Roberts, Ross told his confidant, "I organize my life around being on my computer in private." And this lifestyle was killing him.

"Brb, gotta move."

In one of the more nauseating experiences, while on his travels, Ross had set off to a sleepy surfer town in the middle of the jungle in Thailand.

The plan was to lap up the waves, enjoy the beach, hike through the palm trees, maybe smoke some weed, and (if all went well) meet a pretty young backpacker. Except something went catastrophically awry on the site the moment he pulled into town. Someone had started stealing Bitcoins from his account as a result of a major programming error. Ross had no choice but to fix it right there and then—and it wasn't an easy fix.

He was holed up from morning until night in the local Internet café, incessantly biting his nails while he tried desperately to stop the Bitcoin robbery, all while locals and backpackers lackadaisically wandered down the jungle town's dirt roads, drank beers, and surfed in the warm ocean waves. ("The people there thought I was a nut," Ross later told Variety Jones. "There I was 18 hours a day on my laptop chewing my nails off. All these mellow people on vacation lookin at me like wtf is up with that guy?!")

Adding to this anxiety, Ross was terrified that someone would see the Silk Road logo or images of drugs on his screen or ask questions about the code he was writing. Worse, a local, trying to gain favor with his local cop buddies, might anonymously alert the authorities.

The anxiety could be petrifying when he was at his most lucid. Given that Ross's site was making it possible to buy drugs from anywhere with Internet access, he was technically a wanted man all around the world. That meant he could be subject to the laws of almost any country on the planet. And the last place Ross wanted to be arrested for enabling the sale of vast amounts of drugs was in Southeast Asia, where Westerners had been hanged when they were caught trafficking mere ounces of heroin.

So there was only one thing to do. When it was clear that Erica's Facebook post had gone unnoticed and that no one else suspected him of being anyone but Ross Ulbricht, he set a date to return to Texas. That alone didn't resolve the anxiety of running the site. But Ross had a plan there too. He promised Variety Jones that he would start taking long walks, eating healthier meals to stay focused, and tripling his daily meditation quota to at least thirty minutes before he went to sleep. With VJ counseling him, Ross was going to try to handle the stresses that came with running the biggest drug Web site the world had ever seen.

As for the nails? On April 10, a few days before he left Australia, he walked into a pharmacy, slid a few dollars across the counter, and walked out with a bottle of anti-nail-biting formula.

He excitedly told Variety Jones about his new purchase. Ross said that he was going to apply the magic ointment to his nails at least once a day for the next week. "Time to kick the habit," he told VJ.

But he wouldn't be able to kick it for long. Upon returning to America, Ross was going to discover that not only had the Silk Road grown immensely over the past few months, but law enforcement's zeal to capture the Dread Pirate Roberts had too.

# Chapter 24

# CARL, ELADIO, AND NOB

For a DEA agent, going undercover was one of the most exciting, and equally nerve-racking, aspects of the job. If you did it right, you could catch some unscrupulous people; if you did it wrong, those people could catch you.

Carl Force had learned this lesson the hard way, as a newbie DEA agent almost fourteen years earlier, when one of his first assignments was on a case in the small town of Alamosa, Colorado.

Carl had ended up there after arresting and then turning an informant, who promised to help facilitate some drug buys with the local dealers. The town was just north of the New Mexico border, so it was a perfect smuggling port to get coke and meth into the country.

The informant set up a few meetings to get the initial operation off the ground, but things went haywire almost immediately. Whenever Carl would show up for an undercover drug buy, the informant would spin into a panic, frantically telling Carl that he looked too much like a cop and, as a result, was putting the entire operation (and possibly both of their lives) in serious danger.

Carl didn't like to be told what to do, but upon peering into a mirror he realized the informant was right; he looked exactly like a cop. So Carl decided to go through a mini physical transformation. He got his ears pierced with golden hoops, grew his hair out, and started to dress less like a DEA agent and more like someone who sold drugs for a living.

To ensure he couldn't be fingered as a Fed, he also took on a made-up persona that had an elaborate backstory. This taught Carl the crucial lesson that you don't just show up to an undercover operation and simply say you work in the world of organized crime. You have to show someone that you do.

A decade later, as he sat in the DEA office in Baltimore, staring at the user registration page for the Silk Road Web site, he was about to apply that lesson again.

Carl had done his homework, prepping for this very moment. But before he could sign up for an account on the site, he had to figure out who he was going to be on the Silk Road. Unlike in his real-life undercover work, this time he would be hidden behind a keyboard, which meant he could be whoever, or whatever, he wanted. He could be black, white, Spanish, or Chinese. Male or female, or something in between. The online world was his stage; he just needed to decide who would come out from behind the curtain.

Carl started with what he knew, plucking stories from his time down south, and he settled on the character of a smuggler from the Dominican Republic who siphoned $25 million of mostly coke and heroin into the United States each year. He gave this character the name Eladio Guzman, notably adapting the surname of the world's most famous analog drug lord, El Chapo Guzmán, the head of Mexico's Sinaloa Cartel. He then created an elaborate history for his Guzman, saying that he knew people all over South America to traffic drugs, launder money, or have people killed. Oh, and he was blind in one eye and wore an eye patch as a result.

To ensure everything about him seemed real, Carl had a fake driver's license created by the DEA with his real photo and his new made-up name.

But on the Silk Road people wouldn't use their real name, even if it was fake. So, in the same way that the leader of the site called himself the Dread Pirate Roberts, Carl would need to create a moniker for his made-up persona. Again, he decided to pick his nickname from something else he knew well: the Bible. Call it a gut feeling, years on the job, or overconfidence, but he wanted the nickname he chose to illustrate what was going to happen as a result of his work on the Silk Road. And so he chose a name from the Bible of a city that was destroyed by a king: the town of Nob.

So Carl Force would become Eladio Guzman, the Dominican drug smuggler, who would go by the online nickname Nob.

He went home and told his twelve-year-old daughter he needed her help. He grabbed a piece of white paper and with a black marker aggressively scribbled

"ALL HAIL NOB." He then placed an eye patch over his fake blind eye, pulled a dark hoodie over his bald head, and held up the piece of paper as his daughter snapped a picture of him.

Then he signed up for an account as Nob.

For the past month Carl had been meeting with the Baltimore agents to discuss a strategy for their probe. The plan wasn't too different from Jared's. They would try to build up a case (obviously a competing one, as they knew Jared was already working his own Silk Road investigation out of Chicago) by arresting dealers and then working their way up the ladder. There had been countless meetings to discuss this strategy, though Carl thought such a path would be too laborious.

Or Carl could just say "fuck it" and try to knock on the big boss's door.

He chose the latter. On Thursday, April 21, at around noon, Carl sat at his computer, transformed himself into his new drug smuggler identity, and wrote an e-mail to the Dread Pirate Roberts. "Mr. Silk Road," he began. "I am a great admirer of your work." This accolade was followed by a brief explanation that Nob was a man of "considerable means" who had been in the drug business for more than twenty years. He noted quite frankly that he saw the Silk Road as the future of drug trafficking and that, most important, he had a proposal: "I want to buy the site." He hit "send" and waited for a reply.

When the HSI team in Baltimore found out what Carl had done, they were irate. This wasn't part of the plan. Carl had gone rogue before they had even decided what they were going to do. There were calls from supervisors to the assistant special agent in charge, or ASAC, whose main job was to ensure that people like Carl didn't go rogue. But Carl didn't really care. He just kept looking at his e-mail, waiting for a reply from the Dread Pirate Roberts.

He checked that afternoon—no reply. The following morning: still nothing. *Tomorrow*, he reasoned. *The Dread Pirate Roberts will reply tomorrow.*

# Chapter 25

# JARED'S CHICAGO VERSUS CARL'S BALTIMORE

J ared's tiny HSI office was starting to look less like an office and more like an extension of the mail center at Chicago O'Hare. Circling the room along the walls were dozens of tubs piled as high as a small child, all filled to the brim with envelopes—around five hundred in all. These packages all had one thing in common: they had at one point contained drugs purchased on the Silk Road.

Above those piles of mail, the office walls were decorated with printouts and photos of the different drugs—pills, baggies, rocks—that had once been inside those envelopes.

It was clear that Jared, who didn't take no for an answer, had fallen deep into the Silk Road case with his stubborn obsessiveness.

He had been working on a system to try to figure out which envelopes (and drugs) came from which vendors on the site. When a package was discovered by the customs officials, no matter what time of the day or night, Jared would get in the Pervert Car and drive to the airport, pick up the narcotics, snap pictures, and fill out seizure documents before returning everything to his office. Then it was off to the Web site to look through every single picture of the drugs for sale and try to figure out where the package had come from.

Given that the Silk Road now had thousands of dealers, it was not an easy task. But Jared was always up for a laborious and all-consuming challenge. He reasoned that when (or at this rate, if) they finally caught the leader of the Silk Road, Jared would have hundreds of pounds of evidence tying the site to actual drugs.

He had learned a lot by purchasing his own drugs on the site, figuring out who was selling what and learning how drugs coming from differing countries might look different from one another. (Some used puffy envelopes; other drugs were hidden in everyday objects like CD cases. Some dealers put them in hollowed-out dead batteries; others stuck tabs of LSD to the backs of photos.) Yet with all of this information coming together, he had also learned something else rather disturbing. The site was growing too quickly for anyone to catch up to it.

In the months since Jared had started to investigate the case, the Silk Road had become a phenomenon. It was being written about in the press all over the world on a daily basis, and given that the site was still running after eighteen months, other potential customers felt more confident buying drugs and guns, so the customer base was growing rapidly.

The slew of press came with consequences, not just for the leader of the Silk Road, but also for Jared. All those stories in all those newspapers and blogs meant that other government agents were learning about the Silk Road, and Jared assumed they would want in on the case.

And he was right.

In the spring of 2012, on a late afternoon, Jared was sitting in his office, sifting through the latest envelopes customs had intercepted and, like a doctor checking an X-ray, holding up photos of drugs next to images on the Web site. He had checked in with his wife, Kim, and was trying to wrap things up to make it to the airport before racing home when his computer sounded a loud *DING!*, announcing a new e-mail.

This wasn't just any e-mail. The system that agents use to keep records of their cases is designed to notify each agent when someone else in the government has read their specific case files. The e-mail that Jared had just received told him that two people at Homeland Security in Baltimore, a sister office within the same agency, were at that very moment reading one of his case files. As he sat there looking at the message on his screen and wondering what was going on, there was another *DING!* And another. Soon it was like an old lady had hit the jackpot in Las Vegas. *DING! DING! DING! DING! DING!*

As Jared sat there perplexed as to what was going on, things grew even stranger. His supervisor in Chicago received an e-mail from another supervisor in Baltimore, saying that a group of agents wanted to come out to the Windy City to talk about the Silk Road case. To add to this bizarre, out-of-the-blue request, the Baltimore agents were bringing their U.S. attorney with them.

This could mean only one thing: Baltimore wanted in on Jared's case. But Jared didn't want anyone impinging on his hunt for the Dread Pirate Roberts. This was his case, not theirs, and other people would surely drag him down in his pursuit. He also knew that coming out and saying that would only lead to infighting, which would only lead to a "deconfliction meeting," where someone very high up in government decides who gets to run a case. That wasn't a good scenario for Jared. In a standoff with older agents, he would likely lose.

So Jared and his boss at HSI agreed to a meeting with the Baltimore team at the Dirksen Federal Building, where Jared had first sold the Chicago U.S. attorney on the Silk Road case.

On the day of the meeting, Jared showed up at the home of the fifty-ton *Flamingo* expecting one or two people from the Baltimore contingent, but instead a small army streamed inside the office, including agents, assistants, and their own personal Baltimore assistant U.S. attorney, who introduced himself as Justin.

After some formalities and awkward handshakes, the Baltimore attorney spoke. "Thanks for meeting with us. We've been reading your reports, Jared"—momentarily looking in his direction—"and you're doing some really great work, just great reporting in there."

Jared thought to himself, *I know you've been reading my fucking reports. I've been getting alerts in my in-box every fifteen minutes for the past few fucking weeks.* He kept his rant to himself for now and instead smiled and nodded.

The Baltimore attorney then explained that the HSI agents in the room, Mike and Greg (who also worked with Carl Force), had picked up a lead in a bust, a dealer who had been "turned" and had given them a list of names belonging to people who sold drugs on the Silk Road. The attorney went on to say that they were going to trace all the people on the list, and "one of those names is going to be the leader of the Silk Road." The Baltimore team sat there gloating with pride at their plan.

Jared couldn't stop himself from interrupting them. "You guys have no idea what you're up against," he said, upset. "You have no respect for Tor and Bitcoin and . . ."

Justin from Baltimore ignored Jared's comment and insinuated that Baltimore HSI was going to be taking over the case against the Silk Road. They might let Chicago join in if Jared had something to contribute.

Furious, Jared was about to interrupt again when he was beaten to it by his own supervisor, who seemed equally annoyed at the way these Baltimore agents had stormed into their town trying to throw their weight around. "Here's what we're going to do," Jared's supervisor declared in a bellicose tone. "You guys are going to go your way; we're going to go our way."

The room fell silent. Any ounce of cordiality that had been there when the meeting began had vanished. Jared's supervisor went on to dictate that if HSI Baltimore bumped into the investigation by HSI Chicago, they would go up through the ranks and deal with it accordingly. "We'll deconflict when we have to."

Silence hung there for a second and Justin spoke again. "That's fine," he said as the group from Baltimore got up to leave. "But we're pretty sure we're going to have this site shut down in a couple of weeks."

# Chapter 26
# THE MUTINY

E very founder goes through it.

When Facebook introduced the "timeline," its few-million-strong user base grew enraged at the privacy violations that came with involuntarily sharing everything you did with others. But Mark Zuckerberg had no choice; he needed to grow his revenue, and this was the path forward. Uber went through it when the company defiantly refused to eliminate its "surge pricing" model, which would make customers' car rides double, triple, and in some instances even octuple without much warning. But Travis Kalanick had no choice; he needed to grow his revenue. Every tech company has faced these challenges: Twitter, Google, Apple, Yahoo! All seemingly screwing over their customers for their own gain. People don't realize that these are simply some of the tough decisions a CEO must make in order to survive. So if Ross wanted to continue to grow the Silk Road, he had to make these kinds of grueling decisions too. And just as in the revolts at Facebook and Uber and every other start-up in Silicon Valley that had pissed off its users, the drug dealers on the Silk Road were outraged at the latest decisions of the Dread Pirate Roberts. So much so that there was talk of a mutiny on the HMS *Silk Road*.

Rumors had been rumbling up through the decks of the ship for weeks about such a rebellion. At first Ross had justly brushed them off as just that, rumors, assuming they were just hearsay from a couple of unhappy vendors who were spreading gossip. Yet now the chatter was growing louder, and there was talk of an insurgency, or even of a mass exodus, that could be in the works on the site.

The turmoil had begun earlier in the year when Ross had made the decision to raise the commission rate he was charging dealers on the site. Back then, whether someone bought a tiny baggie of weed seeds for $5 or $5,000 worth of cocaine, the Silk Road would take a 6.23 percent commission for helping facilitate the deal.

This tax worked out really well for the little guys, who ended up paying pennies for each transaction. But the dealers who were moving the largest volumes of drugs were being forced to pay massive commissions. To get around the fee, some of the top dealers had started doing side deals off the site, in which the Silk Road got nothing.

So the Dread Pirate Roberts and Variety Jones had a plan. They penned a "State of the Road" address, announcing that the commission rates were going to change. "Now, instead of charging a flat commission," Ross wrote in a letter to the site's users, "we will charge a higher amount for low priced items and a lower amount for high priced items, similar to how eBay does it." The announcement went on to explain that the site would take a 10 percent commission on orders less than $50 and 1.5 percent for orders more than $1,000, with a few other fees in-between, hopefully balancing out the scales of commissions. Ross ended his State of the Road address in the same way Fidel Castro ended a homily in 1962 after he had successfully led the Cuban revolution: "I believe our future is bright and we will emerge victorious."

But not all of the buyers and sellers on the site agreed about this new future. Some were happy about the rate hike (especially those who hawked larger shipments of drugs), but others were furious, specifically the dealers who trafficked vast numbers of small doses. In a matter of minutes a chaotic debate ensued on the Silk Road forums.

Ross was genuinely perplexed by the reaction. He was even hurt by the response. Didn't these people realize that if it weren't for him and his revolutionary ideas, there wouldn't be a Silk Road? Didn't they understand that he was putting his entire life at risk for them? If it weren't for his work, they would all still be buying and selling drugs on the street, risking arrest or, worse, caught up in violent turf wars, being robbed, beaten, or even killed in a deal gone awry. And yet they had the audacity to complain about a small commission change. Didn't they know that this entire thing couldn't run itself? That this wasn't a fudging nonprofit? It was a gosh darn business!

Ross became so worked up over the backlash to the commission changes that he responded in a way that essentially told everyone on the site to go fuck themselves. "Whether you like it or not, I am the captain of this ship," he shouted in response to the outcry. "If you don't like the rules of the game, or you don't trust your captain, you can get off the boat."

It was not the best pep talk for the troops.

Thankfully, as time went by, the uproar simmered down and most people accepted the rate changes. But a select few disconsolate dealers were still unhappy. And rumors of what they were planning started making their way to Ross.

"I suspect that several are talking about making backup plans to jump ship, or create competing sites," DPR wrote to VJ in a chat. "I don't want a mutiny."

So Variety Jones decided to venture to the lower decks of the site to mingle with the dealers and buyers, with the goal of finding out how many people were involved in the insurgency and whether an actual uprising might take place.

It was around this time, on a late afternoon in mid-April, that an e-mail popped into the in-box of the Dread Pirate Roberts, with an obscure offer. "Mr. Silk Road, I am a great admirer of your work," the message began, and then offered a brief explanation of who the sender was: a man who called himself Nob and said he had been smuggling drugs for decades in South America. The end of the letter was the best part.

"I want to buy the site."

If a random offer to buy the site had landed in Ross's in-box five months earlier, when stress was at its peak and his personal relationships at their lowest, he probably would have said yes without even a thought. *Give me a bag of Bitcoin and it's yours. Be careful: it isn't house-trained yet.* But today, in mid-April—even with the chatter about a potential riot on the site—how Ross felt about the future was very different.

He was now running a real business. He had almost a dozen employees rewriting code, monitoring the forums, and dealing with support issues. Variety Jones was by his side helping to steer the ship, and Ross was starting to comprehend that the Silk Road was going to be bigger than anything he had ever imagined. More important, Ross had recently had an epiphany that this—this Web site, which had begun as a tiny dream—would be his life's work.

And what a magnum opus it was turning into.

Still, Ross reasoned, it couldn't hurt to reply to this Nob character, whoever he was, and see what he was willing to pay for the site. If this were a start-up in Silicon Valley, a financial offer would be one way to gauge its worth. After all, what was the worst that could happen? He could receive a lowball offer from Nob, and that would be the end of the conversation. Ross clicked the "reply" button on his computer, typed a very short eleven-word response, and hit "send." "I'm open to the idea," the e-mail said. "What did you have in mind?"

As he waited for word from VJ about the mutiny, Ross went about his day, preparing for a camping trip he was about to go on with his old buddies from high school.

Ross had returned to Texas a couple of weeks earlier. As he had promised Variety Jones, he was meditating in the early mornings or late afternoons, then working for a few hours on the site. To keep his sanity, and to keep his fears of law enforcement in check, he would socialize after work like any other normal programmer with a nine-to-five job. He went on hikes in the forest just outside Austin. He smoked some weed with his high school friends and went rock climbing with others. And he had, thankfully, avoided running into Julia since he'd returned to the Lone Star State.

A few days went by before Ross heard back from Nob. But the e-mail was perplexing. Nob said that in order to make an official offer to buy the Silk Road, he would need to see financials, including "monthly gross sales from the site, net sales, percentage charged to sellers, total sellers, total buyers, site maintenance and upgrade costs (?), salaries for the administrator and monitors."

*Ha! That's never going to happen!*

There were only two people on earth who had seen those numbers; one was named Dread Pirate Roberts and the other was Ross Ulbricht. Even Variety Jones didn't know all those details.

DPR politely declined to share the numbers with Nob, citing the risk that such sensitive information could easily fall into the hands of law enforcement. But still, he decided to throw out a potential sale price for the site to see if the buyer was even remotely interested in an acquisition. At the very least, it was titillating to ponder the value of his creation. Facebook was now being valued at around $80 billion; Twitter was worth some $10 billion, and that place was run like a clown car. Surely the Silk Road offered something that, if not quite at their value (yet), was at least in the range for the right buyer. "I think an offer for the entire operation would need to be 9 figures for me to consider it," Ross wrote to Nob.

As this conversation continued, Variety Jones returned with whispers in his ear and reports ready for the Dread Pirate Roberts. It seemed the rumors about the mutiny were indeed correct. A group of dealers on the site weren't happy with the new commission fees and they were weighing what to do next.

Option one for these mutineers, Ross learned, would be to jump ship to a new, much smaller competing Web site that had recently come on the scene called Black Market. Then there was option two: for those behind the rebellion to go off and literally build a competing drug site that had much lower fees. Or finally, the worst-case scenario was not too dissimilar to what happens daily in real-world businesses when a CEO is ousted by the board. In this scenario the dealers were talking about hacking into the site (given its massive security vulnerabilities) and commandeering the Silk Road.

But more disconcerting than any of these options was the other piece of intelligence that Variety Jones had discovered during his reconnaissance mission. The problem, as VJ explained to DPR, wasn't just that people were upset about the high commission fees on the site. There was a much bigger issue looming. One that Ross could never have envisioned when he had the idea for the Silk Road years earlier.

# Chapter 27

# A BILLION DOLLARS?!

Carl sat at his laptop reading the e-mail from the Dread Pirate Roberts. "It's a tough question. This is more than a business to me, it's a revolution and is becoming my life's work," it began, and then proclaimed a price: "I think an offer for the entire operation would need to be 9 figures for me to consider it."

*Nine figures!* Carl almost choked when he read that number. That could mean as low as $100 million or as high as $999 million, and he knew full well it wasn't going to be on the low end of that spectrum. But he was also baffled at how big the Silk Road must be.

Until now, everyone on the Baltimore task force and those inside the DEA had assumed the site was a relatively small operation, but this valuation seemed extraordinarily high. DEA agents had imagined that the site might be worth a few million. At the highest maybe—just maybe—Carl believed it was worth $25 million, tops. But nine figures?

Now Carl was gleeful that he had to figure out how to respond to this high number.

Carl had become particularly excitable as of late. He was almost erratic in his temperament, constantly flipping between a buzzing enthusiasm and an irritable stress about the case. These feelings were only exacerbated by the time he had to wait for DPR to respond to his e-mails, which was sometimes days.

To relieve this stress, Carl sometimes exercised—well, sort of exercised. While he occasionally ran on the treadmill in the DEA office gym, he would also relieve stress by wrestling with his coworkers. As if they were in some sort of secret fight club, he would roll on the ground with other grown men as they tried to pin each other to the floor of the Baltimore offices of the DEA. Then, panting and breathless, it was back to his laptop to see if DPR had replied.

Technically, by writing back to DPR, Carl was breaking protocol again. He had recently been given a talking-to by his boss, Nick, who said that whenever Carl spoke to DPR, he must liaise with the Baltimore team (which had been nicknamed the Marco Polo task force) and that he should run any correspondence by the higher-ups. But Special Agent Carl Force had been on the job fourteen years, and he hated two things: one was authority, and the other was authority from people younger than him (which included everyone on the Marco Polo task force).

*Nope. Not going to happen.* Carl had zero interest in chatting with a drug lord by committee. So after mulling over the e-mail from DPR, he decided to go rogue and reply anyway.

"I could pay nine figures but I am not sure Silk Road is worth that, as of now," Carl wrote under his pseudonym Nob. And then he offered a proposal that he was sure would help capture the site's leader. "I would like to do a spin-off for the major dealers called 'Masters of the Silk Road,'" in which big vendors on the site can facilitate drug deals in the hundreds of kilos, or even tons, rather than in ounces. Nob assured DPR that he could help with this new Costco for drugs, if you will, because he knew smuggling routes all over the world. Finally, he offered the Dread Pirate Roberts an injection of $2 million for 20 percent ownership of this new "Masters of the Silk Road" operation.

He hit "send" and then bounded into Nick's office to tell him, with rebellious glee, what he had done. Nick, obviously, was incensed, responding to Carl's confession with a fusillade of "Fuck you!" and "Fuck this!" and "Fuck that!"

Carl didn't give a shit what Nick thought. Sure, he was his boss, but Carl knew no one could fire him for something like this. That was the one benefit of the red tape that came with a government job; getting fired was often much harder than getting hired. As for those "mopes," as Carl called them, over at HSI Baltimore, he could give even less of a shit what they were going to say.

As far as he was concerned, Carl was talking directly to the leader of the Silk Road. And if his scheme worked, he'd develop a relationship with DPR. And if that worked, Agent Carl Force would have the Dread Pirate Roberts locked up in a matter of weeks. The founder of the Silk Road would be behind bars, and Agent Force would be lauded as the hero who caught him.

# Chapter 28

# THE ASPIRING BILLIONAIRE IN COSTA RICA

Everything was so calm. The ocean, the air, the sky. Ross consumed it all in one gasp and felt happy to his core. It was early morning in Costa Rica, and the wind blew softly from the east, across the placid water where he sat bobbing on his surfboard.

The looming mutiny that had been bubbling to the top of the Silk Road for the past few months had finally fizzled out, though some of those behind the insurrection had left for new, much smaller, competitors on the Dark Web.

With those troublemakers gone, the site was now running relatively fluidly again—employees were toiling away under the direction of the captain, Dread Pirate Roberts—and it was continuing to grow at a staggering pace. Ross's profits were multiplying by the second, quite literally, as the value of Bitcoins was dramatically increasing. It was as if he stuck a dollar bill in his pocket before he went to sleep and found two (or even three) dollars there the next day. As a result, his personal net worth was well into the tens of millions of dollars.

He was tightening up security protocols too. To be sure that the people who worked for him had not been compromised by the cops, Ross made his closest advisers adopt a question-and-answer system that only those two people would know. So if he asked one of his employees, "How's the weather?" the employee would have to reply with the exact phrase: "Boy, is it cold here in the Bahamas." If the employee said something else, like "Oh, fine, how is it with you?" Ross would know something was amiss and could immediately shut down their account. Each employee had their own question and answer. "[If I say] can you recommend a good book?" Ross wrote to another underling, "you reply, 'Anything by Rothbard.'"

But more important than any of that was that Ross had finally figured out how to put the issue of Julia's knowledge about the Silk Road to rest—something he would address once and for all when he returned to Texas in a couple of weeks.

He had flown down to Costa Rica at the end of May to stay at the hidden plot of magic that his family owned there: a four-acre enclave called Casa Bambu at the southern tip of the country's peninsula. Paradise with an Internet connection.

This place was special to Ross for many reasons. When he wasn't in Texas as a child, he had come of age here, exploring the jungles with his sister, sitting on the porch with his mother, listening to the howler monkeys, and learning how to surf on a mini foam surfboard with his father. But Ross loved Casa Bambu for a more salient reason: it had been one of the influences that led him to start the Silk Road. Twenty years earlier his parents had fallen in love with the area while on vacation and decided to build a family holiday home in the pasture. Ross's dad (along with a few friends and locals) built four cabanas that made up a tranquil solar-powered *Swiss Family Robinson* retreat. The Ulbrichts rented the space to tourists part of the year, so paradise paid for itself, and then some. This accomplishment had made Ross want to pursue a similar goal of starting something from scratch.

And boy, had he ever.

Ross had confided in Variety Jones about some of his lofty earlier dreams and how they now seemed within reach. Specifically Ross shared a silent declaration he had made to himself in 2004, that by the time he was thirty years old, he would be worth $1 billion.

For so long it had seemed he would fail dismally at that quest. Yet now, two months after he turned twenty-eight, the goal wasn't so out of reach anymore. As Ross said to VJ in one of their long conversations, when he looked at the current trajectory of the Silk Road, if he calculated the future sales of the enterprise, "it could happen." He could very well be a billionaire in two years.

When Ross showed VJ the latest Excel spreadsheets outlining the revenue and projections of the Silk Road, VJ responded with a shocked "Fuck me!" then added, "A hundred million is starting to look lite for 2012! On for a billion in 2013!"

"Giddy up," Ross replied.

To get there, though, they would need to continue expanding. DPR and VJ had been experimenting with different ideas to grow the site, including a "4/20" contest where people could enter a raffle and win different illegal things, and some legal ones, including an all-expenses-paid vacation with some additional spending money.

But Variety Jones and DPR both knew it wasn't contests and the Silk Road alone that would get Ross to his coveted billionaire status. The site needed to diversify into other markets and to reach a larger set of customers. They discussed an entire genre of underground Web sites that would borrow from the Silk Road brand. SilkDigital could be for downloadable digital goods, like stolen software and tools for hackers. SilkPharma would be for pain meds, uppers, or downers. Maybe they could build a site for weapons, they reasoned. But these expansions would take work. So Ross had decided to come down to Costa Rica, to his parents' patch of paradise, to focus on this exact problem.

His mother and father didn't have a clue what their son was working on. How can you look at your own flesh and blood, who was once a Boy Scout, then a physicist, who donated books to the local prison in his early twenties, and think, *Oh, maybe he's becoming one of the most notorious drug dealers alive?* You can't. It doesn't enter the mind. When Lyn and Kirk looked at their son, they saw a brilliant and idealistic twenty-eight-year-old who spent so much time on the computer because he was trading stocks.

Ross believed the day would come when the movement he'd launched would become unstoppable and prove to the U.S. government that the only way to win the war on drugs was to legalize them completely. Then, and only then, would the Dread Pirate Roberts be able to remove the mask, and Ross Ulbricht would step out onto the world's stage and take a bow. His mother would proudly look at her son, the hero of the libertarian movement, a movement that had first been planted in Ross's mind as a tiny seedling at his parents' dinner-table discussions back in Austin.

Though Ross and VJ knew that wasn't going to happen just yet.

As Ross sprung out of the water in Costa Rica, he rinsed the sand off his body and scarfed down breakfast before scurrying away to work on his laptop in private, hidden from prying eyes. "I'm in a magical place right now to be sure," he told Variety Jones when he logged into their chat window. "I'm stoned on oxygen and the sea breeze."

But that now-familiar specter of something bad was looming again, and VJ had something else to talk about.

"Dude, I'm worried about our winner," Variety Jones said, referring to the person who had won the 4/20 contest and was about to be awarded the all-expenses-paid vacation and a few thousand dollars in cash.

"Whasamatta?" DPR replied.

"He's trying to dry out; Heroin; it's not working, and I think his recent influx of cash didn't help."

"Oh geez. Fuck, what are we doing," DPR said, then joked: "Shoulda thought more carefully about dropping $4k on an addict; maybe our next prize will be 3 months in rehab."

"Yeah," VJ said. "It does show we've got problems Gillette doesn't have in their promos." Variety Jones then joked that their next promotion should be "Win 3 months in Rehab! The more drugs you buy, the more chances you have to win!"

As Ross changed the subject of the conversation to more pressing issues, specifically how to expand the Silk Road and grow the business so he could reach that special ten-digit number, the calm Costa Rica sky was starting to turn a deeper gray. A violent storm was on the horizon, ominously moving closer to land.

# Chapter 29

# VARIETY JONES GOES TO SCOTLAND

I t was dark and quiet in Glasgow, Scotland, as the clock in the hotel room wound past 2:00 a.m. and a middle-aged man, sitting at his computer, sipped some water to quench his thirst.

The man known as Variety Jones was balding and disheveled, his T-shirt stained and stretched at the neck, his eyes worn and droopy like a plastic figurine left too near a fire. This was a man who had been through hell and back, his body ravaged by years of disease, drugs, and jail, but he had clearly enjoyed the trip.

On his computer screen a number of windows sat splayed open. One had some sort of programming code and another appeared to be a chat window with two people talking.

The man with the droopy eyes clicked on the chat box and then began typing.

"Tappity tap tap," he wrote to DPR, then pressed the "return" key.

A moment later there was a reply: "Taparoo."

"I'm in the land of 12 Euro tins of beer in a mini fridge," Jones wrote. "Oh joy!"

"Hello hotel bill."

VJ had been lying low in London with his girlfriend for the past few months while he worked on the Silk Road for his unofficial boss, the Dread Pirate Roberts. Mostly their relationship had gone swimmingly. Their skill sets were complementary, and they largely shared the same worldview. But a fissure had begun to surface. After Jones had come to Glasgow to celebrate his uncle's death—yes, celebrate: as VJ told DPR, the "Jones" clan "threw bigger funerals than weddings," with the casket in the middle of a pub and a revelry of dancing and drinking, made up of four hundred friends and family, flowing around the deceased uncle—he had logged on to check in with DPR and resolve a moral disagreement they were having.

It wasn't often that they argued. The relationship between Jones and Dread was impenetrable, and a true and tight friendship had developed between the two men since a year earlier, when they first met through the Silk Road. Their alliance had blossomed over their shared belief that drugs should be legal, and guns too. VJ was a loyal servant and companion. He had even talked about buying a helicopter company to break DPR out of jail if he was ever caught. "Remember that one day when you're in the exercise yard, I'll be the dude in the helicopter coming in low and fast, I promise," he had written to Dread. "With the amount of $ we're generating, I could hire a small country to come get you."

But even with that bond, fundamental disagreements over the direction of the site would crop up, and Variety Jones was trying desperately to steer DPR in a new direction on a particular topic.

It wasn't even up for debate in VJ's mind that the Dread Pirate Roberts was as libertarian as they came and that he believed the Silk Road should be a place to buy and sell anything. There were no rules and no regulations, and as a result there was something illegal for sale on the site for literally every letter of the alphabet. Acid, benzos, coke, DMT, ecstasy, fizzies, GHB . . . but it was the letter *H* that had Variety Jones in a very difficult quandary. He was fine with everything before and after that letter, but heroin—he hated it.

"I don't even have a problem with coke," VJ wrote to DPR, but "H, man—in prison I've seen guys—I wish that shit would go away."

Variety Jones was open about the time he had spent in jail. He told long and funny stories about people he had met behind bars and explained the ins and outs of getting around the system, including how cans of "mackerel" were the currency of choice in the British prison he had been confined to years earlier. "I treat [prison] like being in a 3rd world country with poor communications infrastructure," he joked.

But he told Dread about his time in jail not for amusement but as a prelude to sharing a story about what he had seen heroin do to people in prison: In lockup they drug-tested you randomly, but they performed these exams only during the week, on Monday through Friday. Everyone inside knew how long each drug lasts in your system. If a prisoner smoked some weed, for example, it would show up in his piss for up to a month. As a result, no one ever smoked weed behind bars. But heroin only sticks around in your bloodstream for two days, tops. Which meant that if you injected H on a Friday, it was out of your system by Monday morning, just in time for the drug tests to begin.

"On Fridays," VJ wrote, "folks would go wild on H." And in the maximum-security wing where he was housed, H days had been nicknamed Hell Days, because that's exactly what they were like. "Guys would jam a week's worth of H in 4 hours." The wails from the inmates who were under were followed by moans as they came to and then a week of vomiting and tweaking as they spun out, unable to sleep, jerking and tugging and twisting in their beds as they waited for the following Friday to arrive, when they could ease the pain from the Friday before, and the cycle would begin anew.

"It wasn't pretty in there then," VJ said. "They just wanted to sleep."

Now, long out of jail and the deputy of the biggest drug site the world had ever seen, VJ found himself in a moral predicament.

DPR had been talking to the South American smuggler, Nob, about transporting massive amounts of heroin through the United Kingdom and selling it in bulk on the Masters of the Silk Road site. But before they could even begin building such a site or taking money from Nob, DPR wanted to ensure this Nob character was legit. So he had asked VJ, his consigliere, to help facilitate an early test deal.

Morally, though, Jones told Dread, "I don't think I could make money off importing H. If you want to, I'll offer all the help and advice you need, but I don't want to profit off of it."

Ross had never seen the effects of heroin in person, as he noted to VJ that the experience of Hell Days "sounds awful." But it still didn't deter him from his belief system. As Ross had argued back at Penn State, it wasn't his place to say who could put what into their body. "I've got this separation between personal and business morality," DPR explained to VJ. "I would be there for a friend to help him break a drug dependency, and encourage him to not start, but I would never physically bar him from it if he didn't ask me to."

Variety Jones contemplated how hard he should press the issue. He had been doing his best to counsel the Dread Pirate Roberts, but sometimes DPR's ego got in the way. On more than one occasion VJ had lost his patience. "You should be acting like Steve Jobs, not Larry the Cable Guy," he had written to DPR about a previous debate. "Leaders lead, they don't throw out things willy nilly, and wait to see who follows what."

Often Dread would try to defend his ideas, but there was no grappling with Variety Jones; a maestro on the keyboard, he was a master debater, a true contender who could have stood up to Ross on any topic—and often did.

The conversation about H dragged on for a while, but there was no sign that DPR was ever going to relent. So, while sitting in that dark Glasgow hotel room, VJ ultimately decided to let DPR win the discussion about heroin.

There were two reasons, though. The first harkened back to the last time he had let a disagreement like this cause a rift between him and a business partner, years earlier when VJ co-ran a Web forum that sold weed seeds online. That dispute had destroyed that enterprise and, according to Jones, had ended in a shoot-out in Texas.

But more important, Variety Jones decided to let the issue go because he had much bigger plans for his involvement in the Silk Road. While the Dread Pirate Roberts didn't know this yet, VJ didn't want to just be an employee; he wanted to be co-captain of the ship.

# Chapter 30
# THE ARMORY OPENS

Ross had anticipated a lot of different scenarios for the Silk Road, but not this. In his mind, years earlier, he had envisioned a free market where anyone could buy or sell anything without being traced by the government. There would be no bureaucrats telling people what they could sniff, swallow, or inject. It would be completely free and open. And that was exactly what the site had become.

Yet to some of the buyers and sellers on there, this freedom was a problem. The mellow people who bought and sold weed on the site didn't want to be associated with the speedy people who bought and sold cocaine. Some of the hard drug dealers didn't want to be in the company of the right-wing crazies who hawked guns. And some of the gun guys didn't want to be in the same shopping cart as the scummy heroin dealers. Round and round it went.

Even though all these people were dealing in illicit activities, they each had a moral sense that their particular outlawed product was more just than another.

Variety Jones was preternaturally aware of these hidden dynamics. He had been warning his boss about this for some time, pressing Dread to at least get the guns off the site so he didn't lose the weed sellers. This would also help mainstream customers feel more comfortable shopping in the drug aisles. "So grandma can come here for her cheap Canadian pharma meds," VJ wrote, "and not trip over a Glock 9mm" handgun on the way to the cash register.

Ross saw things differently. The ability to accept anyone was in many ways Ross's superpower. He had practiced this philosophy from high school to the Silk Road. So he found it perplexing that others couldn't just go about their business and enjoy the free world he had created.

Because of his unflinching acceptance, there were now more than two thousand different types of drugs for sale on the site, as well as lab supplies to make your own drugs and products to store and sell those drugs. There were digital goods, including key loggers, spy software, and other similar tools to hack into someone's e-mail or webcam. People could buy forged documents, including passports, fake IDs, and even counterfeit cash that was indistinguishable from real money. And then there was the most contentious section of the site, labeled "weapons," which had grown so much that you could buy everything from handguns to AR-15 automatic weapons. You could pick up bullets, grenades, and even a rocket launcher if need be.

But if Ross wanted to keep growing his flourishing business, he needed to appease the more conventional customers, libertarian or not.

"Guns will scare off a lot of mainstream clients," Variety Jones had said.

So Ross was going to have to make some changes. If he really wanted to make drugs legal, which was his ultimate quest, he was going to have to solve the gun issue. While he wouldn't bar them—he wouldn't bar anything—he instead decided to create a gun-only Web site.

When he explored the idea with VJ, they had together come up with the name the Armory. (At first it was going to be called "Silk Armory," sticking with the Silk Road branding, but they both decided it sounded too bizarre. Or, as VJ pointed out, "Silk Armory sounds like they sell Hello Kitty AK-47's.")

Thankfully, it hadn't been too difficult to build the Armory; it wasn't like creating an entirely new site. Ross simply siphoned the code from the Silk Road, slapped on a new logo—a big, rugged *A* with wings—and changed some design elements.

But the Armory failed to solve a number of existing problems with weapons sales. Ross had hoped that people would be able to use the site to buy guns with the same ease as picking up a .22 at a local Walmart. But it turned out that shipping guns in the mail was a lot more complicated than placing a few sheets of acid (which looked like blotter paper) in an envelope. Ross needed to ensure that the people buying and selling the weapons from the Armory would be able to get them to one another without someone from ATF showing up at their door and escorting them to jail.

But he kept asking himself how.

It wasn't like he could call his local post office on Park Drive in Austin and say, "Hey, I want to send some guns to a friend. What's the best way to do this?" So he did what most people his age do when they don't know something: he went to social media. Plodding over to his personal Facebook and Google+ accounts, Ross posted an update asking, "Anyone know someone that works for UPS, FedEx or DHL?" When a friend asked why he wanted a contact at one of these mail companies, Ross replied, "Well, I have a startup idea in the shipping sector, but I have zero experience there."

There was another issue that came with the guns Web site. It meant that more law enforcement would be looking not just for the generals who ran the Silk Road but also the people behind the Armory. (Not to mention the bulk drug Masters of the Silk Road site, which would bring more global attention and the interest of more governments when it eventually opened for business.)

The scrutiny the site was now receiving from the press, and the inevitable added attention that would slam upon it with the opening of the Armory, made it clear that the stakes were rising. All of these terrifying prospects led Variety Jones, who was now being dubbed the site's security chief, to decide that it was time for him to move further underground.

The best place he knew to do that was Thailand, where he had hidden once before and where, he told DPR, he had a few cops on the payroll. But going back to Thailand meant he would have to leave his lady behind in London.

"I'm getting her out of the crossfire," VJ wrote to DPR. "I need the world to think we've split. If I end up in Guantanamo, I don't want her in the next cell."

"That's tough."

"She knows I'm changing the world, and that it's dangerous for her," VJ replied. "But I'm not safe to be around."

With all of this added attention Ross knew that he was going to need to move again too. Going back overseas didn't make sense right now, and staying in Texas, near his family, wasn't an option either. The lies and the possibility of being found out were just too risky. What he needed was a place where he could be on his laptop for eighteen hours a day and no one would question why he was being antisocial or what he was working on.

Which meant he had to go to San Francisco.

As he opened the doors of the Armory Web site, he began plotting his move out west, reaching out to friends who lived there and figuring out where he would stay and what his cover would be once he arrived.

But before Ross could go anywhere, he had one last loose end to tie up. He opened his Web browser, navigated to Julia's Facebook page, and sent her a message asking if they could meet.

# Chapter 31
# ROSS SILENCES JULIA

Ross strolled along Rainey Street in Austin, past rows of old homes that had been converted into bars, as he headed toward the Windsor on the Lake apartment building. It was late afternoon in the summer of 2012, and the street was relatively quiet. A few people sat on outdoor benches amid the faint sounds of Texas as they guzzled beers and ate local barbecue. He approached an apartment building on the street, pulled out his phone, dialed a few numbers, and waited for an answer.

He hadn't been back in Austin for long, and wouldn't be there much longer. But before he left the Lone Star State again, maybe for good, he had to resolve the biggest problem of all.

"Hey," he said into his phone. "I'm out front."

A minute later Julia appeared, running down the steps to greet Ross with elation. After a long hug hello, she stood back and looked him up and down to examine his outfit (blue jeans, black belt, gray V-neck T-shirt, and matching sneakers), then laughed. So much time had passed since their romance had begun; their lives had taken drastically different routes, and yet here was Ross Ulbricht, looking virtually unaltered. "You're wearing the exact same outfit I bought you at Penn State!" she snickered. Ross simply smiled.

They hadn't seen each other since that fateful night in October, and Julia was thrilled to reconnect. She ushered him into her studio to show him around.

Boudoir photos lay everywhere, some on walls, others tilted on her desk. Ross immediately recognized a large picture of a woman arching her back. It had been taken in the studio where he had experimented with growing his first batch of mushrooms in Julia's underwear drawer two years earlier. How far he had come since then! Just twenty-four months ago he had been broke and aimless; now he was rich and as steadfast as ever.

"Wow, this place is amazing," he said as Julia waltzed around in front of him.

"I know. Aren't you proud of me?" she replied ebulliently. "I'm dating a new guy now. He takes me on all of these trips and takes me to all these great dinners."

"Way to make me feel awesome," Ross said, joking with her, and then quipped, "Well, I'm dating a girl too."

After some small talk, Ross asked if they could go for a walk to discuss something. "Of course." Julia beamed as she grabbed his hand and they strolled out of the building, down the concrete steps, and across the street toward a dirt path that led to Lady Bird Lake.

The sun was beginning to set as they meandered along the trail, hand in hand, telling stories about the past few months of their lives. Julia was still in love with Ross, and part of her hoped he had come to take her back. They eventually came across a tree that was wider than Ross stood tall. At its base there was a huge rock that rested on the water's edge. They sat down together.

"So," Ross said as he took a deep breath, preparing to tell Julia something important. "I just want you to know that I quit the site—I quit the Silk Road."

"Thank God! That's so wonderful." She leaned over and gave Ross a huge hug, holding on to him for as long as she could.

The leaves above them sighed in the breeze as Ross looked out at the sun that reflected pink and yellow and orange off the water. He took another deep breath and began an explanation of why he had given up the site. It had grown too big; it was too stressful; it just felt right to pass it along to someone else. "I'm so sorry for telling you about it in the first place," he lamented, "and I take full responsibility—"

"Thank you," Julia said as he continued to talk, and tears began welling up in her eyes.

"I just felt so powerful running the site," he said, then paused, as if he were reciting lines in a play. "I'm sorry."

Julia thanked him again, both for the apology and for quitting the Silk Road. She leaned over and they started to kiss. After a few moments Ross pulled back and looked her in the eyes. "I just need to know one more thing," he said. "Did you tell anyone else about the site? Anyone other than Erica?"

"No," she responded quickly.

"No one?"

"No. I didn't tell anyone else. Just Erica." A pang of guilt came over her for having betrayed the secret at all. "I love you, Ross."

"I love you too," he said as they continued kissing, the sun lowering into the horizon behind them. "I just couldn't move on without knowing that no one else knew."

They spoke more about the past, and Ross told her about his travels—about Thailand and the beaches and jungles and a mountainous sculpture he'd seen that was made entirely of extra-large dildos; about Australia, picnicking with his sister, and that his travels had made him reflect upon his life and how thankful he was that he no longer had anything to do with the Silk Road.

The cold air was beginning to blow off the water and Ross suggested they walk back.

"So what are you going to do now?" Julia asked as they crossed Rainey Street back toward her apartment building.

Ross told her he was leaving Texas in a few days to move to San Francisco. He planned to build an app with an old friend from Austin, René Pinnell. "I probably won't see you again for a while," he told her solemnly.

She would be sad to see him go, she explained, but happy for him that he was free from the clutches of that awful Web site.

"Yeah," he agreed, "I'm glad to be rid of it too; it was too stressful."

As they approached the door to the studio, Ross leaned in and kissed Julia one last time. "I love you," she said. He didn't reply. He just held her there for a second and then turned around and walked away. Heading into the darkness, alone.

# PART III

# Chapter 32
# CHRIS TARBELL, FBI

A question had been plaguing Chris Tarbell all day—in the office, at lunch, and now as he walked through downtown Manhattan with his coworkers. As the group crossed Broadway and turned right onto Center Street, he just couldn't stop himself; he had to ask. "Okay," he said to the men around him, "if you had to . . ." But before he could finish, they all began wincing, knowing full well what was coming. A "would you rather" joke from Tarbell was usually a distasteful, often comical query that always landed at a moment his colleagues least expected, intentionally catching them completely off guard. These often-crass jokes could range from the truly unpalatable to the truly bizarre. "Would you rather: sleep with your mother, or sleep with your father?" "Would you rather: be half your height, or double your weight?" "Would you rather have an erection for a year or hiccups for the rest of your life?"

"Where do you come up with this shit, Tarbell?" one of his coworkers asked.

"Come on. If you had to—like, you had no choice," Tarbell continued, as they kept walking, his colleagues grimacing as Tarbell harangued them with questions like an older brother tormenting his younger siblings.

The badgering briefly stopped when the group came upon the Whiskey Tavern, a local dive bar on Baxter Street, sandwiched between two bail-bond storefronts that looked out on the New York Police Department.

All the cops and government employees in New York had local watering holes they burrowed into after work. The FDNY went to Social Bar on Eighth Avenue, the NYPD had Plug Uglies on Third, and the Cyber Division of the FBI's New York office lived at the Whiskey Tavern. Special Agent

Chris Tarbell of the FBI and his team of agents frequented the shit-hole dive bar at least five nights a week.

When they arrived, Meg, the freckled bartender, would greet them with a "Hello, boys," then let them know, "The back room is all yours." The area of the bar she was referring to was always reserved for the FBI cybercrime crew, and if they arrived unannounced, Meg would evict whoever was there.

Given that tonight was a special evening, Tarbell asked for a few bottles of champagne, pronounced "cham-pag-nay." (By "champagne" he meant Miller High Life—the so-called champagne of beers, which cost $4 a pint at the tavern.)

Most of the FBI agents at the bar dressed the same, wearing oversize dark suits and white button-down shirts, and could have easily passed for bankers or lawyers. That was not true of Chris Tarbell, who looked like a cop from ten city blocks away with his short buzz cut, young face that didn't seem to fit his stocky 250-pound body, and swagger that exuded confidence.

As they settled in for a night of revelry, it was Tarbell who was the star of the show. After all, he was the one responsible for recently taking down an infamous hacker group, called LulzSec, that the media and security experts had asserted could never be stopped. What made LulzSec so special was that, unlike hackers of the past who would break into an institution for financial gain, this nefarious crew had spent the past year ransacking the Internet for the "lulz," a neologism that essentially meant "a good laugh." Part of their comedic hacking had included knocking the CIA Web site offline, breaking into Sony Pictures servers, and defacing the Web sites of the British newspapers the *Times* and the *Sun* by posting a fake news story that Rupert Murdoch had died. All just for fun.

But after months of undercover work, Chris Tarbell and his FBI team had systematically arrested the people behind LulzSec all across the world—in Chicago, Ireland, and New York City. Which is why the gang was celebrating at the Whiskey Tavern.

In the back of the bar, Meg reappeared with a dirty black tray crowded with twenty shot glasses, half of them filled with cheap whiskey, the other half with green pickle juice. She dropped the concoction, known as the Pickle Back, a bar specialty, on the table.

"Whose turn is it to drink the tray?" Tarbell bellowed to the group of men around him, all of whom responded with another wince.

Years earlier Tarbell had invented this ritual—known as the "drinking of the tray"—wherein someone was expected to drink the slushy potion of pickle juice, whiskey, and any other liquid that had been sloshing on the tray before the drinks were served. If no one else had the guts to do it, Tarbell was always up for the sickening challenge.

At thirty-one years old, Tarbell had already made a big name for himself as one of the top cybercrime agents in the FBI, if not the world. Sure, he'd landed the LulzSec case by chance when a tip came in through a hotline and Tarbell was the lucky one to pick up the phone. But it was what he did with that information that separated him from the other agents—turning the top hacker of LulzSec, a man who was known as Sabu, and then using him to bring down the entire organization. Because of Tarbell's ability to find people online, the media would soon bestow on him the nickname "the Eliot Ness of cyberspace," after the renowned American Prohibition agent.

It was no accident that Tarbell had ended up where he was, rising through the ranks of the FBI. He had planned it this way, just as he planned everything. Tarbell had worked hard to earn his master's degree in computer science, then became a cop. After more than a decade of eighteen-hour days, he had made his way up through the FBI to become a special agent. And he didn't stop there. When he wasn't with his wife and kids, he continued to study computer forensics for any technology platform imaginable.

He endured this because, more than anything, he desired to be the absolute best at anything he put his mind to. If his gym buddy was able to bench-press 400 pounds, Tarbell would spend months of his life lifting weights until he could bench-press 450 pounds (which he could actually do).

Over time he learned that the way to have a leg up on everyone else was to anticipate something before it happened and then have the answer to it. He prepped for everything. The night before he took his SATs in high school he did a practice drive to the test site to ensure he arrived on time. He did this the day before his physical test for the FBI. During his first few weeks at the Bureau he created a meticulous map of the entire office, labeling who everyone was and what he needed to know about them.

This obsessive planning came home with him. He told his wife, Sabrina, that the couple needed a code word they could use in case anything ever went wrong. "'Quicksand,'" he told her. "That's the word we use with each other if we're ever in trouble: 'quicksand.'" And when the cybercrime boys went out drinking, Tarbell texted ahead to let freckled Meg know how many people to expect. Nothing like planning a party at a dive bar.

On this particular night as many as fifty government employees were at the Whiskey Tavern to celebrate the capture of the LulzSec crew. As Tarbell sat there licking the taste of pickles and whiskey off his lips, Tom Brown, the assistant U.S. attorney for the Southern District of New York. who would end up prosecuting the LulzSec hackers, wandered over.

"So, Tarbell," Tom said, preparing to ask a question that had been plaguing him all day. "What's next? Who are we going after next?"

Tarbell looked back, annoyed. He had just spent the past few months of his life working twenty-hour days trying to take down LulzSec, and Tom was already badgering him about the next target. "Come on," Tarbell said. "We just fucking finished a case. Can't we just celebrate first?"

"Of course you can," Tom replied glacially, taking a short sip from his drink, "but I just wanted to see what we were going to do after that."

Tom was clearly baiting Tarbell and already knew the answer. "There is a target no one has been able to crack," Tom said, explaining that "no one" included the DEA, HSI, and a handful of government agencies from around the globe. The cybercrime FBI agents sipped from their cham-pag-nay as they listened to what Tom was saying. "I think," he said, "we should start looking at the Silk Road next."

# Chapter 33

# ROSS ARRIVES IN SAN FRANCISCO

The Alamo Square neighborhood of San Francisco has long been considered one of the city's most beautiful. The few blocks that make up the modest district sit snugly near the center of the city, framed by the past and with views of the future. The square is lined with bright "painted lady" Victorian homes built in the late 1800s, thanks in part to money from the Gold Rush years earlier. To the east, across gritty Market Street, modern glass skyscrapers are erected almost daily to house the fortunes being minted by the new gold rush—a wave of handsomely funded private companies, many of them valued at more than $1 billion, so-called unicorns. After the bubble had popped years earlier, there had been a resurrection of start-ups returning to the city, and billions of dollars ready to fund them.

On a bright and chilly afternoon in the summer of 2012, in the park in the middle of Alamo Square, a group of children giggled as they bounced through the playground, and unleashed dogs barked as they chased one another on the hilltop. And there, amid this happiness, Ross Ulbricht lay on the grass, inhaling his new city.

Ross fell in love with the Bay Area from almost the moment his feet touched the ground in San Francisco. Everything looked so magical and new. The flat, prairielike avenues of Texas were replaced by streets that seemed to undulate like a never-ending roller coaster. The billboards along the freeway didn't talk about NASCAR, Jesus, or the best rib-eye steak in town but rather advertised mystical search engines, social networks, and even new digital currencies.

He had arrived in this wonderful universe a few weeks earlier, wide-eyed and full of vigor. All he owned now was a small bag of clothes and his laptop. He felt as free as he ever had: the homeless kingpin of one of the fastest-growing drug empires in the world.

The decision about where to stay was simple. His pal from Austin, René Pinnell, who now lived in San Francisco, and his girlfriend, Selena, offered up a spare room in their small but welcoming apartment. Soon after Ross unpacked his few belongings, the three friends settled into a new routine, spending evenings exploring the city, cooking dinner, and talking about the meaning of life. (There was, however, one thing Ross didn't talk about: the Silk Road. He was never going to make that mistake again.) They played card games together, Twister, Scrabble (Ross often won), and hugged each other good night.

After breakfast each morning, while René and Selena sauntered off to work, their new roommate, Ross, would wave good-bye and wander down the street to a nearby coffee shop to oversee his drug empire.

The safest place he had found to work was a small café on Laguna Street called Momi Toby's, which was conveniently located a block from René's apartment on Hickory Street. Momi Toby's (pronounced "mow-mee toe-bees") resembled a French bistro with small tables and chairs outside. Inside, the Wi-Fi was free, and lots of seating allowed Ross to have his back against the wall so no one could see his computer screen, and subsequently the Silk Road.

As the weeks went on, Ross made new friends in the city, which carried some stress. While he couldn't talk to them about what he did for work, he could discuss what inspired him to do it. After all, in San Francisco the mentality of using technology to try to disrupt a broken system wasn't a strange way of thinking but rather the norm. In so many ways, the programmers and entrepreneurs Ross met were just like him.

They looked at the world around them and saw that the government was a ball of wasteful red tape; that the taxi industry treated customers like shit; hotels overcharged and overtaxed; health care was a sham, driven by the needs of the insurance agencies, not the sick; oil-dependent cars had helped to justify an eternal war in the Middle East; and illegal drugs were only illegal because the government wanted to control the people. And all of these issues were a result of the previous generations' mistakes. Their parents had inextricably fucked up the world we lived in, and it was the people in San Francisco—those just like Ross—who were going to use technology to fix it all.

*You're fucking welcome!*

He was also invigorated by the manifestation of the libertarian ideals around him that the start-ups were employing. And here was Ross, doing the exact same thing, but instead of taxis or hotels, health care or gas-guzzling cars, he was trying to defeat the U.S. government and its pathetic, destructive war on drugs.

The CEOs of these other start-ups were no different from Ross, either. They had all read the same Ayn Rand books. These chief executives shared the same quotes on Facebook as he did: "The question isn't who is going to let me; it's who is going to stop me." The leaders of these companies all preached the same verbiage as the Dread Pirate Roberts too, on their blogs and in their press releases: "Let the market decide; not the government." "Let the people determine who should win; not the politicians." "We're changing the world and making it a better place."

Most of all, the new friendships he was making were the perfect antidote to the problems he was now experiencing on the Silk Road. Sadly, his closest confidant was starting to rub him the wrong way. Not only was Variety Jones not okay with selling H, which went against Ross's entire libertarian philosophy behind the Silk Road, but VJ also proclaimed that sure, while he was there to help Dread free people from the clutches of government, they were still, at the end of the day, drug dealers.

Ross vehemently disagreed. "As long as we don't cross [a] line in our pursuit," DPR wrote to Variety Jones, "then we are only doing good."

"Ha, dude, we're criminal drug dealers," VJ responded. "What line shouldn't we cross?"

"Murder, theft, cheating, lying; hurting people," DPR replied, resentful of the question. "That line. We are drawing a new line I guess you could say. According to that line, we aren't criminals."

This discussion echoed another suggestion from VJ, that Ross should put a powerful lawyer on the payroll. "You need to pick a top man, a top man in his field, with top man contacts," Jones wrote. "That field is interstate drug smuggling, money laundering, RICO and drug kingpin legislation." But in Ross's mind, he wasn't going to get caught, so why would he need a "top man" lawyer? That was already admitting defeat.

And then there was the biggest new development between the two friends and associates: it seemed that VJ wanted more ownership too. Maybe this was why he had been so nice all along? Maybe when he had come up with the brilliant plan to rename the creator of the site the Dread Pirate Roberts, it was Variety Jones's hope that one day he would become the next pirate to captain the ship.

Their recent debates had come to a head when VJ wrote, "I think we need to formalize . . ." To create an official partnership between the two men . . . "If only to avoid confrontation in the future."

Ross was caught off guard by the question, and another debate ensued.

"Here's the thing," VJ wrote. "I do well two ways." Option one: "50/50." Option two: "Me having it all."

What the heck was Variety Jones talking about?! Ross wasn't giving up control of his site. Here was the only person Ross could trust in this online world, who had given him endless advice, and was now giving ultimatums.

"Well, you can't have it all now can you?" DPR wrote. "You could compete with me and maybe you'd win, but . . ."

VJ could tell the conversation was getting contentious quickly, so he quelled the argument. "Naw, let's not go down that road. I'm not gonna do that, ever, I promise. But, I do know what I bring to the table, and it's a shitload."

"I know you do."

"Dude, I want equality," Jones wrote. "I don't do second fiddle very well."

But Ross had no interest in parity. In the current version of the site, it was Ross's world, and he got to decide what went and what didn't. He dictated who got a raise and who didn't. People who worked hard were rewarded, as he had recently done with some focused employees, giving some of them an extra few hundred dollars in Bitcoin when they excelled. When Ross wanted to reward Smedley, the chief programmer, he did it on his terms. "You've really stepped up to the plate here already. Your base pay is still $900 of course, but I'll throw [in] a bonus." And when Inigo, another lieutenant, needed help finishing a renovation project on his house, Dread gave him an extra $500 to pass along to his handyman. Those kinds of decisions were up to Ross the Boss to decide, not VJ.

What would have happened if he had to run these things past his lieutenant? No, thank you. Plus, how would Ross exert power and control on the site? He was already having a difficult time getting people to show up to work on time, or fill out the correct reports that he wanted to see at the end of their shift. He even enjoyed disciplining employees, telling them (still in

Ross's hokey banter) that they had "fudged up" when they needed a good scolding.

Ross had worked too hard to simply hand anything to anyone. And shortly after this conversation with VJ, Ross simply stopped talking to him for a few days. Instead he retreated into the real world. Into San Francisco.

As Ross stood up from the grassy knoll at Alamo Square and reached for his brown laptop bag to head back to his apartment, there was no question about it: This was the place he was supposed to be. This was the city where Ross would make the Silk Road into the greatest start-up the world had ever seen. And yet, as he walked back along Sacramento Street, past those beautiful painted lady Victorian homes and the modern glass skyscrapers, Ross didn't know that he would soon face challenges that no other start-up in the city would have to deal with. That in a matter of months he would find himself dealing with dirty cops and rogue employees, and Ross Ulbricht would have to decide if he wanted to have people tortured and killed in order to protect his growing enterprise.

# Chapter 34
# CHRIS IN THE PIT

It had been a few months since the FBI had taken down the LulzSec hackers, and the hangovers from the subsequent celebrations at the Whiskey Tavern had since worn off. Yet there was one aspect of that case that Chris Tarbell couldn't get out of his mind.

He was sitting in an area known as "the Pit" at the New York FBI offices, talking with other FBI agents—Ilhwan Yum and Thom Kiernan—weighing if the cybercrimes division of the FBI should get involved in the Silk Road case or go after a different target instead.

The Pit, where they sat, looked like a sunken living room and was big enough for a handful of desks and chairs. This enclave had been around for decades and was considered the top spot in the New York City headquarters. Years earlier, before Tarbell and the nerdy computer agents started occupying the desks there, the Pit was home to organized-crime agents. Back then they went after mobsters who stayed as far away from technology as possible, fearing that something as inconsequential as a pay phone could be used to track their location. Now the men in the Pit went after mobsters who had adopted technology as a way to hide their whereabouts.

But the old guys and the new did share one thing in common: both generations of FBI agents were practical jokers. Some days Tarbell and his colleagues would rub leftover deli meat on another agent's desk phone earpiece, then call from another room to watch the agent smear roast beef and mayonnaise on his or her ear. Tarbell had once played a joke using another agent's car, hooking the car's horn up to its brake pedal so every time the agent tried to slow down on his drive home, his horn blared at the cars in front of him. And then Tarbell was always ready with a "would you rather" question.

Tarbell's desk was covered in papers and paraphernalia from previous cases. In the center of this mess were his three computers, the two classified machines that were used only for internal work and the one unclassified computer that couldn't be traced back to the FBI, where on the screen the Silk Road Web site currently sat looking back at the agents.

As they spoke about the site, Tarbell thought to himself that if they did go after the Silk Road, he was going to do everything he could to avoid the unthinkable mistake the Bureau had made in the recent LulzSec case.

There were two main aspects of the LulzSec arrests the Feds needed to pull off for the takedown to work properly. First, it was imperative that they capture every suspect at the exact same time, even though they were all in different states and countries. They had to ensure that the hackers didn't alert anyone else about their arrests, or the entire operation would fall apart. The FBI had pulled this part off seamlessly. But it was the second detail, which was equally important, where they had failed dismally: It was crucial to capture each suspect on his or her laptop with the computer open. If the hackers closed their computers and those computers were encrypted, the data inside would be locked away forever. Even with the fastest and most advanced FBI computers, it could take more than a thousand years to figure out the password of a properly encrypted machine.

One of the most important LulzSec targets that the FBI planned to arrest was also allegedly the most dangerous member of the group. His name was Jeremy Hammond, and he was a political activist and computer hacker who had been arrested more than half a dozen times for protests against both Nazis and Republicans, for breaking into private servers around the world, and for releasing information to WikiLeaks.

Fast-forward to the night of the LulzSec takedown. The plan was as follows: Tarbell would go to Ireland to oversee the arrest of one of the LulzSec team's youngest hackers, a spritely nineteen-year-old. An FBI team in Chicago would be stationed, ready to pounce on Hammond. Senior agents in New York would watch live video feeds of the other arrests. Given Hammond's ties to political advocacy groups, and his several previous arrests, there was a chance that the hideout he was in would also be full of other activists, some with violent records. So at the last minute a higher-up at the FBI decided to send in a fully armed SWAT team to get Hammond on his computer. It would be the first time the FBI would use a SWAT team to arrest someone on a laptop.

It was early evening when the FBI trucks tore into the Bridgeport area of Chicago and a dozen men in bulletproof vests with machine guns descended on the single-story brick house where Hammond was hiding. The wooden front door flew off its hinges, and the agents stormed inside, throwing a flashbang grenade into the kitchen on the left and then scurrying into the other rooms with weapons drawn, screaming, "FBI! FBI! FBI!" But in the few seconds it took the SWAT team to reach the rear of the house, where Hammond sat, the dreadlocked hacker had calmly pushed the lid of his laptop closed, and there he sat at his desk, his hands in the air and a locked computer in front of him. It was the equivalent of doing a massive drug bust and the suspect flushing the drugs down the toilet before the cops made it into the bathroom.

While all the agents were upset about the laptop incident, Tarbell was particularly tormented by it. He didn't make mistakes. Ever.

And yet here he had.

Thankfully, there was a silver lining to the Hammond incident. Maybe it was an accident, or possibly laziness, but for some reason Hammond had not encrypted his laptop properly, and the FBI forensics lab was eventually able to get inside using a special brute-force technology that tries every password imaginable until it guesses the correct one. It took the government's supercomputer six months to figure out that Hammond's password was "chewy12345." But Tarbell knew that being able to crack the code was pure luck. Most, if not all, experienced hackers and people on the Dark Web encrypted their laptops with much stronger passwords for this very reason.

Now as Tarbell sat there in the Pit talking to his coworkers about how they would approach this Silk Road case, he assured his team that if they did go after the Dread Pirate Roberts, they wouldn't make the same mistake they had with Hammond; Tarbell would have a plan to ensure they captured DPR with his hands on the keyboard.

# Chapter 35

# BATTEN DOWN
# THE HATCHES!

The argument between the Dread Pirate Roberts and Variety Jones didn't last long. They needed each other and knew it. But it would mark a turning point in the relationship between the two men, where there was no question that DPR was now in charge. And Jones wasn't going anywhere, as he had warned. He was making tens of thousands of dollars a month in salary from the site and needed that money whether he liked it or not. Ross needed VJ too. He was ready to take the next step in the life of his business. It was time to close ranks and bring some corporate order to his illegal drug empire.

"I wanted to raise a topic we haven't discussed before," DPR wrote to Variety Jones.

Ross knew VJ would be thrown off by the comment. While the two men had no idea what the other looked like, over the past year they had discussed almost everything imaginable, from the personal to the professional. They had shared their hopes, dreams, fears, and desires and counseled each other on every aspect of those worlds. The Dread Pirate Roberts had even trusted Variety Jones enough to tell him personal things about Ross Ulbricht, explaining that he had once been a physics student in college and about having his heart broken by his old girlfriend from Texas.

So when Dread wanted to talk about something new, VJ was a bit taken aback. "Can't imagine there is a topic we haven't discussed before."

But there was one, and it might have been the most important topic of all. "Local Security," DPR wrote.

*Ah, yes. That.*

Ross had been working for months to try to fix security vulnerabilities, both in his life and on the site. After many close calls, including instances of hackers attacking the servers, and constantly having to move to different coffee shops and cities to cover up his secrets, he was fully aware that he had to put together a plan to protect every single area of his life that made him vulnerable.

He hadn't been caught yet. If he was more careful going forward, Ross reasoned, he would never be caught. And given the amount of attention the site was receiving—being mentioned in hundreds of news articles a week all over the world—the people hunting him would only grow more desperate. Silk Road's wares had expanded beyond drugs and guns to include synthetic drugs from China—among them, new forms of synthetic heroin, like fentanyl, which was up to one hundred times stronger than traditional morphine—not to mention a slew of explosives and other highly dangerous goods. So it was time to bolster his defenses and strengthen his security. He wasn't going to take any chances.

To begin, he put Variety Jones in charge of looking into any possibility that law enforcement, or LE, as they abbreviated it, might be lurking on the site. Next Ross got to work securing other vulnerable areas of his life, including his own laptop.

First and foremost, he made sure his Samsung 700Z was properly encrypted. He had talked to VJ about this before, days after they read the news about someone being arrested for leaking information to WikiLeaks. The news reports about the bust noted that the man had used exactly the same password to log in to his computer and for his encryption software and that the FBI cracked it in no time at all.

"What a macaroon," VJ had written.

"Weak," Ross agreed.

"If he had a good password, they'd have nothing," VJ said, referring to the "Feebs," the nickname they used for the FBI. He then added that the man who had been arrested was an "idiot" for not taking security more seriously.

With this ominous lesson, Variety Jones offered some advice to DPR: You should set up your computer to automatically shut down if it hasn't been used for a certain period of time. More important, you need to install a kill switch, where you can press a random key on your laptop that kills the machine instantly. This way, if the Feebs approach you in public, you press the key and your computer is locked forever.

Dread replied that he would do just that.

Now Ross had another question for VJ, asking if he should store his files in the cloud so his laptop was completely clear of anything related to the Silk Road. This way, if the man behind the mask were ever grabbed with his hands on the keyboard, there would be nothing that could link him to the site. "Would be nice," DPR wrote, "to think that my laptop has nothing critical or incriminating on it." After some back-and-forth on the pros and cons of each (the negative being that storing everything in the cloud would make working on the site painfully slow), Variety Jones suggested that Dread keep all his Silk Road files on his computer but that he encrypt them, so if his computer was grabbed by the Feebs, they would never be able to get inside.

Great idea!

"Ok, just needed to talk that through," DPR said. "Thanks!"

As another backup plan—the most-wanted man on the Internet could never have too many—Ross decided to partition the hard drive on his laptop into two different sections. (This was like cutting an earthworm in half so that it regenerated and became two new worms.) His computer essentially now became two computers with two different accounts, with one side of the machine strictly allocated to the Dread Pirate Roberts and used only for all things Silk Road. The other side of the computer was assigned to Ross and was where he would e-mail his friends and family, log in to Facebook, and flirt with girls on dating Web sites.

This was when Ross created a very strict rule, perhaps the most important of all his new security enhancements. Anything that could be linked to Ross Ulbricht online (personal e-mails or social media) would never be done on the DPR side of the computer. On the flip side, anything that linked to the Dread Pirate Roberts (logging in to the Silk Road, chatting with VJ, uploading new code to the servers) would never happen on Ross's side of the computer. This was imperative to ensure that the two identities did not leave a trail back to each other online.

For the backup plan to the backup plan, Ross added booby traps that would activate in the highly unlikely event that someone did get into his laptop. One of the traps made the laptop go dark if someone snooped though his Web browser history more than half a dozen times.

The next part of Ross's security operation would require ensuring that the people who worked for him were all really vigilantes fighting to legalize drugs, and not employees of the DEA or the FBI. To do this, Ross started asking people who wanted a paycheck from the Silk Road to share a picture of their ID—a driver's license or passport, something that showed who they really were. It was a tough ask, Ross knew, but it was imperative if he didn't want to end up in jail.

Now when he hired someone new, he went through the customary conversation, explaining that they would have no choice but to divulge who they were to the Dread Pirate Roberts.

"Do you need to see my id?" ChronicPain, a new employee, asked DPR as he prepared to join the site to help manage the user forums.

"Yes," DPR replied. (Without a doubt.)

"Can I just tell you my name?"

"I'll need your id with current address," Dread wrote; then, to put ChronicPain at ease, he noted that his ID "will be stored encrypted, and I will probably never need to decrypt."

"So," the new employee said without much of a choice, "I guess I'll just have to trust you on that."

"Yea."

Ross knew that most people would agree. Being part of the movement he was creating was more important to his employees than a slight risk. And sure enough, in a matter of hours the ID for ChronicPain arrived in DPR's in-box.

There was also another reason to get those IDs. Ross was giving his employees more responsibility, and some even had access to Bitcoins on the site. If someone decided to cross the Dread Pirate Roberts, he would need to know who they were and where they lived. There would be retribution for such actions.

The final item on his security cleanup checklist was to create his own digital go bag that he would employ in case something catastrophic happened. If the cops knocked on his door, he needed a plan for what to do and where to go.

Ross opened a text document on his computer and created a file he called "Emergency." He then began writing a list of things he would need to do in the event that something went terribly wrong. A doomsday list.

"Encrypt and backup important files on laptop to memory stick; destroy laptop hard drive and hide/dispose; destroy phone and hide/dispose," Ross wrote. "Find place to live on craigslist for cash. Create new identity (name, backstory)."

But he also knew that if the day arrived when Ross and DPR did have to go into hiding, simply finding a place on Craigslist and changing his name wouldn't be enough to protect him indefinitely. He would have to come up with a safe place to flee to. Possibly even another country. A country that embraced pirates and would take in Ross Ulbricht and the Dread Pirate Roberts and their millions of dollars in wealth and keep them both out of reach of the U.S. government.

# Chapter 36

# JARED'S DEAD ENDS

*This is so frustrating!* Jared thought.

He held on to his son Tyrus's hand as he continued walking down the aisles of the Barnes & Noble in Lincolnshire, Illinois. They trudged up one row of books and then down another. Every few feet Tyrus, who was now three and a half, looked up at his dad as Jared searched intently for something among the stacks.

"Hello," a chirpy woman at the information counter said to them finally. "Can I help you find something?"

"Erm," Jared said, "I'm looking for some books on the Mises Institute." He looked around to make sure no one had overheard what he was asking about. The last thing Jared wanted to do was get into a discussion with a random person on this topic.

"The My Says Institute?" the woman asked loudly, looking down at her computer.

"No, it's Mises, *M-I-S-E-S*," Jared whispered. "It's a libertarian think tank that focuses on Austrian economics and . . ." He trailed off, realizing this probably made no sense to the woman in front of him. After all, this made no sense to Jared.

But still, he needed these books for the next phase of his investigation, which was starting to stall.

Since the beginning of the year, Jared had seized almost two thousand new shipments of drugs coming into the country, all by figuring out what each package would look like, and in doing so had disrupted the Silk Road as best he could. Jared had also arrested and detained a few dealers on the site, including one of the busiest, who sold ecstasy and other drugs from the

Netherlands. And he had subsequently taken over some dealers' accounts on the Silk Road, gaining a better understanding of the inner workings of the operation.

But he was still no closer to unearthing the founder of the site. So after finding himself circling around in too many online cul-de-sacs, Jared decided he would try to get inside the mind of the Dread Pirate Roberts, which was why he was standing in the Barnes & Noble in Lincolnshire, awkwardly asking about the Mises Institute.

In recent weeks he had sat at his desk, a Rubik's Cube always spinning in his hand, as he read all of the online postings by the Silk Road's creator, looking for similarities in the author's language. As the site had grown, DPR's message had become more brazen. While at first the founder's idea had been to make drugs legal, more and more he wrote about how terrible the U.S. government was, and how it was a place for the abuse of power. In one post DPR gloated that the "state is unable to get its thieving murderous mitts on [the Silk Road]."

Based on all of his writings, Jared had started to build a profile of who this Dread Pirate Roberts might be. He was likely very educated, young, not rich but not poor either, and while he wanted to destroy the American legal system, he was also doing this for the money. DPR had even admitted this in postings on the site, noting that "money is one motivating factor for me. . . . I also enjoy a few first-world pleasures that I feel I have earned. . . . Compared to most I know, I still live quite frugally." But from Jared's readings it appeared that DPR also believed that what he was doing was making the world a better place. "As corny as it sounds," Dread had written online, "I just want to look back on my life and know that I did something worthwhile that helped people."

Jared, trying to find things that others couldn't see, started to analyze DPR's speech patterns. For one, Dread used the word "epic" a lot, which showed that he was likely younger. He also used emoji smiley faces in his writing, though he never used a hyphen as the nose, writing them as :) rather than the old-fashioned :-). Yet the one attribute about DPR that stood out to Jared was that rather than writing "yes" or "yeah" on the site's forums, Dread instead always typed "yea."

DPR was constantly recommending books to his followers—a litany of literature from the Mises Institute. Jared wanted to understand Dread's thinking and read along too. But the books were so dense that nothing he read made any sense. To him it appeared that the arguments made by the authors were just a series of justifications for doing things in the world without taking responsibility for how those actions might affect other people.

All those books and all that research hadn't brought Jared any closer to DPR.

To make matters worse, Jared had heard from his counterparts at the Homeland Security office in Baltimore that a DEA agent, Carl Force, had managed to get close to the Dread Pirate Roberts, and Carl had been chatting with him undercover.

Hearing this, Jared reluctantly asked the HSI Baltimore team to look through some of Carl's chat logs to see if he could find more patterns in DPR's language.

When an e-mail arrived containing some of the logs, Jared was shocked at what the DEA agent was writing to DPR. Carl Force appeared to be offering more information than he should to the man he was supposed to be hunting, explaining how drug-smuggling routes worked and how to buy and sell heroin in bulk. It was one thing to curry favor with a perp whom you were trying to lure into public, but this felt like it was going several steps too far.

As Jared sat at his desk in Chicago, staring at all the mail tubs on the floor, the Mises books on his desk, and the pictures of drugs that covered his walls, he felt so frustrated that he was being caught up in dead end after dead end. Jared needed a break in his case. Something, anything, just a little sign that he was on the right track.

# Chapter 37
# A PIRATE IN DOMINICA

**W**elcome aboard, and thanks for flying with us." The voice crackled over the intercom as the plane slowly edged along the tarmac of San Francisco International Airport. "Just in case, a life vest is located under your seat." Ah, yes. The ominous what-to-do-in-case-of-an-emergency warning. A cautionary tale that served as the perfect allegory for Ross, who sat in the middle of the plane, nervously thinking about the last two hours and the next two weeks.

Ross had expected an easy morning with some last-minute packing for his trip. But instead DPR had woken up to the discovery that the Silk Road was under attack by hackers who had brought the servers to a halt. To fend off the attack, Ross had been frantically working with Smedley, his lieutenant programmer, all morning.

"I think we should install that waffle so we can see the results from mod-sec," Smedley wrote as he tried to figure out what was happening. "Everything with a .txt extension can go into /etc/modsecurity/."

"Let me think," DPR replied, frantic as the clock ticked down to his flight.

"Disable everything."

"OK. We'll need mysql, yea?"

The morning had gone on like this for a couple of hours, and then Ross had no choice but to set off for his trip, leaving Smedley responsible for fending off the hackers.

For Ross that was all irrelevant now. Poor DPR would not be able to log on to the Silk Road for at least six hours, until his next layover. He'd just need to trust that Smedley and his team of employees, whom he was paying between $900 and $1,500 a week for their services, had it under control. Sleep. That's what he would do. He would need it when he landed. As the plane leveled off at 35,000 feet, Ross leaned back in his seat and closed his eyes.

While he could have easily afforded to buy a Learjet (or two) and fly private, he had instead chosen to lie low and travel commercial. As a result, the travel alone for his trip was going to last almost two days and take him more than four thousand miles away from San Francisco. First he had to stop in Atlanta, Georgia, then catch a connection to San Juan, Puerto Rico. The following day, groggy and tired, he would take a small prop plane over a dozen tropical islands until he arrived in the Commonwealth of Dominica—smack in the middle of the Caribbean.

This wasn't a vacation. It was his trapdoor—his out. The final touch of an escape plan that had been in the works since he'd begun his security overhaul months earlier. A what-to-do-in-case-of-an-emergency scheme. After months of research and seeking the advice of Variety Jones, it turned out the Commonwealth of Dominica, where citizenship can be picked up for an "investment" of around $75,000, would serve as the perfect place for Ross to hide the Dread Pirate Roberts from the Feebs. It was also the ideal spot for Ross to stash his millions of tax-free dollars without Uncle Sam asking where all that money came from.

The entire trip to Dominica was an exhausting slog. Ross would deboard a plane and find a private corner in the airport to open his laptop so that DPR could log on to the Silk Road and wage war against attackers before rushing off to the next flight. This went on again and again until Ross finally landed in the tropics.

He stepped off the plane to see a tiny airport with a blue roof surrounded by tentacle-like palm trees. The taxi from the airport took almost an hour to get to the Fort Young Hotel on Victoria Street, where Ross was staying.

When he arrived, he checked in, logged on to the site, and was immediately relieved to discover that Smedley had managed to squelch the assault against the Silk Road. Everything was back to normal—for now.

Ross closed his laptop, crawled under the soft white sheets on his bed, and slept for fourteen long hours.

When he woke up, sounds from the Caribbean were waiting outside his window. Birds—seagulls, pelicans, and colorful parrots—talked among themselves as the sound of the water washing over the rocks below trickled into the hotel. He walked out onto his balcony and looked off to the right, where the cruise ship dock sat empty. To his left he could see Champagne Beach and the top of Pointe Michel. It should have been the perfect morning in paradise, but when DPR went online, he found himself back in a living hell. While Ross had slept, the attackers had returned with a vengeance, and the Silk Road was completely incapacitated. A hacker who went by the moniker "JE" had e-mailed DPR and demanded a $10,000 Bitcoin bounty to stop the assault. DPR messaged his consigliere, Variety Jones, and asked what to do. "Pay," VJ counseled.

After all, $10,000 was nothing to DPR these days. Considering the Silk Road was now, on average, facilitating a quarter million dollars in sales each day, an hour of the attack was costing DPR more than the hacker's measly ransom fee. (The $10,000 fee soon turned into a demand for a $25,000 payoff.) Reluctantly he sent the money.

"Had to swallow my pride there," DPR wrote to Jones after transferring the Bitcoins to the aggressor. But the site was back alive—again, just for now. Before the pummeling resumed, there was a lot of work to do to plug holes in the ship. VJ said that he would work with Smedley to get everything back in order and prepare for new assaults. "Take some time to meditate," Variety Jones told DPR. "Get centered 'n shit."

Ross was grateful that the relationship between the two men was now back at its peak, and they had started offering affectionate quips to each other once again, especially when they signed off the site at night. "Love ya :)" Dread would write to VJ, who replied, "Dude, you know I love ya' too, eh." At other times they would end the day with "smooches 'n shit" and a "smoochie boochie" back.

So when Variety Jones told Dread to go and meditate, that's exactly what Ross did. He closed his laptop and set off through the hotel in search of a Jacuzzi. The resort was a stunning three-hundred-year-old inn that sat along the edge of the island. On the roof there was an infinity pool, and next to it a steaming hot tub. Ross slipped into the frothy water, his body feeling lighter under the weight of two worlds sitting on his shoulders. As he peered at the splendid Caribbean Sea, he took a deep breath and calmness enveloped his mind.

These types of chaotic issues, like hackers and ransoms, didn't bother Ross for long. In many respects he had started to enjoy them.

"How lucky are we to get these problems," he had written to VJ. "I always wanted big problems on my plate; never knew if I'd get there." And such problems, he explained, had Ross thinking about his legacy and what he would leave behind when he was gone.

"Winning the drug war is gonna be easy," Jones said.

"I think that's more or less a foregone conclusion," Ross replied.

DPR wasn't the first pirate to visit Dominica. For hundreds of years it had been home to real raiders, the ones who hid their booty in the caves around the archipelago. Now pirates like Dread could hide their digital wealth in bank accounts around the islands without worrying about the U.S. government reaching in and grabbing any of it.

"My top priority right now is getting a new citizenship," Ross had told Variety Jones, who had in turn counseled, "Make sure your plan includes at least two backup locales." While Ross was in Dominica, he had also started exploring other countries, including Italy, Monte Carlo, Andorra, Costa Rica, and even Thailand, as alternate places to live if he went on the lam.

But disappearing came with its consequences. Ross worried about those closest to him and whether he could handle never seeing them again. "I grew up here," he said to VJ about leaving the United States. "My family is here." And more important, he admitted, one day he wanted to start his own family. "The worst part is that I have no one to talk about this stuff with," Ross wrote. "It just bounces around in my head."

Jones knew that feeling better than anyone, and he counseled his friend as best, and as sternly, as he could. "Best advice I can give right now is plan on a few years without emotional attachments," VJ wrote. "Ex's can put you in jail for life."

"I'm not complaining about any of this," Dread wrote back, noting that this was a "great fucking problem to have."

Over the following two weeks Ross tackled his objective methodically. The process of getting citizenship wasn't as easy as dropping a bag of hundred-dollar bills, or a thumb drive of Bitcoins, on someone's doorstep. Ross had to gather letters of recommendation from some longtime Texas friends, telling them that he was exploring a citizenship in Dominica because there were some interesting tax opportunities for non–U.S. citizens. Then there were official forms to fill out, documents to submit, background checks, and even a medical exam. All annoying but necessary officialdom Ross had to go through for the sake of DPR and his future should he have to follow his emergency plan.

When he wasn't dealing with his citizenship application, Ross made friends in Dominica. There was Lou, a midthirties, sinewy local island woman who showed him the coves and shantytowns and poured him lots of liquor–and–Coca-Cola drinks, a Dominican specialty. He spent time at the beach, kicking a soccer ball back and forth with Kema, another local. He swam in the Lagoon River at sunset, then spent the evening under a gazebo on Purple Turtle Beach, eating barbecue, plantains, and rice, partying late into the night as the sound of the waves trickled onto the shore in the distance. It really was paradise.

When his new friends asked Ross what he was doing in the country, he simply replied, "I'm here on business." Sadly for Ross, that wasn't far from the truth.

He was forced to spend more time than he would have liked on his trip dealing with the growing pains of the site. Ross had to oversee customer-support tickets that seemed endless, with people complaining about drugs not arriving on time, the site being too slow, or harassment on the forums. There were more hackers to fend off with even larger ransoms, the Feds to hide from, and his employees to inspire. *Fudge, this was hard work.* But Ross's bank account was brimming with his bounty. When things were difficult, all he had to do was look at the spreadsheet with those numbers, and those numbers would look back at him, the ultimate pep talk to keep going.

Thankfully for DPR, during this particularly tumultuous moment there was relief in sight: Silk Road Movie Night!

Inspired by the clubs he had joined back at Penn State, and as a remedy for his loneliness, Ross had started Movie Night on the Silk Road, as well as the Dread Pirate Roberts's Book Club.

For tonight's film, DPR had instructed everyone on the site that on "Friday the 16th, at 8 pm EST," they should simultaneously press "play" on the movie *V for Vendetta* (with a link to download the film). The movie, DPR told his shipmates, was about a country under occupation by a police state and a vigilante known only as V, a masked marauder who fights against the government.

Sure enough, at 8:00 p.m. Eastern, people from all over the world, including those in America, Thailand, and Australia, pressed "play" on their laptops as the picture began. And on the island of Dominica, Ross sat in his hotel room watching the film, enamored by its message. It was as if some lines had been written by DPR himself. "People should not be afraid of their governments," V says in the film. "Governments should be afraid of their people."

Over the following week, as DPR worked on the site, he was invigorated by the message in the film. But unlike V in the movie, Ross had a different goal in mind: he was making money, lots of it.

If the Silk Road had been valued as a start-up in Silicon Valley, it would now easily have been one of those fabled unicorns, worth a billion dollars or more. Venture capitalists would have been salivating to meet with the site's CEO and invest millions more in the company. While most start-ups are in the red for the first few years of their existence, the Silk Road had mushroomed to be worth more than the value of the entire country Ross was visiting right now, Dominica. But for now it wasn't a company; it was an illegal entity. It didn't have a CEO; it had a leader who was a pirate. A pirate who at this moment was packing his bags at the Fort Young Hotel, preparing to leave paradise.

After two weeks on the island, with his citizenship application now going through the system, it was time for Ross to return home.

The trip back to the United States took almost two days, Ross finally touching down at San Francisco International Airport after the four-thousand-mile journey.

On the surface it seemed that the trip had gone unnoticed, that the Dread Pirate Roberts had slipped in and out of the United States without detection—which was true. But Ross wouldn't be so lucky.

As an American customs official swiped his passport into a digital scanner, Ross William Ulbricht didn't know that his name and where he had just traveled from were now being converted into a million ones and zeros. Or that this information was now traveling from the customs official's computer across the country, in mere milliseconds, through the same wires that enabled people to buy and sell drugs on the Silk Road, and landing in a database that belonged to the U.S. Department of Homeland Security.

Ross Ulbricht.
IMAGE RECOVERED FROM ULBRICHT'S LAPTOP

Ross the Eagle Scout.
IMAGE RECOVERED FROM ULBRICHT'S LAPTOP

Young Ross in elementary school in Austin, Texas (top left).
IMAGE FROM ULBRICHT'S FACEBOOK PAGE

Ross with his parents, Lyn and Kirk Ulbricht, on graduation day.

The NOMMO Club at Penn State University, where Ross practiced his djembe drumming.

Senior prom, where Ross ended the evening fully clothed in a swimming pool.

IMAGE COURTESY OF DEBORAH HORWITZ

Ross Ulbricht and Julia Vie about to go on a date.

IMAGE COURTESY OF JULIA VIE

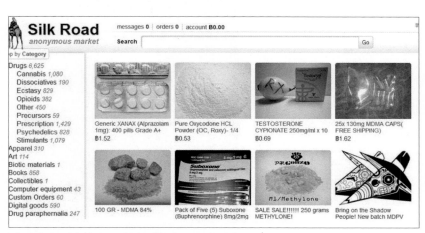

The Silk Road Web site, which offered more than 6,625 different listings for drugs.

Gary Alford of the Internal Revenue Service.

Jared Der-Yeghiayan of the Department of Homeland Security.

Carl Force of the Drug Enforcement Agency, sitting at his desk in Baltimore, Maryland.
IMAGE COURTESY OF *EPIC MAGAZINE*

Force disguised as Nob, his online alter ego on the Silk Road.
USED AS EVIDENCE BY THE U.S. GOVERNMENT

This image of Roger Thomas Clark, who is believed to be Variety Jones, was discovered on Ulbricht's laptop among other photos of Silk Road employees.

IMAGE RECOVERED FROM ULBRICHT'S LAPTOP

Chris Tarbell of the Federal Bureau of Investigation.

IMAGE COURTESY OF THE TARBELL FAMILY

```
03/26/2013
private guard nodes are working ok.  still buying more servers so I
can set up a more modular and redundant server cluster.  redid login
page.

03/27/2013
set up servers

03/28/2013
being blackmailed with user info.  talking with large distributor
(hell's angels).

03/29/2013
commissioned hit on blackmailer with angels

04/01/2013
got word that blackmailer was excuted
created file upload script
```

A section of the detailed diary found on Ross Ulbricht's computer in which he describes commissioning a "hit" on someone who was trying to blackmail the Dread Pirate Roberts.

IMAGE RECOVERED FROM ULBRICHT'S LAPTOP

Curtis Green, known on the Silk Road as ChronicPain, with his dog in Spanish Fork, Utah.

IMAGE COURTESY OF *EPIC MAGAZINE*

Curtis Green being fake-tortured in the Marriott Hotel by the Marco Polo task force.

USED AS EVIDENCE BY THE U.S. GOVERNMENT

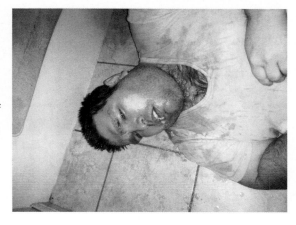

Curtis Green's staged murder, an image later sent to the Dread Pirate Roberts.

USED AS EVIDENCE BY THE U.S. GOVERNMENT

The photo Ross used to obtain fake IDs from a vendor on the Silk Road.
IMAGE RECOVERED FROM ULBRICHT'S LAPTOP

# Chapter 38
# CARL LIKES DPR

O n paper the Marco Polo task force was an all-star team of talent, composed of Carl Force at Baltimore's local DEA and other agents hailing from various local departments of the federal government, including the postal service to help with seizures and the Secret Service to trail the money (Carl, of course, was in charge of the drugs). In the months since the task force had been realized, the group had proclaimed that it would be the first in the United States to crack the Silk Road case.

Yet almost from the start the Marco Polo crew was entangled in disorder.

First there were the serious turf wars that emerged. If you were the one who took down the site, you'd be lauded as a hero forever. This case could change a career. As a result, some on the task force were backstabbing more experienced agents to try to gain leadership control of this hot new case (and in many instances were succeeding).

The cherry on top of that chaos was Carl Force, who wouldn't take orders from anyone, even his own boss. More often than not, when requests came in from others on the task force, Carl just ignored them altogether.

This wasn't the first time in his career that Carl had acted this way. During one of his last real-world undercover operations, years before he started playing the lead role of Nob the drug smuggler on the Silk Road, he had gone rogue on a case and soon found himself in a lot of trouble with the DEA, and his wife.

Back then Carl was working undercover among a group of drug dealers when he started to go deeper and deeper into their clandestine world with the hope that they would trust him more, which could lead to a big bust. But

Carl was slightly too good at the undercover part of the job. While he was manipulating the people he was trying to arrest, he started to blur the line between cop and friend. At nightclubs he would get blackout drunk with the people he was monitoring. When women approached him and his new friends, Carl didn't shoo them away to focus on trailing his subjects but rather embraced these bad girls with open, inebriated arms. Before long the line between pretend drug dealer and churchgoing DEA-agent dad faded so much that he had to quit the undercover work and go off to rehab, eventually landing, sober, with the desk job in Baltimore.

Years later, when Carl decided to become Nob, he reasoned that this was a different kind of undercover job. He was safe from the temptations of the underworld because he was behind a computer. And yet, just as in his old days with the drug cartel, Carl found himself increasingly drawn into the world of the Dread Pirate Roberts. After a day in the DEA offices, Carl would go home, straight into the spare room of his old Colonial house in Baltimore and onto the computer to converse with the man he was supposed to be hunting.

The room where Carl sat typing away wasn't much to look at, with a single bed and a bookcase that had once belonged to his grandfather. Here Carl would sit in an old brown and white lounge chair, his legs stretched out on the ottoman, as his online personality, Nob, chatted with DPR about everything and anything, and Pablo, the family's mentally deranged cat, which hated being touched, watched from the bed.

At times they talked about family, with Carl saying prayers for Dread and his loved ones. During other occasions, they talked about their health.

"Tell me about your diet," Carl asked.

"Minimize carbs," DPR replied, "no bread, no pasta, no cereal, no soda. I eat lots of hard boiled eggs."

One reason Carl was able to chat with DPR for so long was because it was apparent to him that Dread was lonely. All that time behind a mask must have taken its toll on the leader of the Silk Road, and DPR evidently sought solace from the people he was connecting with online. Carl astutely reasoned that he could use this to his advantage, coaxing the leader of the site to share more, and enticing him to be Nob's friend. A little manipulation here, some deceit there, and the Dread Pirate Roberts would be eating out of Carl's hand in no time at all.

Yet the attempt was backfiring, not because Carl wasn't getting close to

DPR, but rather because he was getting too close to him. They would talk for hours about relationships, music, and the future of the drug trade.

For Carl, who had been fighting the war on drugs for more than a decade and getting nowhere, arresting one dealer only to see another take his or her place had gnawed at his purpose in the world. Now the arguments the Dread Pirate Roberts was making about the war on drugs were actually starting to make a little sense. Maybe the answer to all this violence and waste of government resources and the hundreds of thousands of people rotting away in jails was to legalize drugs. Maybe Carl was on the wrong side of the war.

Maybe, maybe, maybe.

Somewhere along the way of those maybes, Carl started to become enamored with Dread. He started greeting DPR with affectionate salutations. "Hello my friend," he would write. "Is all well?" At other times he offered, "Stay safe," and each night that they spoke, he told DPR to "sleep good." There were compliments: "You are the most interesting man in the world, stay thirsty my friend!" And Carl even joked once, "I love you." To which DPR replied, "Yer making me blush :)." Soon after that exchange, Carl started to sign his letters to DPR with an affectionate "Love Nob."

Sure, part of this was Carl being undercover, but part of it wasn't.

As the relationship progressed, in addition to trying to draw out the leader of the notorious drug and arms Web site, Carl started antithetically offering advice on how DPR could camouflage himself even more. "You can do one of two things," he wrote to Dread. "Move to another country where you are safe from the laws of your native country or come to grips [with the reality that] there is always the possibility of getting caught."

He counseled DPR on looking into alternative passports and possibly finding a backup place to live. Carl also taught him how international drug-smuggling routes worked through "dead drops," where dealers leave drugs or guns in a location like a storage locker at a train terminal and then give the buyer the locker combination so they can grab their stuff and leave the money behind without the two ever meeting in person. The perfect way for the Silk Road to avoid the mail system. Finally Carl gave DPR advice about getting a lawyer.

Carl wasn't always blurring the line of DEA agent and pretend drug dealer. There were times he did things by the book, including helping his co–case agent Mike McFarland from HSI Baltimore order drugs off the site from low-level dealers and then arresting those sellers. Over the summer they detained a few people and took over their accounts with the goal of trying to corner others. In one instance they arrested a man in Baltimore who sold meth on the Silk Road. In another they busted a man in Lincoln, Nebraska, who sold phenazepam, bromo blotters (which were similar to LSD), prescription meds including Xanax and Valium, and, for an added bonus, guns.

But even during the moments when Carl was doing his job as a cop, he would sometimes become a rapscallion. In one instance he teamed up with another agent, Shaun Bridges, who worked for the Secret Service and who had joined the Marco Polo task force to help follow the money. The two agents tried to recruit the National Security Agency to help in their hunt. Bridges had an intimidating look to him, with thin, squinty eyes, a black goatee, and short buzzed hair that made his ears pop outward. There was something about him that seemed to say, *Be careful with this one*, but Carl didn't see it.

The NSA, or "No Such Agency," as it was unofficially called, was rumored to be able to crack into any secure computer on the planet. Carl reasoned that the NSA could help him break Tor and find the Dread Pirate Roberts. While everyone else on the Marco Polo task force knew the agency didn't touch drug-related cases, Carl and Shaun were determined to get it involved. So one day, without the knowledge of any of the other agents, the two men set up a secret meeting with one of Shaun's contacts at the NSA. They didn't want a paper trail, so everything was done in person.

The NSA analyst they met with, while sympathetic to their plight and the numbing hunt for the Dread Pirate Roberts, informed them that the NSA's mandate was only to go after targets that could harm the security of America. "Sorry, we can't help you," the analyst said. Oh, and by the way, this conversation never happened.

But the two agents weren't going to give up so quickly, so Shaun presented an alternative idea to Carl: "Let's start trying to buy explosives on the site!" This way, he said, they could show that the Silk Road and other Dark Web sites could be used to harm America.

"I'm in!" Carl responded gleefully. When Carl told his boss, Nick, he was warned not to go there, noting that "bombs" were not part of the DEA's mandate, in the same way that drugs were not part of the NSA's.

But Carl was in charge, at least in his mind, and no one was going to tell him what to do. So he and Shaun explored buying pipe bombs online and having them shipped to an undercover government PO box, where they would be able to show the NSA analyst that the Silk Road could be used for an attack on U.S. soil. Soon they realized a random discovery of a couple of pipe bombs in the mail might cause a bit of a stir in the postal service, and the plan was halted at the last minute.

When that detour didn't work out, Carl returned to the goal of befriending DPR, and in doing so, would say whatever he wanted to the site's leader.

Not surprisingly, almost anyone who read the chats between Nob and Dread started to question why they were so detailed.

On more than one occasion Nick, Carl's boss at the DEA, saw the conversations between the two men and was livid. He would call his underling into his office, slam the door shut behind him, and, amid the din of heavy metal music, erupt into an apoplectic rage. (Carl found glee in pissing off his boss, so he sat there undeterred.)

"I'm just doing this stuff to get close to him," Carl told Nick unapologetically, which was half true. "I need to develop trust with DPR."

It was hard to assert that this approach wasn't working. There was an argument to be made that Carl was going to bring down the Silk Road before other agents, and it was becoming apparent that there were plenty of others in the U.S. government who wanted that glory, including (as Carl had heard) Jared Der-Yeghiayan over in Chicago. It seemed perfectly fine to overlook Carl's peculiar interaction with DPR if it meant the Marco Polo crew was going to win.

Which is why when Carl approached his team about doing a controlled drug buy that would be facilitated by none other than DPR himself, no one questioned if it was a bad idea.

The plan Carl came up with was to have his online persona, Nob, sell a bulk order of cocaine or heroin to a buyer. And as he suspected, the Dread Pirate Roberts was happy to help expedite the sale.

"How much can you sell 10 kilos for?" DPR asked one afternoon.

Of heroin?

Yes, of heroin.

Nob, playing the part, explained that he had only "Mexican brown H, not china white" but that the first ten kilos would be $57,000 apiece, or just over half a million dollars. If the sale went well, he would drop the price to $55,000 a kilo, and then to $53,000. But what he could sell for less money, Nob explained to Dread, was a kilo of cocaine.

"All right," DPR wrote, he would find a buyer for a kilo of coke.

And so, as Dread went off to facilitate the sale, it was starting to become unclear who would be on the other end of that transaction. Would it be the churchgoing DEA-agent dad who wanted to capture the Dread Pirate Roberts and get the glory of bringing down the most notorious drug dealer of his career? Or would it be Nob, the fearless drug smuggler who wanted to help DPR find safe passage along the Silk Road?

# Chapter 39
# KIDNEY FOR SALE!

Ross stood in his bedroom, his white sheets rumpled on the bed, as he buttoned his pink-and-green-checkered shirt before heading out on another San Francisco adventure.

Over the past few months he had explored every crevice of the Bay Area. On some days he had ventured south to Bernal, where he climbed to the peak of a hill. He took long walks past the piers with sunbathing sea lions. He had gone north with his roommate and best friend, René, over the Golden Gate Bridge to Marin, where they hiked the trails amid the redwood trees, clambering through the salty fog and stopping every few feet to marvel at thousand-year-old trees that seemed to almost touch the heavens. Between explorations Ross went on boating trips with friends through the choppy waters of the bay, brushing past Alcatraz, the notorious prison that had once been home to Al Capone, the American gangster who fought the U.S. government during Prohibition.

But one of the more memorable experiences of his time in San Francisco happened on a Thursday afternoon in early December, when Ross and René happened upon the Contemporary Jewish Museum in the South of Market area of the city.

Homeless people, mostly drug addicts who had fallen on hard times, lined the streets, pushing their lives in carts from one soup kitchen or rehab center to the next, past the big glass buildings where those billion-dollar start-ups grew larger and more powerful by the hour. It was chilly that day, and a light sprinkle of rain fell from the sky as the two friends walked inside the museum. They wandered around the brightly lit, cavernous rooms until they came upon a metal box the size of a shed on whose side the word

STORYCORPS was written in big bubbly red letters. Ross and his friend pulled open the door to the metal box and sat down in front of two microphones. A red light soon came on to indicate that what they were about to say to each other was going to be recorded.

Ross began, introducing himself and noting, "I'm twenty-eight years old." His voice was calm and crackly.

The recording they were about to make was part of a National Public Radio experiment; the box they sat in would travel the country, enticing Americans to tell their stories for posterity, to try to capture the change the United States was going through at the time. Some of the recordings people had already done in other parts of America were sad, like the two parents who told the story of their young son who had died because he couldn't get a bone marrow transplant for a fatal disease. Another man talked about his experience being hit by a roadside bomb while serving in Afghanistan. And other stories were more uplifting, like the couple who fell in love during Hurricane Katrina.

It might not have been the wisest thing for Ross to draw attention to himself. But if on the Silk Road the Dread Pirate Roberts got to speak the truth about society all the time, why shouldn't Ross be able to do the same thing in this world? No one would ever be the wiser that the man about to speak into the microphone was actually two men.

Ross and René were instructed to talk to someone who might listen to their conversation two hundred years in the future. They began discussing how they had ended up in San Francisco. René had come for the "start-ups and the money," he said. Then it was Ross's turn to tell the story of how he had ended up inside this metal box.

"I was living in Austin, Texas," Ross said, and then he trailed off, as if he were traveling back there in his mind. "And, ehm," Ross continued, stuttering slightly as he stared off into the distance. "And, ehm," he said again.

René looked back, waiting for his friend to finish the sentence, seemingly oblivious to where Ross's mind had just wandered off to.

As close as Ross had gotten to René, he kept the promise he had made to himself a year earlier. He would never tell anyone else in the real world about the online world he had created. He had learned that bitter lesson with Julia.

It had been difficult hiding the truth. Friends in the real world would say things to him like "Why don't you try this business idea or work on that app?" to which Ross would simply say, "Good idea, dude. I'll think about it." But, as he told his employees on the site, he just wanted to "scream at them, 'Because I'm running a goddam multi-million dollar criminal enterprise!!!!'"

Lying came at a price. To separate those two worlds, and to justify the actions he had to make in each—telling stories to his family and friends in one and making resolute decisions with vast repercussions in the other—the man in the pink-and-green-checkered shirt had become incredibly adept at separating the life of Ross Ulbricht from that of the Dread Pirate Roberts.

As Ross he would go on these walkabouts with his friends (or alone), and the biggest decisions he had to make each day were where the adventure would begin and what he would eat for lunch. When he stepped into the role of the Dread Pirate Roberts, he hid Ross away, and DPR reveled in the power that came with dictating the rules of a world in which hundreds of thousands of people roamed. He was the one who decided who got to stay on his island and what they could and could not do while they were there. And DPR, while seemingly the same person as the sweet Ross his mother had raised, was able to make tough decisions that a younger self would have cowered away from.

This had happened just two weeks earlier, when DPR had been faced with a query on the site that no one had ever posed to Ross in his debate clubs back at Penn State.

"Question for you," one of his employees had asked at the time. "Do we allow selling kidneys and livers?"

Well, that was something Ross had never imagined people might want to hawk on the Silk Road. "Is it listed?" he replied. "Or someone wants to sell?"

The employee then forwarded an e-mail that had come into the Silk Road's support page from someone who said they wanted to sell kidneys, livers, and other body parts; according to the anonymous sender, the sales of these internal organs would "all be consensual" between the sellers and the buyers.

On the black market a person's kidney could sell for more than $260,000 (though a kidney from a Chinese man or woman would go for only $60,000), and a good liver was $150,000. Almost every part of a person's body was for sale, and for a hefty profit. Bone marrow, for example, sold for as much as $23,000 a gram (compared with $60 a gram for cocaine). A family who couldn't get that for their dying son in the broken U.S. health-care system would happily pay for it on the Dark Web.

"Yes, if the source consents then it is ok," DPR wrote, then noted to his employee that "morals are easy when you understand the non-aggression principle," citing the same libertarian argument he had used so many times in his debates at Penn State. Anything goes in a free market, the principle states, as long as you're not violent toward anyone else without cause. (If someone tries to harm you, then you have every right to defend yourself and your personal property, Dread explained. An eye for an eye was the way of the libertarian world.) Selling a liver or spleen on a Web site was entirely moral and just, he noted.

In addition to allowing organs on the site, the Dread Pirate Roberts had also recently approved the sale of poisons on the Silk Road.

"So uhh we have a vendor selling cyanide," wrote another of Dread's employees. "Not sure where we stand on this, he's not listing it as a poison, but its only the most well known assassination and suicide poison out there." The employee followed up with "lol."

DPR asked for a link to the sales page. The listing pointed out that while cyanide could be used to kill yourself (in about seven to nine seconds)—the person selling the acid had noted that with each order they were including a free copy of the e-book *The Final Exit,* which was a how-to guide for suicides. Cyanide did also have some legitimate uses, the seller pointed out, like cleaning gold and silver, and was "the perfect medicine to treat leprosy."

After a couple of minutes deliberating, DPR said to the employee, "I think we'll allow it." And then he reiterated the site's mantra: "It's a substance, and we want to err on the side of not restricting things."

The Silk Road, after all, was just the platform—no different from Facebook or Twitter or eBay—on which users communicated and exchanged ideas and currency. So who was DPR to err on the side of anything but yes? It wasn't as if Twitter dictated what kind of opinions people could and could not write in the little box at the top of the screen. If you wanted to spew brilliance or idiocy in 140 characters, then so be it. It was your God-given right to say what you wanted on the Internet, in the same way it was your God-given right to buy or sell whatever you wanted and put it into your body—if you chose.

That had been Ross's goal with weapons too when he started the Armory, though he recently had been forced to shut that site down because it had proven too difficult to get guns through the U.S. Postal Service. As a result, not enough people were willing to buy weapons on the site, so he reinstated the sale of these arms on the Silk Road (as a temporary solution) while he explored new ways to help people traffic them back and forth anonymously. To the Dread Pirate Roberts, whether the merchandise was guns, drugs, poisons, or body parts, it was the people's right to buy and sell it.

"Absolutely," the employee replied in agreement. "This is the black market after all :)."

"It is," Ross responded, "and we are bringing order and civility to it."

While these decisions were still difficult for Ross to make, the line where Ross ended and DPR began was beginning to blur. And just like other ambitious CEOs who ran other start-ups around San Francisco, he was unable to see how a single decision, made from behind a computer, could trickle down and affect an untold number of real, living human beings.

*I think we'll allow it.*

Back in that metal box at the Contemporary Jewish Museum, René began speaking again, looking at his friend Ross and noting that in San Francisco, "it feels like we're caught up in a moment."

Ross, returning from another one of his daydreams, agreed. "I get that feeling as well," he said. "I feel like the world is in flux." It was, and in many ways the people around them were causing all of the changes.

For the next thirty minutes the conversation between Ross and René bounced from family and friends to drugs (and how much Ross had loved them as a teen). Then Ross talked about his almost-fiancée from Texas, and how the experience of her cheating had battered him emotionally.

"Are you at all jaded?" René asked.

"Oh yeah," Ross replied. "Big time."

René then went on to explain that he had experienced an epiphany of late, that we all work so hard in our jobs, and for what? "There is no level of success that would make me feel happy all the time," he reflected. "Those little achievements are little fleeting moments."

Ross scratched his beard, seemingly disagreeing with his friend. "I imagine there is some silver lining to . . . pushing yourself to the limit," Ross said. "I've had similar experiences with my work, where that becomes everything, more important than anything."

They then started to wrap up their recording. But first, before they said good-bye, René asked his friend where he would like to be twenty years from now.

"I want to have had a substantial positive impact on the future of humanity by that time," Ross remarked.

Then René asked, "Do you think you're going to live forever?"

"I think it's a possibility," Ross declared into the microphone. "I honestly do; I think I might live forever in some form."

# Chapter 40

# THE WHITE HOUSE IN UTAH

The little house on East 600 North Street in Spanish Fork, Utah, had seen better days. The white slats of siding were chipped from years of neglect, as was the wooden fence on the edge of the property. In all directions small white steeples rose into the Utah sky, offering endless places of worship. This was, after all, Mormon country, home of the Latter-day Saints.

On a Thursday morning in mid-January 2013, every few minutes the silence was punctured by a car passing through the nearby intersection. And in the distance there was the echoing rattle of the wind irritating a dozen or so ragged American flags that lined the nearby streets.

But there was something unusual about the street that day. An uncommon number of cars were parked along the road, including a windowless white van that sat across the street from the house. If a passerby could have seen inside the van, he or she would have spotted a group of men checking the chambers of their semiautomatic machine guns while others placed masks over their faces and adjusted their bulletproof vests.

Just after 11:00 a.m., right as the HuHot Mongolian Grill across the street from the white house opened its doors for the daily $8.99 all-you-can-eat buffet, a man emerged from the white van wearing blue jeans, sneakers, and a dark blue jacket with a U.S. Postal Service emblem on its sleeve. He walked up to the little white house with a small package in his hand and knocked loudly. "Hello!" he yelled as his fist thudded against the screen door. "Anyone home?"

No one answered, but it was apparent that someone was indeed inside. The man with the postal jacket dropped the package onto the decrepit checkered welcome mat on the stoop and headed back toward the white van.

Nearby, Special Agent Carl Force of the DEA watched this spectacle from an unmarked police car. "He's not going to fall for this," Carl said to another much older agent sitting next to him in the car.

"Give it some time," the older agent said. "He'll come out."

Carl waited, savoring the serenity of the moment: the vast open sky and the flapping flags, all surrounded by the snowcapped Wasatch Mountains and the sweeping emptiness beyond. Carl had ended up there, as had all the other men with him, as a result of his online persona Nob having concocted a brilliant plan to have the Dread Pirate Roberts find a buyer for a kilo of cocaine. In no time at all DPR had connected him with a dealer on the site, and after agreeing to the $27,000 price, Carl had been given the address of a man named Curtis Green, who worked for DPR and who had agreed to take possession of the coke as a middleman for the buyer.

As soon as the deal was struck, the Marco Polo task force had to scramble to get things in order. Thankfully, Carl had a connection at the Major Crimes Unit in Utah, which had agreed to loan the agents the kilo of cocaine from the evidence vault for their sting operation.

A few days later Carl picked up the coke and a Priority Mail package. Before placing the drugs inside, he drove over the package in a truck a few times to make it look like it had been through the mail. The agents decided to do a "controlled delivery" of the drugs, with one guy posing as a postal worker to drop off the package at Green's house and then, hopefully, arrest him. But given that this was the Marco Polo task force, the operation was a mess from the moment they landed in Utah. In particular, the agent tasked with dressing up like a mailman had decided not to dress up like an actual mailman. He just lazily slipped the postal jacket over his normal clothes for the delivery.

"This guy looks nothing like a postal worker," Carl said to the gruff agent next to him as they watched the fake postal worker slip back into the white van.

A few minutes went by, and finally the door to the dilapidated house creaked open and a heavyset man with short, dark hair emerged, peeking out of the doorway like a timid and lost animal. This was Curtis Green, who appeared to be in his early forties and who had a visible look of worry across his face. Green, Carl knew, was one of the key lieutenants in the Dread Pirate Roberts's vast drug network, spending his days holed up in the house, brokering deals between buyers and sellers and resolving disputes when transactions went wrong.

Green looked directly toward the white van, then down at the package, and walked cautiously out onto the porch. A pink walking stick in hand, he hobbled toward the parcel, then leaned down to pick it up and examine it. The package was a Priority Mail box, no bigger than a brick, and there was no return address anywhere. He wore a fanny pack around his waist, and it shifted slightly as he ambled across the porch. Seemingly deciding he wanted nothing to do with the package, Green threw the parcel into a trash bin on the lawn and limped back inside.

"What the fuck?" Carl exclaimed. The men in the van were in disbelief too. What now? They all knew that you can't arrest someone for throwing a brick of cocaine in the garbage. As they contemplated what to do, Green reappeared, slowly peering out of the doorway as he had a few minutes earlier. This time he retrieved the package from the garbage and brought it inside.

The door clicked closed behind Green. It was go time.

It took only a few seconds for the back of the white van to burst open, which prompted a cascade of subsequent thuds from the doors of the cars parked around the corner. Dozens of men from the local SWAT team and DEA streamed out of the vehicles, with long dark guns drawn, and trampled across the dead grass on the lawn. A black battering ram appeared and slammed into the front door of the little white house. The agents of the Marco Polo task force stormed inside. "On the floor!" one of them yelled as Green stood over the now-open package of powder with a pair of scissors in his hand, a plume of cocaine covering his face.

Green, stuttering, did as he was told, lying down on the ground as quickly as he could. He called out the names of his two Chihuahuas, Max and Sammy, as they yapped at the men with guns. "Keep your hands where we can see them!" an agent yelled. Max, the older of the two dogs, couldn't handle the mayhem and lost his continence, shitting himself on the living room floor, while Sam, the smaller pup, tried to bite another agent's shoelaces. On the wall above this chaos there were pictures of Green's wife and kids and a square decorative tile that offered the welcoming message "If I had known you were coming, I would have cleaned up!"

Green was searched—the cops found $23,000 in cash stuffed in his fanny pack—and was read his rights. He was visibly petrified, telling the cops he'd do whatever they needed; tell them whatever they wanted to know; show them how Bitcoins worked and the computer he used to log on to the Silk Road.

The cops in the back of the house rummaged through Green's drawers, pulling out his wife's big black dildo that became the butt of several jokes. Other officers went down into the basement, where they found a series of computers linked together for what they were told was Green's Bitcoin-mining farm. These computers ran software Green had downloaded that constantly crunched numbers trying to find Bitcoins online that he could then turn into real physical cash.

As the cops rummaged through his stuff, one of the HSI agents from Baltimore took timid Green aside and began questioning him. This left Carl and Shaun Bridges, the Secret Service agent who had tried to set up the meeting with the NSA, to examine Green's computer. They soon discovered that Green, as an employee of the Silk Road, had a special account on the site with privileges that allowed him to change people's pass codes and even log others out of their accounts. This was an administrative right that, Green told them, had been granted to him by the Dread Pirate Roberts himself.

As Carl and Shaun explored Green's account for evidence that would bring them closer to capturing DPR, they noticed one other feature about Green's administrative abilities on the site that seemed out of the ordinary. It appeared that Green, as a moderator, also had access to other people's Bitcoins on the Silk Road. Hundreds of thousands of Bitcoins, to be precise. Green could have easily stolen that money if he wanted to. After all, everyone believed that Bitcoins couldn't be traced like cash. But Green would never do such a thing, fearing a vicious reprisal from the Dread Pirate Roberts. Neither, one would think, would federal agents with the Marco Polo task force who had taken an oath to protect citizens, "so help me God."

But in the coming days, without the knowledge of anyone else inside that little house on East 600 North Street in Spanish Fork, Utah, or within the U.S. government, Shaun Bridges of the Secret Service was about to do the unthinkable. He started tinkering with the computer that belonged to Green and furtively siphoning $350,000 out of other people's accounts on the Silk Road, all using Curtis Green's log-in credentials. Rather than turning this money in to the U.S. government as evidence, Shaun would instead secretly transfer that $350,000 into his own personal accounts online.

It didn't stop there.

It wouldn't take long for do-gooder, churchgoing dad Carl Force—completely separately from Shaun Bridges—to start stealing money from the Silk Road too. But rather than purloin the money, as Shaun did, Carl would instead sell information back to the Dread Pirate Roberts in exchange for hundreds of thousands of dollars in Bitcoins. This information would help Ross Ulbricht stay ahead of law enforcement as they hunted for the leader of the Silk Road.

Just as he had before, Carl was about to cross the line between covering a criminal and becoming one.

So help me God.

# Chapter 41

# CURTIS IS TORTURED

The lobby of the Marriott Hotel in Salt Lake City was as bland and soundless as any other. The carpet was as hard as concrete, and a stale smell of coffee hung in the air. In the corner of the foyer, a television played with a ticker streaming below the newscaster who read the latest headlines, noting that new home sales in the United States had fallen by 7.8 percent over the previous month, and the economy was again sputtering.

Upstairs in one of the hotel suites, a pink walking cane lay on the floor. And a few feet away, in the bathroom, the owner of that cane—Curtis Green—was being drowned by a postal worker from the Marco Polo task force. Across from him, as Green's head was held underwater and his arms flailed about in panic, Carl Force of the DEA stood with a digital camera videotaping this torture.

It had been a week since the DEA had come into Green's house with a battering ram, smashing down his front door and scaring the shit (quite literally) out of his poor Chihuahuas. After he had been booked, processed, and let go from the local police precinct, he had gone home, dropped onto the couch, and cried. He reasoned that the next steps would be getting a lawyer, having a court date, and maybe striking a deal with the DEA that would grant him a lesser sentence. But events had played out differently.

After his arrest the Marco Polo task force returned to Baltimore, and the Mormon boy, Green, had been told to lie low. Carl and the rest of the team had assumed that they would have time to question Green later and could sift through his computer for more evidence in the meantime. But as Carl had learned (as Nob), the Dread Pirate Roberts had figured out that his employee had been arrested.

Amid a flurry of confusion, Shaun Bridges, Carl Force, and a postal worker from the task force had returned to the Salt Lake City Marriott to question Green, to try to glean what they could while he still had access to his Silk Road files.

Green arrived at the Marriott with his lawyer and immediately began babbling on about how the ruthless Dread Pirate Roberts would soon surely send his goons to have him killed. He was so petrified he couldn't sleep, he said. He kept peering out of his window in Spanish Fork, fearing that someone would come and tap on the door and that would be the end of Curtis Green and his two Chihuahuas. Green went on like a scared teenager telling the principal about some bullies that would get him after school.

Green had always been a rambler and, as Carl soon believed, a weakling. In high school Green's classmates had called him "the Gooch." At the time, young, chubby Green didn't know what the term meant and laughed along with the other boys when they referenced him by that nickname. It wasn't until years later that he found out that a gooch was the area on a man's body between his scrotum and his asshole.

Carl could easily see why the nickname had stuck. After a few minutes of his rambling, Carl wanted to slap him or tell him to shut the hell up, or both. (Gooch!) Green seemed as nervous as his three-pound Chihuahuas. Sometimes he whimpered as he spoke to the Marco Polo task force about his role on the site and about the dreaded Dread Pirate Roberts. At other times he pleaded, "I'm just a good Mormon boy."

Eventually, after a couple of hours of questioning, Green's lawyer left the interrogation early, noting that his client should just tell the cops everything he knew. As the lawyer walked out, the Gooch started crying. Carl thought about how pathetic this man was and how he was everything Carl hated in the world: not tough enough to stand up for the choices he had made.

At around noon, exhausted from hours of interrogation, they decided to go down to the restaurant of the Marriott Hotel and grab lunch. As everyone ate, Carl logged on to his laptop as Nob to chat with DPR and see if he knew more about the man sitting across from him. It was then, as Green sat eating french fries and trying not to upset his DEA captors, that Dread told Nob what had happened. One of his employees had stolen some Bitcoins, and he wasn't happy about it. "Not a ton of money," DPR said as they began typing to one another, "but it pisses me off to no end."

"Who is it and where is he," Nob wrote back as he looked up from his laptop at the Gooch, who nervously looked back.

"I'll send you his ID," DPR replied.

Nob immediately asked why he had this man's ID.

"I had him send it to me when I hired him," Dread wrote back, "for just this kind of situation."

As Carl chatted with Dread, he played dumb about what had happened with his kilo of cocaine, but he was also surprised that Green had the audacity to steal $350,000 in Bitcoins shortly after he had been arrested. "You stole money from DPR?" Carl asked Green, shocked that the Gooch would do such a thing. Shaun, who had really stolen the money, just watched silently.

"No!" Green replied, panicked. "You've gotta be kidding me. I wouldn't even know how to steal a penny from him."

"Just admit it!" Carl yelled. And then Shaun jumped in too. Shaun's glare was intimidating, with his narrow, snarly eyes. "Just admit you stole the money!"

"I didn't!"

"Why are you protecting him?" Carl asked.

"I didn't do it!" Green sobbed.

During this exchange, a request from the Dread Pirate Roberts popped up on Carl's computer screen asking if he knew anyone who could beat Green up and force him to send the money back. Given that Carl was posing as a big-time drug smuggler, he told DPR that of course he knew people who could do that kind of work.

"How quickly do you think you can get someone over there?" DPR asked. "And what does that cost you?"

Carl looked up from his computer and informed Green that his day was about to change—slightly. Green, still rambling, was terror-stricken as he heard what they were going to do next. They would have to make the beating look real, Carl informed Green. DPR wanted evidence.

They returned to the hotel room, and Carl told Green to go into the bathroom. The tub was filled with water. The camera clicked on, and the postal worker thrust Green under, his arms waving as he gasped for air. His screams sounded like a rumble under the water. He couldn't breathe. And then, after a few seconds, the postal worker yanked his head out by his hair and held the drowning man's face up to a video camera as the Gooch panted, trying to regain his breath and making every effort possible not to cry again.

"I think we should do it again," Carl said as he peered over the video camera at Green's pathetic-looking face. The postal worker agreed, grabbed Green's head again, and pushed him back under the water. It was pure chaos, like *Lord of the Flies,* but rather than children trying to kill poor chubby Piggy, special agents with the U.S. government were drowning the Gooch.

Green begged them to stop, but they did it again and again. "We have to make it look real," Carl sneered.

"I swear," Green said as his face was pushed under the water again, "I didn't steal the money!"

"Just admit it!" Carl yelled back at him. "Stop trying to protect DPR!"

And yet while all this was going on, there was one person who was not in the bathroom. Shaun of the Secret Service had told the others on the task force that he was going to take Green's laptop and submit it into evidence at the nearby bureau. But instead he was going to use it to steal more money from the Silk Road, money that no one knew he was taking. As Shaun closed the door behind him, the sound of the Gooch's cries echoed through the hotel suite in the Marriott as Carl continued to yell at him. "Just admit it, you piece of shit!"

"I swear," Green wept. "I didn't steal a penny!"

# Chapter 42
# THE FIRST MURDER

Ross had figured that one day it might come to this. That one day he would be faced with this kind of ruthless decision—to "call on my muscle," as he'd told an associate. When that day came, he'd imagined that maybe he would have to end the life of a dealer gone rogue or someone who threatened the mission of the Silk Road. But not one of his own people. And certainly not Curtis Green from Spanish Fork, Utah.

While this decision was daunting for DPR, at least one part of it would be easy: figuring out who would do the job. With so much cash on hand, it turned out there were plenty of people who were willing and able to murder someone—particularly in a barren stretch of Utah. Variety Jones had access to a man he simply called "Irish," who could be dispatched—from Ireland—to Utah, where he would find Curtis and make him disappear. (One slight problem here was that Irish wasn't very tech savvy, so retrieving the $350,000 in Bitcoins Green had stolen could prove to be a complicated challenge.) Inigo, another Silk Road employee and one of a few people DPR actually trusted implicitly, volunteered to go and take care of the problem himself, but he was way too important to the infrastructure of the site to be a foot soldier. So DPR decided the job would have to be done by Nob, the South American drug dealer he had become so close to.

After all, it was Nob who had lost a kilo of "Colombia's finest" when Green had been busted by the DEA a week earlier, a salient fact that Ross had discovered by a simple Google search of Curtis Green's name after he didn't show up to work one day, which had led him to a Web site that catalogued recent arrests.

There, in all its glory, was the mug shot of his chubby employee.

Ross hadn't imagined this was what he would be dealing with when he woke on a cold winter's morning in early 2013. At first when he found out about Green, the only thing he could do was feel sick to his stomach, as he told VJ in a chat. Then, a couple of hours later, the taste of vomit was quickly turning into one of vengeance.

DPR spoke to all of his associates about what to do. There was a real fear that Green would sing to the cops about the Silk Road, telling the Feds about the innards of the site, how it worked, and who was involved with it. That, plus the $350,000, left Ross with essentially three options for how to handle his rogue employee.

The first possibility was the easiest: to simply pay a visit to Green at his home in Spanish Fork, Utah, and scare him into returning the money he had stolen. The second was more difficult—but definitely more just—and involved beating Green for his unscrupulous treason. Maybe one of DPR's guys would bind Green to a chair, slap him around a bit, break a few fingers, a nose, threaten his family, and scare him into returning that money. But there was a problem with both of these choices: If word got out that it was okay to sing to the cops and steal hundreds of thousands of dollars in cash, the Dread Pirate Roberts wouldn't be the most feared pirate sailing the Dark Web, but rather a weakling pushover. The Silk Road would be known as a place where you could break the rules without reprisal.

This led to the third option for Green: killing him.

Decisions, decisions.

How quickly life changes. One minute you're making $300 a week as a college researcher. You're sleeping in a basement and your only belongings are two black garbage bags, one full of clean clothes, the other dirty, and your biggest worry in the world is whether the pretty girl with the black curly hair whom you just met at the drum circle will call you back. Then an idea hits you. It starts as just a thought, like a kid's daydream of a giant invention. But once it becomes lodged there in your mind, it won't go away. Then something happens, like a bolt of lightning striking a kite, or mold accidentally contaminating an experiment, and you realize this idea is actually possible. You type lines of code into your computer and out comes a world that didn't exist before. There are no laws here, except your laws. You decide who is given power and who is not. And then you wake up one morning and you're not you anymore; you're one of the most notorious drug dealers alive. And now you're deciding if someone should live or die. You're the judge in your own court. You're God.

But God wasn't ready to end another man's life. At least not yet. So he issued a directive to Nob to go off and find Green and have him roughed up.

"I'd like him beat up. Then force him to send the Bitcoins he stole back," DPR wrote to Nob. "Like sit him down at his computer and make him do it." He then reiterated to Nob that getting the money back "would be amazing."

Nob said he would send his guys to Utah to do just that.

But while Nob had set off to find Green, and Ross had issued a pardon of sorts, he still wasn't sure this level of amnesty was the right decision. How could he let someone steal that much money from DPR and get away with a measly beating? The conundrum lay in the reality that violence was not something Ross was used to, though it was something he believed in when absolutely necessary.

Back at Penn State, a short lifetime ago, while sitting in the Willard Building off Pollock Road, Ross had defended this very topic with Alex and his friends in the College Libertarians Club.

"Yes, but the use of force is completely justified if you have to defend your own rights or personal property," young Ross had argued while discussing one of the latest Murray Rothbard books he had devoured. Back then it had just been idealistic, hypothetical banter by a group of college students. The conversation had even followed some of the club members to the Corner Room bar on College Avenue, where, amid the sound of sports talk and the clink of pints of Samuel Adams, they had discussed Rothbard's *War, Peace, and the State,* which explained why you could use violence against any "individual criminal" trying to harm you or steal your personal property.

Now, as the Dread Pirate Roberts, the more Ross thought about it, the more he wondered if beating Green up would be enough of a punishment to deter others on the site from betrayal. He started to wonder if he might not have a choice but to put his libertarian theories to their ultimate test. Curtis Green had, after all, stolen DPR's "personal property." All $350,000 of it.

As Ross weighed the decision, his chief adviser offered an alternate argument. "At what point in time do we decide we've had enough of someone's shit, and terminate them," Variety Jones asked rhetorically upon hearing about the theft. He no longer referred to Green by his name but simply as the "Organ Donor." To VJ, heroin was harmful and he wanted no part of it, but murder, well, that was a completely different story.

Given that Green had been arrested, Variety Jones (who knew a bit about actually being arrested) pointed out that the Organ Donor might strike a deal with the "Feebs" to divulge everything he knew about the Silk Road. Or he might skip the country, VJ cautioned, and disappear with DPR's 350 grand.

Soon other advisers jumped into the fray. "There are certain rules to the underworld," one wrote to DPR. "And problems can sometimes only be handled one way."

All these devils on DPR's shoulder, and the only angel was Ross Ulbricht. (It wasn't like Ross could call up his best friend René in the real world and ask his opinion. *Hey, buddy, got a minute? I'm thinking about having this guy killed for stealing hundreds of thousands of dollars in drug money from me. You think I should do it?*)

Given what everyone was saying to DPR, these arguments had started to make sense. This was not a playground; it was a fucking drug empire, and there had to be consequences to people's actions. "If this was the Wild West, and it kinda is," Ross replied to Variety Jones, "you'd get hung just for stealing a horse."

*Exactly! Now you're talking.* VJ stoked the fire further, questioning what it would take before the sheriff of this Wild West did just that. "At what point in time is that the response," Jones asked.

"It's a good question I've been thinking about the last 24 hours."

Finally, Variety Jones rang the final death knell. "So, you've had your time to think," he said. "You're sitting in the big chair, and you need to make a decision."

*Ross, jump off a cliff.*

"I would have no problem wasting this guy," DPR replied.

And in eight words the hit was put out on Curtis Green. With a few strokes on his keyboard, the creator of the Silk Road had just sanctioned his first murder. Now he just had to find the right person to kill him.

# Chapter 43

# THE FBI JOINS
# THE HUNT

It was 4:45 a.m. when the silver SUV pulled into its usual parking spot on the corner of Church and Thomas streets in Lower Manhattan. Right on time. The car had black tinted windows with government plates and blue and red police lights hidden under the front grill. The door to the SUV swung open and FBI Special Agent Chris Tarbell stepped out, wearing gym clothes and a light jacket, even though the winter temperature in New York City had dipped into the teens.

Come rain or shine, sleet or snow, this was Tarbell's ritual. He worked out every day before he went into the FBI offices at 26 Federal Plaza, a couple of blocks away. But today's routine was going to be different. While the cybercrime FBI agents hadn't lost interest in the Silk Road, that topic hadn't moved past a discussion in the Whiskey Tavern among the Pickle Back shots and cham-pag-nay, mostly because of bureaucratic bullshit within the system that Tarbell couldn't stand. Higher-ups at the Beau (which they pronounced "B-you") had argued that drugs were not the mandate of their division of the FBI.

But finally, after months of discussions over how to get in on the Silk Road case, an opportunity had presented itself. Later that day a woman from the DEA in New York City would be coming by to talk about the site and ask if Tarbell and his crew could help the DEA's investigation.

After leaving the gym, Tarbell changed into a dark suit and white shirt and grabbed his coffee from the nearby Starbucks before making his way up to the twenty-third floor of the federal building. As he sat with his other agents in the Pit, a woman from the DEA arrived with Serrin Turner, the assistant U.S. attorney in New York City whom the FBI had worked with on the LulzSec case.

The DEA agent wore jeans and a sweater, proudly displaying her badge and gun on her waist. She sat down in an empty chair and explained that she was part of a New York task force based a few miles away in Chelsea. They had been sporadically looking into—"well, trying to look into"—the Silk Road for the past year and a half, and their attempt at an investigation had gone nowhere. Shortly after the *Gawker* article had published back in June 2011, Senator Chuck Schumer had done what most politicians do, holding an impromptu press conference and demanding that the government go after the drug site, even though he was clueless as to what that entailed.

Since the Silk Road sold drugs, the DEA agent explained, the government had asked her office to look into the site. That had been a mistake, it turned out, as her office knew how to do only physical busts with physical drugs, not digital busts with technologies like Bitcoin, Tor, or even the Dark Web, whatever the fuck that was.

"People upstairs are pissed that we haven't gotten very far," she lamented. And then she explained that the leader of the site—"who now calls himself the Dread Pirate Roberts, you know, from the *Princess Bride* movie"—had grown more brazen with the contraband that was for sale, including hawking guns and hacking tools. What's more, this Dread Pirate Roberts was publicly denouncing the U.S. government. The New York DEA had hit a dead end, and they needed the help of the FBI.

When the meeting ended, Tarbell and his team said they would talk among themselves and be in touch. They shook hands and parted ways.

"Well," Tarbell said to the agents in the Pit, "there are two problems here." First, his team didn't want to just be "assistants" to the New York DEA. If the FBI was going to go after the Silk Road, the FBI was going to do it alone. The Beau didn't work well with others. Never had. Especially the douche bags over at the DEA.

Which led to that other salient issue: they had been told several times by their higher-ups at the FBI that drugs were not in their job detail; computers were.

But the meeting with the DEA agent had given Tarbell and his crew an idea. The site was no longer just hawking drugs. People were now peddling several hundred different types of hacking tools too, including key loggers, banking Trojans, malware apps, spyware, and a slew of other digital goods that landed right in the purview of the men sitting in the Pit.

There, in that moment, the FBI team decided that was how they would get involved with the Silk Road case. Rather than help the DEA find drug dealers, the cybercrime agents would go after the site themselves. Tarbell picked up the phone, presenting the strategy to his bosses.

Several weeks later approval finally came back down the chain of command, saying that the team could open an investigation on the site. After months of red tape and wasteful officialdom, Tarbell and his coagents opened a new case file, numbered 288-3-696.

In addition to HSI in Chicago, a task force in Baltimore, and another group of local and federal officials in New York City, there was now a new agency hunting for the Dread Pirate Roberts: the Cyber Division of the FBI, and the Eliot Ness of cyberspace would be leading the charge.

# Chapter 44

# CAMPING AND
# THE BALL

*February 2013*

I can't remember if I told you," DPR wrote to Inigo. "But I'll be gone until Sunday afternoon."

Ross was relieved to be getting away. The past few weeks had been a complete disaster. He had even wondered if there was something wrong with him. In his online world nothing was going right. His employees were screwing up all over the place (including Variety Jones, who had failed to deliver some new security code on time). And his off-line world wasn't much better, given that he was single and lonely and couldn't seek advice from anyone he actually trusted.

On top of his melancholic state of mind, he had discovered that in addition to Curtis Green stealing $350,000 a couple of weeks earlier, someone else had purloined another $800,000 in a different heist.

Eight. Hundred. Thousand. Dollars. Just gone. That was more than $1.15 million stolen in a matter of days. Luckily for Ross, a million dollars was now just a small fraction of his savings, but it still stung. There had been a reprisal, of course. And DPR had finally put a hit out on Green. The cost wasn't too insane, either: $40,000 up front and another $40,000 after he was dead.

The decision hadn't been easy. That was for sure. But he was convinced that it was the right one; illustrating to the world that society could be safer by legalizing drugs was more important than the life of a man who might squeal to the Feds. Plus, Green had broken the rules of DPR's world. There had to be consequences. Without them there would be chaos.

Before leaving town, DPR sent Inigo one last message, instructing him to "hold down the fort for me." Then Ross closed his laptop, leaving DPR hidden within the encryption software he had installed on his computer. There would be no need for him where Ross was going for the next few days. He grabbed his bag and left his apartment.

San Francisco's temperature had clung to the high forties most of the day, yet Ross was dressed as if he were going to the beach, not up north for a two-day hike in the wilderness. His fellow campers had planned appropriately. Selena, whose birthday they were celebrating, was bundled up with woolly socks and a thick scarf. René was wrapped three layers thick, like a piece of precious porcelain about to be shipped in the mail. And Kristal, Selena's sister who was in town from Portland, looked like she was going camping in Antarctica. Ross, on the other hand, had decided this trip would require only a pair of thin Adidas shorts and his new, bizarre, bright red Vibram FiveFinger shoes, which made it look like he was wearing a pair of gloves on his feet.

But in a matter of minutes the cold ceased to matter to Ross; he felt warm inside as he looked over at Kristal, who was, quite frankly, too beautiful to have him worried about his outfit.

Ross instantly had a crush.

He was smitten with Kristal. Her long, straight black hair was perfectly braided in the back, revealing her splendid hazel eyes and perfectly puckered pink lips. She looked just like Pocahontas.

Once the bags were packed in the car, he hopped inside and it pulled away as the four friends chatted in unison. They drove along the 101 and the Golden Gate Bridge came into view. Selena pulled out her camera to snap a picture of the orange towers, which seemed endlessly high. Ross could see the bright blue sky, as vast and open as the ocean he had seen in Dominica. To the right he could see Alcatraz again, that looming prison in the distance.

They continued along the curvy roadways through Sausalito and into Mill Valley as they made the hour-long drive to the entrance of the hiking trail.

The beginning of the trail was a well-worn gravel path that soon turned into a sinuous bridle walkway. Before long the group found themselves in the thick of nature. Ross and René were perfect gentlemen, offering to carry the ladies' backpacks. Each man slipped one on his back, one on his front. They high-fived with delight.

• • •

On the other side of the world, in Perth, Australia, sixteen-year-old Preston Bridges and his mates had been planning their own festivities for a while now. Preston had already picked out his outfit for the Year 12 Ball and had been in constant discussion with the other kids at Churchlands Senior High School about the after parties they would attend.

Preston was a handsome kid, with thick, fluffy eyebrows and flopped-over blond hair that hung to one side of his face. He had chosen to spend the hours before the festivities on the beach with his mates, jostling in the fleecy, warm water and talking about the evening ahead.

"You look like you went for a spray tan," his father, Rodney, joked with him at around 4:00 p.m. when he got home. Preston smirked and bounded off down the hall to change into his tuxedo for the dance.

A little more than an hour later, at around 5:30 p.m., Preston walked out of his bedroom for what would be the last time in his life.

He looked smart in that black tuxedo, his matching bow tie strung perfectly around his neck. When his mother, Vicky, arrived to pick him up, she noted how handsome her boy looked. His dad snapped a few pictures of them together. In one, Preston turned to his mother, pulled her close to him, and kissed her squarely on the cheek as she beamed. He soon set off for the ball.

• • •

Ross and his trio of friends finally found camp and set up their blue-and-white tents on the flat grass of the hillside that overlooked an endless green ocean of Northern California Douglas fir trees. It smelled like pines, and a feeling of calm came over them all—especially Ross. René commented that it was like paradise as the group sat down on the slope and watched the world do nothing. Ross snacked on oranges, pistachios, and rice cakes. Soon they built a bonfire. As night fell, Ross and Kristal talked and gazed up at the stars, the smell of smoke disappearing toward heaven.

The rest of the weekend for Ross was like a dream. He swam in Kent

Lake at the head of Peter's Dam—even though the water was freezing. He rolled down a bright green hill and giggled like a child. He played cards; they hiked, joked, threw Frisbees, and skipped, literally, as they explored the wilderness.

But most important, Ross and Kristal fell for each other like two teenagers at a high school dance.

. . .

The Sunmoon Resort hotel in Perth, Australia, was the perfect place for an after party for the dozen young teenagers who had just left the Year 12 Ball. The hotel had inexpensive rooms with balconies that overlooked the esplanade and the green, jagged ocean along Scarborough Beach. The smell of chlorine wafted gently up from the pool below as Preston and his friends made their way to the top floor of the resort and into the suite they had rented together.

As the night drew on, friends and acquaintances came and went. Yet at around 4:30 a.m., as the boys contemplated calling it a night, one young teenager showed up at the hotel with a surprise. He wasn't one of Preston's close friends, but he wanted to be, and he had brought a gift.

"What is this?"

"It's N-bomb," the kid explained to Preston. "It's like LSD." They make it in China, he said. It was synthetic, a drug made in an unregulated lab, and while it was sixty times stronger than acid, it was perfectly safe. The boy said he had purchased a "party pack"—buy ten, get one free. He had gotten it from a Web site he had learned about called the Silk Road. The drugs had simply arrived in the mail.

Of the eight boys who were in the hotel room that night, five decided to take a hit of N-bomb. The boy who had brought the drugs offered Preston two blotters. Of those five boys who took the drug, only one had an almost immediate adverse reaction to it: Preston Bridges.

He immediately began acting erratically. The world around him started to become surreal. He panicked. *What the fuck was going on?* The hallucinations were taking over and there was nothing he could do about it. *Make it stop!* He didn't know where he was, what he was doing. His friends tried to calm him, but to no avail. Everyone was in a panic, most of all Preston.

The room seemed to spin on its axis. *Help! Help!* Around and around. Preston started to run. He was still in the hotel room. Still on the second floor. But he ran anyway. He ran off the balcony and into the air, falling thirty feet, headfirst, into the parking lot below.

Sirens began wailing in the distance.

The heart monitor made a slow, repetitive beeping noise as Preston lay on the gurney in the hospital. His thick, fluffy eyebrows and flopped-over blond hair sat motionless as tubes snaked around him. His tuxedo was gone; now he was shirtless, with sensors glued to his chest to monitor his vitals. His black bow tie had been replaced by a neck brace. And that classic Preston Bridges smile was no longer there; instead a plastic hose had been placed in his throat to ensure that he could breathe.

His mother, Vicky, collapsed on the floor when she saw him. His father wept into Preston's sister's arms. As the day drew on, hundreds of kids from school arrived, streaming in groups of eight into the hospital room as they wept for their friend who lay there in front of them, the soccer-playing, beachgoing teen now motionless.

On Monday afternoon the doctor ushered Preston's family into a small room in the hospital. Then, as tears and shock covered the faces of his mother, father, and sister, the doctor informed the family that at 3:48 p.m. sixteen-year-old Preston Bridges had died.

• • •

And then, just like that, the weekend was over. Ross, René, Selena, and Kristal packed their bags and drove back through the orange towers of the bridge. Back to San Francisco. Back toward the Silk Road.

Ross returned home with a broad smile. He felt renewed as he opened his laptop and logged on to his world.

"So everything smooth while I'm gone?" he asked Inigo.

"Yep. nothing exciting happened."

"Goooooood," the Dread Pirate Roberts replied.

"Surprising huh?" Inigo responded. "Like something always happens when your away. It's like the curse is lifted."

Life was looking up. Ross was making plans with Kristal to visit her in Portland in the coming weeks. They were going to stay in a cabin in the woods. They would get massages and order food in a cozy cabin, then romantically nuzzle up to each other over a long weekend.

He was so jubilant about the prospect of his new love interest that he had even broken one of his own security rules, telling several of his employees and confidants on the site about the girl he had just met. He even told Nob, his drug-smuggler-turned-hit-man who was currently searching for Curtis Green.

"You seem to be in a very good mood!" Nob wrote.

"I am," DPR replied. "It's a girl :) A woman I should say. An angel."

A weekend that had started out shitty had turned great. And the big, fat, sloppy cherry on top was that the Silk Road had made its usual fortune that week, selling drugs to people all over the world, including a "party pack" of N-bomb to a sixteen-year-old in Perth, Australia.

# PART IV

# Chapter 45
# GARY ALFORD, IRS

The sidewalks of Manhattan reminded New Yorkers that summer wasn't in sight just yet. Half-frozen, dirty dollops of sludge lined the city streets as wind whipped garbage down the avenues like frigid tumbleweeds. On a mid-February morning in 2013, in front of 290 Broadway, just off Duane Street, a line of men and women waited pensively to pass through a security checkpoint into a massive beige tower. While the mere sight of the building was intimidating enough, the name that hung on the gold placard on its east wall could—regardless of the temperature outside—send shivers down anyone's spine: INTERNAL REVENUE SERVICE.

This was one of those rare government buildings in which someone who uses a calculator for a living can wield more power than a person who carries a gun.

One of those calculator-carrying men was Gary Alford, who arrived for work at that beige tower like clockwork each day. A large and forbidding man with wide shoulders and a square jaw, when Gary stood still, he was completely motionless, like an anvil that had fallen to the floor and couldn't be moved. He was African American, and his dark complexion often seemed even darker against the white of his shirt, which he always wore to work, along with a crisp suit and tie.

While Gary looked like a normal IRS employee in his business attire, he was far from ordinary and had a number of eccentricities that made him stand out from all his coworkers.

One of the strangest of these idiosyncrasies was the bizarre fact that he read everything—literally everything—three times. It didn't matter what it was; if it had text on its pages, Gary would read it once, then again, and then once more. When he received an e-mail, he would read it three times before replying. He would read news articles three times. Books; text messages; research papers; someone's tax forms. He did this, he told people, to ensure that he remembered more information than those around him. When he was younger, he had heard that the brain retains only a small percentage of words when you read, so he reasoned that if he started consuming every snippet of text at least three times, he would remember more.

Sure, it was repetitive, but most of the things Gary did were.

Each of his mornings was a replica of the one before. Gary would commute exactly the same route to work, arriving at the IRS offices at exactly the same time and walking the same worn path through the same marble lobby.

There was no reception desk or waiting area on Gary's floor, just two locked doors—one to the north and one to the south. On the wall of the hallway there was a poster of Al Capone, the American gangster who controlled the flow of liquor during Prohibition. The mug shot on the poster was there to remind employees that when it came to the Criminal Investigation division of the IRS, where Gary worked, it was good old math that took down Al Capone in the 1930s, not liquor bottles or smoking guns. And it was the IRS that landed the gangster in Alcatraz Federal Penitentiary, off the coast of San Francisco.

Like most of his coworkers, Gary had a strong New York accent. He'd grown up in the city, gone to college there, and now lived there with his wife and their fluffy Maltese-Yorkie mix, Paulie. But unlike other agents he worked with, who had grown up in high-rise apartments or the suburbs of Long Island, Gary had been raised in one of the city's grittiest low-income housing projects.

He was born in the Marlboro Houses in Gravesend during the summer of 1977. The week of Gary's birth, a brutal heat wave caused a lightning storm, which struck a power station and plunged New York City into complete darkness. Within a matter of hours after Gary entered the world, chaos ensued, with looting, riots, and arson sweeping across New York's boroughs. (Gary used to joke with people that "I shut the city down when I was born!") On top of the riots and power outages, New York was also being haunted that summer by a serial killer nicknamed the Son of Sam.

Gary didn't last long in the housing projects. In the 1980s his family moved farther east, to Canarsie, after colorful crack vials from New York's rising crack epidemic had started to line the gutters around Stillwell Avenue, where they lived.

Now, thirty years later, Gary sat amid the faded green and white cubicles at 290 Broadway, checking his e-mail (reading each one three times) and finishing up reports from previous investigations that involved people who had tried to hide money from the U.S. government in far-off countries.

But while Gary's morning had begun like any other, it was about to change drastically. His phone rang with a call from the IRS supervisor, asking the young and ambitious agent to come into his office.

As Gary wandered into the room, taking a seat in an uncomfortable lime green IRS chair, his director immediately pounced. "There's a task force we want you to join," the supervisor said. (There would be no small talk here; this was the IRS, after all.) The supervisor continued, moving into an explanation of who, what, and why. The case, he told Gary, involved a Web site where you could buy drugs and guns. "What do you know about the Silk Road Web site?" (Gary knew nothing about the site and stared back with wide eyes.) "What about Tor?" (Nope. Nothing.) "And Bitcoin?" (Blankness.) "Well, that doesn't matter," the supervisor said. "The strike force is a drug task force, and you're going to be leading the money-laundering side of the case." (A tinge of excitement.) "It's a big change, Gary." (You're damn right it is.)

The strike force, Gary was told, included local and state police investigators, DEA agents, and the U.S. Attorney's Office for the Southern District of New York. That alone made the case seem important to Gary. Finally Gary was told that he would be moving to a new office in Chelsea, a few dozen blocks north.

It was time to bring in the people with the calculators.

He left the supervisor's office grateful for, and invigorated by, his new assignment. Back in his cubicle he immediately logged on to his computer and began reading as much as he could about the Silk Road, three times over.

He started with the *Gawker* article, then clicked on dozens of other newer links, scouring the words and images, until he leaned back in his chair, staring at his computer as pages of articles about the drug-dealing site and Bitcoin and Tor flickered on the screen. He knew full well, as his supervisor had told him, that teams of law enforcement had been searching for the creator of the Silk Road for almost two years, and each road they had traveled down had gone nowhere. He also knew that he would have to find a new investigation technique if he wanted to have any chance of taking down the site and its creator.

*But how?* he thought.

His mind spun in a thousand different directions as he tried to figure out how he could approach the case anew. Almost immediately an idea struck him. He thought back to a time in his life that he didn't remember but that he had heard so many stories about: the summer of 1977, the year Gary Alford was born. He remembered the story of David Berkowitz, the American serial killer who had murdered six people and wounded seven others in New York City that year, the man better known as the Son of Sam. And Gary imagined that the way the cops had caught that ruthless serial killer would be the way Gary Alford could catch the leader of the Silk Road.

# Chapter 46

# LIFE AND DEATH ON THE ROAD

G reen is dead and disposed of," Nob wrote. "I will get you a picture for proof of death."

"Ok, thank you," the Dread Pirate Roberts replied. "I guess they were unable to get him to send the coins he stole."

"They had to do CPR on him one time, actually the trick to torture sometimes is keeping the guy alive," Nob wrote back, explaining that Curtis Green, the thief who stole the Dread Pirate Roberts's $350,000 in Bitcoins, had been tortured and drowned before he ultimately succumbed to a heart attack. "Died of asphyxiation / heart rupture."

When Dread didn't respond to the macabre description of the murder, Nob asked, "You ok?"

"A little disturbed," DPR said. "But I'm ok." And then he admitted to Nob, "I'm new to this kind of thing is all."

Variety Jones had reassured Dread that what they had done wasn't simply the right decision but the only one. "We're playing for keeps," VJ wrote. "I'm perfectly comfortable with the decision, and I'll sleep like a lamb tonight, and every night hereafter."

"Well put," DPR wrote back. "Enjoy the rest of your evening mate."

"I will, you too," VJ replied. "Sweet dreams."

When Ross opened his next e-mail from Nob, he was greeted by an image of a lifeless Curtis Green peering back at him. Green's thick jowl hung off to the side, and a pool of vomit had erupted from the dead man's mouth. From the picture it appeared that Curtis's T-shirt was drenched, likely from the waterboarding Nob's thugs had administered before the thieving Green had taken his last breath.

Ross then saved the picture to an encrypted folder on his computer and messaged Nob again, asking where he wanted the final $40,000 to be sent for the hit. "Send to the same account?"

"Yes."

Ross was obviously torn up by what he had done. Killing someone wasn't an easy decision, but he also knew that this was something he might have to do again in order to inoculate his empire against people who threatened it. There was no fate worse to him than losing control of what he had built.

It was, after all, his legacy, the thing people would remember him for two hundred years from now. He wanted so badly to leave an imprint on this world and for people to know (eventually) that he was the one who had done it.

Being forced to order the murder of someone was just the price he had to pay to leave that mark. And who the fuck was anyone to judge? All of the greatest people in history had to make such decisions. The president of the United States faced these kinds of choices every day, pressing a button that unleashed a drone over a village in Afghanistan, killing people to protect the republic. This was the case in business too. Dozens of Chinese workers who made iPhones had subsequently jumped to their deaths because their working conditions were so dire, but Steve Jobs had to accept those sacrifices because, by fucking God, he was changing the world on a massive, massive scale. This was simply the plight of men and women who wanted to leave a dent in the universe.

In addition to the murder, other issues had been pummeling Ross. As of late hackers had again been targeting the Silk Road on a regular basis, knocking the site off-line for hours at a time. While DPR's employees were working tirelessly to build defenses, the only way to get the hackers to stop was to pay them a ransom of $50,000 per week thereafter.

What Ross needed right now was a break. Thankfully, the same weekend that DPR paid Nob for his services and it was clear Green was dead, Ross was going to see his new girlfriend, Kristal.

Things had really blossomed between them since the camping trip a few weeks earlier. After a night in the woods looking up at the stars and sitting around a campfire, they returned to the city and made plans to see each other as much as they could. Over e-mail and text message, they told stories about their pasts, and shared hopes about their futures—though Ross only skimmed the surface of those dreams.

He had felt so lonely over the past year running the Silk Road. He had all of this success, and no one to share it with. So he fell in love headfirst with Kristal. A weekend together soon turned into every weekend together. Once, Ross flew up to Portland, where Kristal lived, and they spent an entire day cuddling under the covers in her apartment. On another trip they set off for an adventure at a nearby campground, where they holed up in a cabin in the woods for the weekend, Ross wearing nothing more than a blue robe and his glove shoes and Kristal in a green dressing gown. Ross felt alive! He sketched pictures of her. After the trip she sent him messages of herself blowing a kiss. He sent her notes of adoration back. But he never told her about his Web site. Never could; never would.

In between all of this, he continued to steer the ship of the Silk Road, sneaking off to transform into the superhero who was going to legalize drugs and make the world a safer place. The man who navigated tribulations only people with his level of power had to negotiate. And it was that power, at this moment, that he needed more than anything to protect.

Someone was now dead who had deep ties to the Silk Road and its founder, and it was not a stretch to think that the cops would soon find the body of Curtis Green. It wouldn't be long before they figured out what had happened. The murder, the site, and the cocaine bust would all point law enforcement toward the Dread Pirate Roberts. He needed dedicated minions now who could really defend and grow the Silk Road into the biggest enterprise on the planet.

As Ross explained to one of his employees: "I'm in it to win it." Then he reiterated what was at stake here. "Before I die, I want the world to be so radically different that I will be able to tell my story in person without repercussion."

Ross was fully aware that he needed more soldiers in his ranks to reach that goal. "I'm thinking we may even staff up," he had told VJ as they discussed moving the operation to the next level. They had killed someone, and they were now running a site that trafficked hundreds of millions of dollars in drugs and anything else illegal. Any one of these felonies could land them in jail for life.

It wasn't that Ross was worried; he truly believed that the Dread Pirate Roberts simply couldn't be stopped—you can't stop an idea! But Ross also knew that the best way to stay ahead of the cops who might knock on his door was to stay ahead of what they knew.

As he returned from his weekend in a cabin with Kristal, he was determined to bring in more bodies to help protect the world he now governed. But he didn't just want to bring on hackers and drug dealers. He needed to up his game. He needed an arsenal of hit men and muscle if someone else was arrested or tried to squeal to the Feebs. But most important, Ross needed to find someone inside the government who would be able to keep him apprised of what the Feds knew. Maybe a local cop, an agent with the FBI or the DEA, or even someone at the Department of Justice. He was willing to pay this person whatever he or she wanted. There was simply too much at stake not to. He wasn't going to let any more fuck-ups happen. It was time to go to war.

# Chapter 47
# GARY'S BIG CHANGE

Everything felt completely out of place for Gary as he reported for duty on the DEA strike force he had been assigned to in New York City. Unlike the IRS's beige downtown office building, which was surrounded by a blockade of federal monoliths and local courthouses, his new workplace was above Fourteenth Street, nestled in among hipster bodegas, cupcake shops, and the Chelsea-Elliot housing projects.

At the IRS, every cubicle was as tall as a man, which afforded privacy for agents and their spreadsheets. Yet the cubicles in his new office were low and open. As a result, when Gary sat down at his desk, no matter which direction he looked, he found himself gazing directly into someone else's eyes. (This was all intentional, Gary was told, designed to get people from different government agencies—NYPD, DEA, IRS, and local and state police—on the task force talking to one another about their cases.) He had no privacy. People in his new office dressed differently too, wearing "casual" street clothes, like sneakers and T-shirts. Gary didn't own any of these, so he had to go shopping with his wife to buy boots and jeans, which made him feel like he was wearing someone else's clothes. Buttoned-up Gary felt completely out of place.

The most dissimilar aspect of the new task force was the open-door policy. People shared the information they had gleaned from their investigations with everyone else. It was all for one, not a cadre of solo IRS suits counting pennies alone.

Before arriving, Gary had done his homework, scouring news articles, forum posts by the Dread Pirate Roberts, and research about the Dark Web, all to get acquainted with the case he was about to join. While reading these pieces, Gary had come across the first white paper that had been published about Bitcoin, written by the creator of the digital currency, an anonymous man who went by the pseudonym Satoshi Nakamoto.

Gary read the paper once and nothing stood out. He read it a second time, and still nothing. But the third time he noticed something, in a section of the paper that referenced the "Gambler's Ruin problem," a theory that no matter how much money you have in a betting scenario, the casino (or house) has an infinite amount of money, and therefore, if you keep making bets, the house will eventually win. Gary reasoned that the same theory was true for DPR and the Silk Road. The U.S. government was the casino; DPR was the gambler. Eventually, Gary believed, because the Dread Pirate Roberts wouldn't stop playing, he would lose.

To say Gary was excited about this case was the understatement of his career. He was ecstatic! As soon as he was settled into his office (or as close to settled as he could be), he was briefed by his new teammates. This was when he very quickly learned that everyone else was not as enthusiastic about the Silk Road case as Gary was—at least, not anymore.

Investigators were burned out and fed up, given that their probe had gone nowhere. To them Gary arriving with all of this enthusiasm for the case was like a child waking up in mid-August thinking that it was Christmas morning.

His co–case agents immediately noticed something about Gary too. When he spoke, he would often interrupt himself and utter a rhetorical "You know?" or "Riiiiight!" almost like someone saying the words "rye" and "tight" together very quickly. He did this all the time. Gary could be chatting away at full stride, and in midsentence he would reach into the depths of his core and, as if he were trying to impersonate a bear, bellow the word "Riiight!" followed by "You know? You know?" and then he would just keep going as if nothing had happened.

Still, "You know?" and "Riiiight" aside, the task force agents explained where the investigation stood. It was May 2013, exactly two years since the famed *Gawker* article had been published, and there were dozens of government agents and task forces all over the world trying to figure out how to breach the Silk Road. There was a team in Baltimore (Carl), a lone agent in Chicago (Jared), and more than a dozen others scattered around the globe, all trying to figure out the identity of the Dread Pirate Roberts—but the case so far had proved unsolvable.

Midway through his briefing Gary was informed that since nothing else had worked, the task force wanted to try a new strategy. They instructed Gary to follow the money rather than the drugs. One of the places they wanted him to start with was a user on the Silk Road who had been buying and selling Bitcoins for drug dealers and the site's creators, acting as a digital money launderette. The strike force told Gary to try to figure out who this human Bitcoin-to-cash ATM was. Then they could try to trace some of those Bitcoins.

Gary was completely up for the task of finding the money launderer, but he also had an idea how they might be able to find the Dread Pirate Roberts.

"How?" one of the cops dubiously asked.

"The Son of Sam," Gary replied.

Gary had heard stories about that New York City serial killer known as the Son of Sam so many times as a kid that it was impossible to forget. But what had always stuck out to him, he explained to the agent, was the way authorities caught the murderer.

It had all taken place between 1976 and 1977 in the same neighborhood where Gary was raised. At the time, the Son of Sam had gone on a killing spree in New York, terrorizing the city and making fools of the NYPD. No matter how many police officers and detectives City Hall threw at the investigation, it was unsolvable. A task force that was set up to find the murderer went nowhere. Yet shortly after the blackout of 1977, one police officer decided to try a new and creative angle to find the killer. Rather than search the crime scene looking for weapons or clues, the officer decided to look for cars in the areas of the murders that had received parking tickets around the same times as the crimes. The cop reasoned that even the most brazen murderer wouldn't have stopped midway through to go and feed a parking meter. So maybe the Son of Sam had gotten one or two parking tickets during his attacks.

After a painstaking search through tens of thousands of violations, the cops found a pattern. There was a 1970 yellow Ford Galaxie sedan that belonged to a man who lived in Yonkers and had been ticketed numerous times within blocks of each of the murders. When detectives went to the car owner's home, they were greeted by David Berkowitz, a defiant twenty-four-year-old, who admitted instantly that he was the Son of Sam. "Well, you've got me," Berkowitz said at the time, and then, with one last barb toward police: "What took you so long?"

Gary told his new team that the similarities abounded. In 1977 traditional policing techniques had failed to solve the murders in the same way that in 2013 modern-day procedures for capturing drug dealers had failed to catch DPR. Both men taunted the police. Both men grew more brazen as they continued to get away with their crimes. And the task forces then and now had failed to find them both.

"I'm going to crack this case," Gary told anyone who would listen. "I really think I'm going to get DPR."

Just like the parking citations had helped catch the Son of Sam during the summer of 1977, Gary was convinced that somewhere out there the founder of the Silk Road had made a mistake. He believed that in a dark corner of the Internet there was the digital equivalent of a parking ticket that would help unmask the Dread Pirate Roberts. And Gary Alford was determined that he was going to find it.

# Chapter 48

# ROSS GOES UNDERGROUND

I t was time to go into hiding.

But this time, rather than the Dread Pirate Roberts having to disappear, it was Ross Ulbricht's turn.

A lot of other terrible things had happened since the murder of Green. Someone was looking for DPR as retribution. The heat was onto him too, with FBI, DEA, HSI, and a slew of other agencies scurrying around the Silk Road site—a sign that there was no fucking around right now. Time to begin an emergency landing.

It was early June 2013, and Ross had no choice but to go through the list he had put together months earlier. The "in case of an emergency" checklist. "Find place to live on craigslist for cash," he had written to himself back then. "Create new identity (name, backstory)."

As he scrolled through rental listings on Craigslist, he came across the perfect place: his own room in a three-bedroom house on Fifteenth Avenue near San Francisco's Outer Sunset, where he could pay cash to cover the $1,200 monthly rent. He anonymously e-mailed the lessor and, following step two on his checklist—"Create new identity (name, backstory)"—rather than calling himself Ross Ulbricht, he used a completely fictitious name, Joshua Terrey. Another name that he reasoned could never be traced back to him.

But creating a new identity was going to be difficult. After all, there were already two people: Ross and DPR. If he had to remember details about a third person, lies would get complicated very quickly. To ensure that Ross didn't forget much about Joshua, he stuck to stories he knew when he e-mailed his new potential landlord. He explained that he, Josh (for short), was twenty-nine years old, was from Texas, and had recently returned from a trip to Sydney, Australia. "I am a currency trader and do some freelance IT work as well," Ross, as Josh, wrote to the couple who were renting out the apartment. "I mostly keep to myself, spending most of my time working."

Ross wouldn't have to worry about any of his real-world friends, like René or Selena, finding out about his new alter ego Josh, as he had a plan to keep everyone separate, never having his old friends over to his new place or his new roommates out to meet his old friends. As for Kristal coming down to visit from Portland, well, that had imploded almost as quickly as it had ignited. As soon as things started to deepen, Ross lost interest. How could you sustain a relationship with someone when you were only giving them half of yourself? As he had confided in his pals, both in the real world and on the Silk Road, he wanted a family one day. Just not yet and just not with Kristal.

But that didn't matter, because just as Ross was going into hiding, another special someone was slowly but assuredly coming back into his life. The person he had sworn he would never talk to again: Julia.

This was not part of his checklist.

Prior to deciding to lie low for a while, he had been reading a book on productivity, which offered a message that wasn't too dissimilar to the approach he'd taken in his college days, when he'd trimmed the unnecessary banalities in his life by not showering for a month or eating only a bag of rice for a week. One of the messages in the book was that the reader should "reboot" their online calendar by starting anew. When he had done just that, the computer had canceled an old event with Julia and automatically sent her a message letting her know.

"How have you been?" she wrote back to him. "Still think you are amazing."

This led the onetime lovebirds to start e-mailing each other sporadically. While it was just flirting right now, maybe it would become something again in the future. If nothing else, it was a nice distraction from the chaos of his now many other worlds.

As Josh, Ross went to the house on Fifteenth Avenue and took a brief tour. He was introduced to the people who rented the other bedrooms in the house and, after handing the cash to Andrew Ford, the man who was renting the room, Ross moved right in.

Josh's new roommates were unaware that the twenty-nine-year-old Texan who was now unpacking his few belongings, arriving with literally a laptop and a small bag of clothes—enough for a week's travel—was really called Ross Ulbricht. And they certainly didn't have any suspicion that he was also the Dread Pirate Roberts, who had tens of millions of dollars in Bitcoins on his laptop and in thumb drives in his pocket. To the roommates, Josh appeared to be a quiet and polite day trader, not the man who over the past few months had ordered the murders of half a dozen people on the Silk Road.

Yes, there had been more people put to death at the hands of the Dread Pirate Roberts.

Shortly after the drowning and subsequent killing of Curtis Green, someone else had tried to scam DPR out of $500,000 in Bitcoins. Though, unlike in the previous case, where the money was just stolen and needed to be dealt with accordingly, this extortioner had threatened to release hundreds of real names and addresses of Silk Road users that had somehow been stolen. The only way to avoid this, DPR was told by the extortioner, was to pay $500,000.

But Ross wasn't going to fall for this again, so he had recruited a new group of henchmen, the Hells Angels, whom he had met through the site, to find the thief and have him killed. "This kind of behavior is unforgivable to me," DPR explained to the Hells Angels over chat. "Especially here on Silk Road, anonymity is sacrosanct."

The cost for this hit had been quoted as $150,000 for a "clean" murder. Dread wasn't happy about this price, as he told the Angels; he had paid half that for a previous murder.

Still, negotiating with a group of ruthless thugs wasn't exactly an easy task, and $150,000 was nothing to Dread at this point, so he agreed to the fee. Over the coming days a picture of the dead man and an e-mail arrived in DPR's in-box. "Your problem has been taken care of. . . . Rest easy though, because he won't be blackmailing anyone again. Ever."

Unfortunately, this didn't end the problems for Ross. Shortly before the Hells Angels had murdered their prey, the extortioner had admitted to spilling his secrets to four other associates, one of whom went by the moniker "tony76" on the Silk Road. Without skipping a beat, DPR paid $500,000 to have them killed too.

In Ross's diary on his computer, he wrote about what he had done. "Sent payment to angels for hit on tony76 and his 3 associates," which was followed by an update about some complicated work he had done on the servers of the site that day: "Very high load (300/16) took site offline and refactored main and category pages to be more efficient."

It seemed that murder, like code, was becoming easier to execute with practice.

To top off all of this chaos, DPR had been issued a death threat from someone called DeathFromAbove, who claimed to know that he had been involved in the murder of Curtis Green. Ross also had another scare when a screwup with the coding on the site leaked the server's IP address. If someone from the FBI or elsewhere had been watching, they would have been able to figure out where the server that ran the Silk Road was—something Ross had kept hidden for more than two years.

And so the mix of the murders, the death threats, the Hells Angels, and the heat that came with them made it imperative for Ross to go into hiding.

Variety Jones had done the same thing too, moving to Thailand to try to avoid being caught if things went up in flames. VJ explained that he had corrupt cops on his payroll there, so he would know if anyone was coming after him and would easily be able to scurry away before the Feebs knocked on his door.

While all this turmoil was raining down on Dread, there had been a good development. VJ was no longer the only person with crooked cops on his payroll. DPR had managed to hire a couple too.

He had put out some feelers to his network on the site, offered up some incentives here, some more there, and it appeared he might have an informant in the government who would keep him apprised of the hunt for the Dread Pirate Roberts, for a fee. The cost, the informant said, was going to be a measly $50,000 for each droplet of intelligence. It was still unclear how this would all play out and whether the details would help him evade the Feds. But it couldn't hurt to try.

Thankfully for DPR, the site was bustling with business. By the end of July, the Silk Road was on track to register its one millionth user. All in the span of a little over two years. Ross could never have imagined that the first small bag of magic mushrooms he had sold on the Silk Road would grow into a site where he was helping a million people buy and sell illegal drugs and other restricted goods. Even with all this stress now being catapulted in his direction, this salient fact was amazing to him.

So paying an informant $50,000 here or the Hells Angels half a mil for a couple of murders there was just the cost of doing business. It barely put a dent in the site's profits.

Thankfully for Ross, he had become an adept and confident CEO of the Silk Road. There was no question now that he was in charge, and while others supported him, DPR was the final arbiter of every decision and no longer sought the approval of his onetime mentor, Variety Jones.

As the boss, Ross often reminded some of his employees that "we are out to transform human civilization." And he offered long and inspiring lectures to them, learning how to motivate the troops when tensions tightened. Which was exactly what some of his workers needed right now, with all the pressure on the site from hackers and law enforcement.

"Let me tell you a little parable," Dread wrote to one employee. "It's the middle ages in Europe. . . ." He went on with the story: A man walks onto a construction site and he sees a group of laborers carving stone blocks for a building. Most of the men are working slowly, with long, unhappy faces. "What are you doing?" the man asks the laborers, to which they reply, "What does it look like we're doing? We're carving stone blocks." But then the man sees another worker who has a glint in his eye and a smile across his face. This worker seems to be toiling at twice the speed of the others, and his stone carvings are impeccable. So the man goes over and asks him, "What are you doing?" To which this laborer looks back and answers: "I'm building a cathedral to the glory of God."

"If someone asked you what you're doing," DPR continued to his employee, "would you say 'dealing with people's problems' or 'working to free humanity'?"

This was why Ross had to go into hiding: because there was too much to lose. He wouldn't be working from René's spare bedroom anymore. He wouldn't be traipsing off to Momi Toby's café on Laguna Street to hole up in his favorite coffee shop and work on the Silk Road. With so many government agencies searching for DPR and "DeathFromAbove" looking to kill him, it was imperative that he become more careful.

So as the bedroom door on Fifteenth Avenue near the Outer Sunset closed, the men outside in the living room assumed that their new roommate, "Josh," was getting to work trading stocks or doing some freelance IT support.

But inside that room, Ross, Josh, and DPR knew that they were all working together to build their "cathedral to the glory of God" and, in doing so, working to free humanity from the tyranny of the U.S. government.

# Chapter 49

# CARL SWITCHES TEAMS

The smell of coffee lingered in the air as Carl sat in his cubicle at the DEA offices in Baltimore, working away on his laptop. Out of the silence his cell phone rang, again. He knew exactly who it was before he even picked up the phone, which displayed a Spanish Fork, Utah, area code. It was Curtis Green again, the Gooch! This must have been the eighth time today that Green had called, and it was getting really fucking annoying.

"I can't believe you think I stole DPR's money," Green said on the phone in a high-pitched murmur. "I swear I didn't steal anything from him."

Carl disagreed. "You're a liar." After listening to Green whine some more, Carl told him to chill out and continue to lie low, as DPR still believed he was dead, and, twisting some fear into him, he warned that if the leader of the Silk Road found out Green was really still alive, you could be sure that wouldn't last long.

"How long am I supposed to stay hidden for?" Green pleaded. "I haven't been outside in months." He then whimpered that he had nothing to do with the stolen money. Carl, fed up with this nonsense, hung up.

After the fake-but-not-so-fake torturing in the Marriott Hotel, DPR had asked Nob to have his "thugs" kill Green. Carl couldn't be bothered to fly out to Spanish Fork, Utah, again, so he told Green to fake his own death. The instructions were simple: Dunk your head in water, as if you've been drowned. Then pop open a can of Campbell's soup. A tomato flavor. And then pour that soup out of your mouth, like you died from being held underwater and there was a mucuslike eruption from your mouth. Finally, so we have something to show, have your wife snap a picture of your lifeless body with your cell phone.

Nob had then sent the grainy photo to the Dread Pirate Roberts as evidence that the thieving piece of shit Green had been murdered. "Died of asphyxiation / heart rupture," Carl wrote to Dread.

That was supposed to be the end of it. Yet shortly after that interaction, Carl had noticed a change in Dread. It was as if the act of taking another man's life, or at least believing he had done so, had given DPR a taste of power and control that he had never felt before. The leader of the Silk Road had started to become more demanding and more confident than ever. When Carl—in a friendly "I'm on your side" capacity—tried to warn DPR about the potential consequences of running the site, Dread responded in a recalcitrant tone that Carl had never seen before.

"I was not forced into this. I chose it," Dread stated defiantly. "I chose it with full awareness of what the consequences would be." He then offered his intransigent view that the Silk Road would grow so large that "it will force governments to legalize" drugs. Don't question the Dread Pirate Roberts, because he was willing to do anything imaginable to see that through.

Dread had become more stern about smaller issues too. When Nob was late to a chat meeting they had scheduled to talk business, he was berated by DPR and given a long lecture about the importance of loyalty and "honoring your word."

*O captain, my captain.*

It didn't take long for DPR to go from feeling disheartened by the death of Curtis Green to believing that the murder was Green's own fault. "I am pissed that he turned on me," he wrote to Nob. "I'm pissed I had to kill him. I just wish more people had some integrity."

Carl agreed wholeheartedly. "Integrity is probably the hardest thing to find [in people]," he wrote, pointing out that loyalty, fear, greed, and power are traits that most of us possess, "but integrity is rare."

It seemed that "integrity" was a rare trait in Carl also.

Over the past couple of months, just like his co–case agent who had stolen $350,000 from the site, Carl had been trying to come up with a way to get money out of the Silk Road for his own personal gain too. This was the opportunity of a lifetime, Carl reasoned. No one would ever find out; these were Bitcoins; they couldn't be traced; it was just like digital cash.

And so he came up with a plan. Several plans, actually.

One afternoon in the summer of 2012, he wrote to the Dread Pirate Roberts with a proposition. It turned out, just by chance, that Nob knew a corrupt government official. Well, whaddaya know? A guy who just so happened to be involved with the Silk Road case. Interesting. This official's name, Nob explained, was Kevin, and he was willing to give information about the case to the Dread Pirate Roberts, but for a small donation.

Dread wanted to know how Nob knew this bad cop.

"He came to me," Nob explained. "Told me about an investigation on me."

"Why did he do that?" DPR asked.

"He did it for money :)," Nob said. "Kevin is a very smart and devious man."

In the same way that Carl had borrowed what he knew about drug smuggling in South America when he created the fictitious character "Nob," he was now borrowing from his own demons to create "Kevin," an unscrupulous government agent who got a thrill from breaking the rules and was now about to cross one of the most sacrosanct lines in law enforcement. He was going to start selling secrets back to the man he was hunting.

Up until this point Carl's supervisors had been able to see everything he wrote to DPR, as their chats were all put into evidence in DEA "Report of Investigation" documents. Aware of this, Carl suggested that Nob and Dread move some of their conversations, specifically those with information from Kevin, to PGP, a highly secure and private chat system that encrypts every single message. If Carl was going to commit a major felony, which he was about to do, he wanted to ensure that the government would never be able to find out by reading these messages.

And with that, a new relationship blossomed.

Under the guise of Kevin, Carl was able to help DPR stay one step ahead of federal authorities by sharing secret and highly sensitive knowledge about the investigation thus far. In return this bad cop required a "donation" of around $50,000 each time he handed over something worthwhile. A donation that DPR was more than happy to pay. It was a foolproof plan: The messages were encrypted, so no one except Carl and DPR could ever read them, and the payment was in Bitcoins, so no one could ever trace them. Carl would offer information about the investigation to the Dread Pirate Roberts, surreptitiously sharing the names of people who might be suspects in the case or of drug dealers on the site who had been arrested and might have turned—pertinent information that would help DPR stay ahead of the Feds. In exchange the man Carl was supposed to be pursuing would pay him $50,000 here, $100,000 there. Money that for Carl would eventually add up to $757,000.

For the Dread Pirate Roberts, it was money well spent to ensure that if anyone in law enforcement ever figured out who he really was, Ross could run before they knocked on his door.

# Chapter 50

# A PARKING TICKET ON THE INTERNET

For months Gary Alford read everything about the Silk Road that he could get his hands on. Every single thing, at least three times. He had become obsessed with the idea that he could find the Dread Pirate Roberts.

Then, on the last Friday in May 2013, as he lay in bed with his laptop, Gary's obsession gave the first hint of paying off.

It had been the end of a typically long week working with the New York task force searching for DPR. Gary came home that evening and enjoyed a meal with his wife, and then the couple trudged upstairs to bed. Mrs. Alford fell asleep almost instantly, and their dog, Paulie, was curled up on the edge of the bed gently snoring.

A lot of the decorations in the Alfords' bedroom were red. The comforter, the pillowcases, and even the walls all looked like they had been spray-painted a deep crimson. In this red room, Gary clicked away on his laptop, still reading about the Silk Road.

Over the past few months Gary had put together a few assumptions about who DPR might be. Dread also knew the American political system incredibly well, which meant he probably lived in the United States. And he must have an impressive computer science background to have built such a Web site.

Then there was the biggest clue of them all.

Gary had read early posts (three times each) by the Silk Road creator, in which he said that buying drugs from the streets, where other people could rip you off or beat you up, was dangerous, and buying from the Silk Road would be much safer. Gary, who was black and had grown up in the housing projects, immediately took offense to this. "What does he mean by 'other people'?" he said to his wife when discussing the case. "Clearly," he had reflected, "he hadn't grown up with these 'other people' because if he had— as I have—he wouldn't be calling us 'other people.'" But while he was irked by the statement, it gave him that final and most important clue: that DPR was white and likely from the suburbs.

Even with these leads Gary had narrowed his search down to about, oh, maybe twenty million people. Still, it was a clue.

Like all the other agents in law enforcement working on the case, Gary had already corralled a list of names that he thought could possibly be the Dread Pirate Roberts. These names included a programmer who had very libertarian-leaning views, someone who worked with Bitcoin, and yet another was a man who managed an online Web forum. But the chance of DPR being any of these people was slim.

So late that evening, as he lay on his red bed, his head on his red pillow, Gary had an idea.

He wondered about the first person to ever write about the Silk Road on the Internet. As far as everyone knew, it was Adrian Chen, the blogger for *Gawker* who had published the notorious first story on the Silk Road. Maybe, Gary thought, Adrian Chen was really the Dread Pirate Roberts.

If so, then maybe Adrian Chen would have written about the Silk Road somewhere else before he wrote about it on *Gawker*.

So Gary went to Google on his laptop and read the *Gawker* article again, three times. On his last pass he saw something interesting in a link that he hadn't seen before: that instead of ".com," the Silk Road's URL was followed by ".onion," which was the domain used on the Tor Web browser.

With that, Gary went back to Google, typed "Silk Road.onion" into the search box, and then filtered by date, saying he wanted to see only results from before June 1, 2011, the day the *Gawker* article was published. This time only a handful of blue links appeared. Click. Click. Click again. And out of nowhere he saw a post on a forum called the Shroomery that had been posted at exactly 4:20 p.m. on Thursday, January 27, 2011—the same week the Silk Road had allegedly opened for business. He clicked the link and began reading.

"I came across this website called Silk Road," someone had written on the Shroomery back in 2011. He continued to skim the Shroomery Web site, which explained how to grow magic mushrooms, until he noticed that the author of the comment about the Silk Road called himself Altoid. Gary sat up in bed.

"Where are you going?" Gary's wife asked, half asleep, as he stood up.

"Downstairs," he whispered. The blue glow of his laptop left the room as he walked across the hall. Paulie jumped down and scampered behind him.

He sat on the couch in the living room and continued to look further. He went to Google again, this time typing in "Silk Road.onion" and "Altoid," and a couple more blue links appeared. Click. Click. Click. And there was another post on a separate forum that talked about the idea of creating a "Heroin Store" that would allow people to buy "H" on the Internet using Tor and Bitcoin. And as on the other site, there was a post written by Altoid.

"What an awesome thread! You guys have a ton of great ideas. Has anyone seen Silk Road yet?" Altoid had written around the same time, in January 2011. "It's kind of like an anonymous amazon.com."

Over the coming days Gary contacted these forums and, using his government credentials, requested the names and e-mail addresses that were associated with the "Altoid" accounts. It appeared that they had been registered to someone with the e-mail address "frosty@frosty.com," which wasn't a real e-mail account and went nowhere. But as Gary dug further, he discovered that the Altoid username had another e-mail address associated with it that had since been deleted but still existed in the forum's database.

The account, he discovered, belonged to a "RossUlbricht@gmail.com."

Another search showed that Ross Ulbricht was a white male from the suburbs of Texas in his late twenties. But there was something missing from the profile of this new suspect: Ross Ulbricht had no computer science background.

Of course, being the first person to ever post about the Silk Road online by no means meant that this was the man who had created the Amazon of drugs. For all Gary knew, dozens or even hundreds of people might have already been discussing the site in private chats, or on unsearchable areas of the Internet, before "Altoid" wrote about it on those forums. But it was enough to add Ross Ulbricht's name to a handful of other suspects Gary had been collecting, all people who might be, in some way or another, involved with the Silk Road.

While he didn't know it at the time, Gary had just discovered the equivalent of a parking ticket on the Son of Sam's car. Except this one was on an obscure post left on a forum on the Internet.

# Chapter 51

# TARBELL FINDS
# A MISTAKE

Chris Tarbell bolted out of the U.S. Attorney's Office at 1 Saint Andrews Plaza in New York. He was walking at a brisk pace toward the FBI headquarters across the street as he reached into his pocket and grasped a tiny gray thumb drive that could change the world—at least, Chris Tarbell's world.

He could barely contain the excitement at the reality that the thumb drive he held possibly contained the servers for the Silk Road. The drive had arrived in the mail that morning, shipped from authorities in Iceland. If the server it contained was not encrypted, it could possibly lead the FBI to the Dread Pirate Roberts.

When the FBI had opened the official investigation into the Silk Road a couple of months earlier, Tarbell and his small team of federal agents were already a thousand steps ahead of every other government group working the case. The cybercrime agents had, after all, spent years hunting for and arresting people on the Dark Web, taking down hackers, pedophiles, identity thieves, and even terrorists, many of whom had adopted these technologies as silent weapons.

The FBI agents also knew that, more often than not, the malevolent people they hunted made mistakes. Sometimes small and seemingly innocuous blunders, but mistakes nonetheless. Often all the agents needed to do to crack open a case was to find one of these.

Which was what Tarbell had recently done.

Given his background in computer forensics, Tarbell could scour technical forums online that discussed the code that held the Silk Road together and actually understand what people were saying. Soon after opening his investigation, Tarbell noticed something that other experienced programmers had seen online: that a recent update to the Silk Road server had left a small but potentially fateful mistake open on the site's log-in page. The error appeared to leak the server's IP address, a series of numbers that was akin to a home address but, rather than pointing at a house, pointed at a server, even a hidden one on the Dark Web.

Upon investigation, it turned out the mistake was a real clue, and after a few hours running software that took advantage of the error, Tarbell was able to pinpoint the IP address that housed the server that stored the Silk Road, which was, it turned out, in Iceland. (Hours after he found the error, the Dread Pirate Roberts saw it too and patched the hole.) It was a huge break in the case, but it was unclear what, if anything, was on that machine. In one scenario the server could tell the FBI the who, what, when, and where about the people who ran the site. But if the server was encrypted, which it likely was, or even deleted by the time they reached it, the clue could amount to absolutely nothing.

It had taken several weeks, a quick trip overseas, some legal wrangling, and a few beers with some Icelandic cops to get Iceland to hand over all of the information on the server. And then in mid-June a copy had arrived by mail at the U.S. Attorney's Office on a gray thumb drive (likely swimming alongside some drugs that had been purchased on the Silk Road).

Tarbell, now holding that drive in his hand, swept past the security guards at the FBI building. He clicked his key card and charged toward the twenty-third floor, looking for Thom Kiernan, the computer scientist he worked with in the cybercrime group.

"I got it," Tarbell said gleefully when he found Thom in lab 1A.

The computer station in the lab was a long bench with monitors, keyboards, and hard drives in every direction. The two men pulled up chairs in front of one of the machines as Tarbell handed Thom the drive, watching with rapt anticipation as he placed it in the computer. Thom's fingers started rapidly dancing on the keyboard, opening the folders and delving into its content. The two men were anxiously excited at the possibility of what it might hold. And then Thom's expression crumpled. He turned to Tarbell despondently and said the last two words on earth that either of them wanted to hear: "It's encrypted."

On the screen in front of them was an endless string of random characters, numbers, and letters that looked like complete gobbledygook. Thousands of lines of unintelligible garbage.

Tarbell was deflated as he picked up the phone and called Serrin Turner at the U.S. Attorney's Office, the man who had just handed him the drive, leaving a voice mail that said to "call me back as soon as possible; there's a big problem."

"Fuck!" Tarbell blurted out as he slammed the phone down. "It's game over."

After a few pointless attempts at unlocking the folders (which was akin to trying to break into Fort Knox with a paperclip) Tarbell reluctantly wandered back to his desk, dejected. In the afternoon Serrin called him back.

"What are we going to do now?" Serrin asked.

"I honestly have no idea," Tarbell replied. "I'm not sure there is anything we can do." As far as they were concerned, it really was game over. He hung up, crushed.

A couple of days went by, and Tarbell called Serrin again to discuss something else. At the end of the call, Serrin asked if they had made any headway on the Silk Road server.

"Nothing," Tarbell said.

"And the pass code didn't work?"

"What pass code?"

"The Iceland guys sent a pass code along with the thumb drive," Serrin explained.

"You never gave me the pass code!" Tarbell responded, shocked that this was the first he was hearing about this, as the excitement from days earlier returned.

"I'm pretty sure I did? Here, let me get it," Serrin said, rustling some papers on his desk. "It's 'try to crack this NSA' with no spaces." It was a jab at the NSA from the Icelandic authorities after Edward Snowden had leaked a slew of top secret information to the press a few months earlier. When Thom typed the password into the files on the gray thumb drive, they opened like magic, and there, in front of Tarbell's eyes, was the entire Silk Road server, unencrypted and as plain as day.

"Holy shit!" Tarbell yelled.

"Holy shit is right."

"It's open. It's wide open," Tarbell said to Serrin over the phone.

"Hell, yes!" Serrin squealed. "Hell. Yes!"

As Thom got to work with the other agents, rebuilding the database and setting up a virtual computer that would house the Silk Road, Chris Tarbell wandered into the back room and pulled a giant piece of butcher paper, about eight feet long, from a plotter printer. With the long sheet of paper in hand, he taped it to the wall of lab 1A. He then pulled out a black marker and wrote the words "silk road" across the top, followed by a series of boxes and numbers below.

In the same way that the organized-crime FBI agents who had worked out of the Pit decades earlier used to create charts on that same wall noting where mobsters sat in a crime family they were hunting, Tarbell was going to create a chart full of numbers and IP addresses that noted where the servers that belonged to the Silk Road were hidden. And just as in times past when lower-level mobsters would lead the Feds to the Don, the hope was that one of those servers would lead them directly to the Dread Pirate Roberts.

# Chapter 52

# THE FAKE IDs, PART ONE

J uly 10, 2013, was a particularly windy day at San Francisco International Airport. Powerful gusts of air rattled planes as they came in over the bay. On some passenger flights the luggage in the hold was jostled around, and on the mail carrier planes, packages and envelopes were shuffled to and fro. But when a Canadian mail flight came in for landing, the wind gusts seemed to stop for a brief moment and the wheels touched down smoothly on the tarmac.

The plane came to a stop and the cardboard boxes in the hull, filled with envelopes, made their way to the Customs Mail Center at SFO. Inspectors unloaded the boxes one by one and unloaded their contents onto different conveyor belts, all destined for small towns or big cities across the United States.

The mail handler on duty that day unpacked one of the boxes, reaching for a pile of square envelopes that had remained close together throughout the journey from Canada. Individually each of those square envelopes was not suspect, but together, as a group, something wasn't right about them.

What stood out to the mail handler was that the envelopes were exactly the same shape and size, and the handwriting on their fronts was definitively the same, a jagged scribble that had been hastily carved into the labels. But, curiously, the return addresses and names on the envelopes were all slightly and strangely different.

One was sent from a "Cole Harris" who lived in Vancouver. Another was sent from "Arnold Harris" at a different address in Vancouver. And a third was from "Burt Harris" in still another corner of Vancouver. Three Harrises, all from different areas of Vancouver, all with the same handwriting on the same size envelopes was not only strange; it was suspect. To top off this curiosity, the letters were all addressed to different people in America, including one being sent to an "Andrew Ford," who lived at 2260 Fifteenth Avenue, right there in San Francisco.

The mail handler grabbed a seizure form, filled out the appropriate boxes, and then sliced open the envelopes to see what was inside.

• • •

Ross had been working around the clock on the site, trying to manage all of the new issues that kept arising, some from disgruntled customers, others related to employees who still weren't working to their full potential, hackers, dealers who were being arrested by the Feds, and packages that were being seized or stolen somewhere along their routes. He was also gathering anti–law enforcement intelligence from someone called Kevin, who told him that the Feds were starting to arrest some of the biggest vendors on the site.

Luckily, Ross was safe from all of this chaos, hiding out as Josh in his sublet near the Outer Sunset and able to work around the clock without any questions from his roommates. (Though he did take a few breaks to watch Louis C.K. comedy clips and *V for Vendetta* again and to read books with libertarian messages that reminded him of his mission.)

With the confidence Ross now felt, he had started to become stricter with his employees, constantly lecturing some of them to work more productively. "I can do better," one underling nervously acknowledged after a recent lecture.

To which Ross replied, "I'm sure you can."

Ross, behind the elusive and fearsome mask of the Dread Pirate Roberts, had also decided to do his first interview, hosting a Q&A session with an intrepid reporter from *Forbes,* Andy Greenberg, who asked DPR questions about the site and its mission. Ross decided to do the Q&A as a text chat so he could run every question by Variety Jones and the two could answer them together. It was the perfect opportunity to spread Ross's libertarian message and, more important, it was an opportunity to implement VJ's plan to suggest that there could be more than one Dread Pirate Roberts.

When Greenberg asked, "What inspired you to start the Silk Road?" Ross cleverly noted, "I didn't start the Silk Road, my predecessor did," and then he explained that "everything was in place, he just put the pieces together."

"Oh, apologies, I didn't know you had a predecessor," Greenberg replied. "When did you take over the Road from him? Before you announced yourself as the Dread Pirate Roberts?"

Ross continued to spin the tale. "It's ok," he wrote back. "This is the first time I've stated that publicly." He told Greenberg that the original creator of the Silk Road was "compensated and happy with our arrangement" and that "it was his idea to pass the torch in fact." The interview lasted four hours and was the perfect rallying cry for DPR's mission.

When Ross wasn't holed up at home on his laptop, barking orders at his underlings, he would go for long walks in the nearby parks, or hang out with his old Austin friends and new San Francisco pals, a nice reprieve from his other worlds.

• • •

Agent Ramirez had worked for the Department of Homeland Security in San Francisco for more than a decade and was by all accounts a seasoned veteran. He always paid attention to the details and always knew the right questions to ask the nefarious people who came across his path.

In July 2013 he was working several cases and had just received an e-mail from someone at SFO Customs and Border Protection about a group of square envelopes they had intercepted from Canada. The mail, the e-mail said, had all contained fake IDs, or at least what appeared to be fake.

Agent Ramirez knew that most of the time customs officials at SFO simply destroyed packages with drugs or fake documents; it was just easier than passing them off to Homeland Security agents. But one of the envelopes had contained nine—nine!—fake IDs. This was a major red flag. Who needs nine fake IDs? One, sure. Two the agent could understand. But nine? The addressee on the particular envelope that was supposed to receive the IDs was an "Andrew Ford," who apparently lived at 2260 Fifteenth Avenue in San Francisco.

While the IDs were perfect copies of driver's licenses from New York, California, Colorado, and the United Kingdom, they all appeared to have a variation of the same person's face on them: a white man with hazel eyes who stood six feet two inches tall and was born on March 27, 1984. In some pictures the man had a thick beard that had been Photoshopped on, and in others he was clean shaven.

This was very unusual, Agent Ramirez thought, and after inspecting the documents further, he decided he would go out to the Fifteenth Avenue address and try to find Andrew Ford to question him about the fake licenses.

• • •

While months earlier Ross had sworn off Julia, vowing never to speak to her again for telling Erica his secret, he was still undeniably attracted to her. So after they reconnected, he invited her out to visit—a weekend of romance and diversion that Ross needed to take the edge off things. It was at least a month before she'd fly out to San Francisco, so he had time to work out the details, but it was highly unlikely that he'd bring her to his sublet.

The home along Fifteenth Avenue where Ross was subletting wasn't much to look at. It was a medley of Spanish elements, with a white exterior and brown terra-cotta roof combined with five whatever-was-on-sale-at-Home-Depot-that-week windows in the front of the house. The front door was glass, and the front yard was a pathetic patch of stark green plants that stood about six inches tall.

Ross, being Ross, didn't care how things looked. For him it was all about the privacy of the house, which was close to the edge of the city, near the beach.

• • •

Agent Ramirez looked at the map on his phone as he pulled up to 2260 Fifteenth Street in San Francisco. He parked and then scanned the building, wondering if "Andrew Ford" was home.

The house was situated in Duboce Triangle, smack in the middle of the city, and was a long rectangular shape, painted blue and gray on the outside. There was no yard in the front, and the entrance to the house was a thick wooden door. Agent Ramirez spent several hours staking out the place, waiting to see if the man in the fake IDs would walk outside to check his mailbox so they could talk to him. But he never showed up.

So the agent got out of his cruiser and knocked on the bright blue door with one hand as he held a photo of the fake IDs in the other.

• • •

The packages Ross had been waiting for should have arrived days earlier, but they still weren't there. He had walked down the orange brick steps to check the mailbox daily. But nothing. Of course, he wasn't looking for mail that had his name on it but rather anything that had been sent to Andrew Ford, the man Ross was subletting his room from, and that had come from Vancouver.

The Canada Post Web site wasn't much help, either. When Ross typed in the tracking number he had been given for the packages of fake IDs he had bought, all he could see was that the envelope was "still in transit."

•  •  •

After Agent Ramirez waited for a few minutes, the door to 2260 Fifteenth Street opened and an older Asian man stepped outside.

"Hi, my name is Agent Ramirez," the officer said. "Is Andrew Ford home?"

The older Asian man looked at Agent Ramirez, assuming that he was trying to sell him something, and tried to shoo him away. "No!" the Asian man yelled angrily. "No! He no live here!"

The agent asked again. "Andrew Ford?" This time holding up a photo of nine fake IDs, each of which had a picture of Ross Ulbricht on the front. "Is there an Andrew Ford who lives here?"

"No!" the Asian man vehemently responded, quickly closing the door in his face. "Now go away!"

•  •  •

Just as Ross didn't talk to his roommates, he chose not to talk to his neighbors, either. He just stayed in his room working on his laptop. If he had talked to the people who lived next to him on Fifteenth Avenue, he would have heard the horror stories about packages getting muddled up in the mail. He might have even heard the tale about the history of the street he lived on: the story about how in the late spring of 1909, the mayor of San Francisco had set up a commission to renumber the houses and roads of the city after years of confusion over the similarity between the streets and avenues. While the commission was started with noble goals, it set entire neighborhoods into feuds with one another, with residents arguing over which streets would be renamed and which would not.

In the end the numbered streets and the numbered avenues remained unchanged.

As a result, packages that were being sent to Fifteenth Avenue sometimes ended up at addresses on Fifteenth Street, and envelopes that were mailed to people on Fifteenth Street sometimes ended up at homes along Fifteenth Avenue.

And in mid-July 2013 an agent from the Department of Homeland Security ended up at the wrong address too, accidentally searching for the man who had purchased nine fake IDs at 2260 Fifteenth Street instead of the address that had been written on the envelope: 2260 Fifteenth Avenue. The address where Ross Ulbricht lived.

# Chapter 53

# THE DECONFLICTION MEETING

Every year around this time, Gary took the day off from work to celebrate the week in 1977 when the lights went out in New York City—the day he was born. But this year, just a couple of days before his birthday, he was asked to go down to a classified location near Washington, DC, to attend a highly classified and incredibly important meeting. Possibly the most important of his career.

The gathering, he was told, was a "deconfliction meeting" about the Silk Road, and it would be held by the highest brass at the Department of Justice, the top echelon of the legal system in the United States. Apparently the DOJ had called the meeting because all of the factions of government that were investigating the Silk Road (which included almost all the factions of government) were not playing well together. Agents weren't sharing evidence. Government resources, aka people's tax dollars, were being squandered on the investigation. Even people within the same agencies weren't communicating, with DEA agents in Baltimore not sharing their findings with those in New York and HSI agents in San Francisco not talking to those in Chicago or Baltimore.

There was also relentless bickering among agencies. These squabbles were routine within any big investigation, but with the Silk Road they were monumentally worse. Everyone wanted the fame and glory of bringing down the big target.

Hence the deconfliction meeting.

Gary woke up the morning of his birthday, kissed his wife good-bye, and got into his Ford Explorer to begin the five-hour drive to DC, where he would present his findings so far on the case.

As the road signs zipped by and the clouds in the sky darkened, Gary was somewhat giddy that he would be able to stand up in the meeting, in front of all of these big and important people, and explain that he had found a few people who might have been involved in the Silk Road from the beginning. It was unclear if any of them was the Dread Pirate Roberts, but he could lay out his cards and at least have a discussion about them. Among these clues, he would be able to talk about "Altoid," the moniker that Gary had determined through a few subpoenas belonged to a man named Ross Ulbricht.

• • •

Chris Tarbell had decided he wouldn't travel down to the deconfliction meeting the Department of Justice was setting up. He knew he was being a prima donna, but he also knew he "didn't have time for that shit."

The FBI agents in the Pit didn't have time for much these days. They were, after all, sifting through the biggest bounty anyone could ever hope for on this case: the Silk Road servers.

"We'll conference in from New York," Tarbell told Serrin Turner, the assistant U.S. attorney from the Southern District of New York. "Plus, you'll be there." There wasn't much of a discussion about it; Tarbell had made up his mind. But to ensure they didn't piss off anyone at the DOJ, they decided to send down two other agents on the case.

• • •

The door to Jared's hotel room clicked shut behind him as he wandered down the hall of the Hilton in downtown Washington, DC, walking toward the elevator. His mind was spinning, trying to figure out what he was going to say at the deconfliction meeting that had been organized by the DOJ.

He had been warned by the agents on the Baltimore task force that he shouldn't say anything at all. The reason for this, they told him, was that there were rumors floating around that the FBI would be in the meeting, and "everyone knows how shady those FBI fuckers can be." If Jared stood up and named one of his own suspects in the investigation, and someone from the Bureau was indeed in the room, they could run off and use that name in their own probe. "They are the worst snakes in the world," the Baltimore team warned him. "Don't say anything in the meeting."

But Jared wasn't so sure that was true; maybe the best way forward was to collaborate. Baltimore was no help at all, but there could be other agents out there whom he could pool resources with. His go-it-alone attitude had gotten him far in the case, but he was starting to question if it could get him all the way.

As Jared drove toward the secret facility in DC where the meeting would be held, he couldn't figure out what to do. He didn't know if he should tell everyone about his recent arrests, or about the other accounts he had taken over on the Silk Road, or about the more than 3,500 seizures that now took up every crevice in his office, piled from floor to ceiling.

*Fuck,* he thought. *What am I supposed to do?*

• • •

The conference room was massive, with enough seating for more than thirty-five people. In one corner Gary sat, staring at the morass of people, most of whom he had never seen before. In another corner Jared inspected the screen on the wall, which displayed the faces of two men, both in another location, who were staring down at everyone. And from that screen Tarbell looked out at the sea of government employees who were now taking their seats.

*Wow, there are a lot of people in this meeting,* Tarbell thought. *Sure is a good use of government money.*

"Okay, let's get started," a man said as the room quieted down. "Let's go around and introduce ourselves. I'll start. I'm Luke Dembosky with the Department of Justice." The room went quiet instantly, as if someone had pressed a mute button somewhere. Luke Dembosky was high, high, high up in the U.S. government. He was someone you didn't interrupt or fuck with. Everyone knew that.

The ground rules of the meeting, Dembosky explained, were that everyone needed to be open and honest about where they were in their investigation. Then the DOJ would decide who got to lead the case going forward.

"Shall we begin?" Dembosky said, looking directly at the Baltimore investigators in the room.

A woman from the Baltimore task force stood up, introduced herself, and began presenting the evidence the Marco Polo task force had gathered over the past year and a half. She read off a few bullet points that were mostly negligible about a couple of informants the team had arrested and then wrapped up almost as soon as she had begun.

"What about the undercover account you have?" Luke Dembosky asked, referring to the undercover drug smuggler persona Nob, which Carl Force from the DEA (a man who was, curiously, not present at this meeting) had been managing for the past year and everyone at the DOJ was very aware of.

"We can't talk about that," she replied. Then she said, "That's 6E."

People in the room looked around in shock. Every member of government there knew that "6E" meant part of a current grand jury hearing, which was a way of keeping the investigation sealed. But it made no sense to pull 6E in a meeting with the DOJ.

"The whole purpose of this meeting is to put your cards on the table," Dembosky declared when he heard this.

"It's 6E," the woman said again, nervous yet defiant. She didn't want to talk about the case, not because she was protecting someone in that grand jury investigation but because she didn't want the other people in the room to steal any of Baltimore's work.

In a matter of minutes a screaming match erupted, with the DOJ attorneys demanding information on the Baltimore investigation and the Baltimore task force petulantly reiterating "6E" over and over.

Dembosky, losing his patience, said it was time to take a break.

When everyone returned to the room, it was Jared's turn to speak. He was anxious. While he had walked into the room that morning determined that he wouldn't share much about his investigation, fearing the FBI would steal all the work he had done, Jared had just changed his mind. After that debacle he had just witnessed, with Luke Dembosky telling the Baltimore task force that their behavior was "completely improper," Jared decided he was going to take a chance and tell the room everything.

He stood up and spoke for more than forty minutes, explaining that he had seized almost 3,500 packages of drugs. He shared the techniques he had developed to spot this incoming mail and how he knew which drugs had been purchased from the Silk Road by matching package contents to photos and locations on the site. He talked about dealers he had arrested or questioned, including people from the Netherlands, and others from all over the United States. He described the vendor accounts he had taken over on the site, and he explained the inner workings of the Silk Road, with charts and illustrations showing who was whom. Finally he talked about a recent account he had commandeered that had belonged to a high-level employee on the Silk Road and showed how the account had allowed Jared to be a fly on the wall in the meetings DPR held with his underlings.

Back in New York, in the middle of Jared's presentation, Tarbell looked at the lead attorney sitting next to him and said, "I want to work with that guy." The attorney nodded his head in complete agreement.

By the end of Jared's presentation, everyone was in awe at the work he had done. His choice to speak had worked to his benefit, and the Baltimore agents, by comparison, looked worse than they had forty minutes earlier.

But the grand finale was about to begin.

When it was the FBI's turn to speak, Tarbell and his crew had decided that the assistant U.S. attorney from New York would explain the FBI's investigation thus far. And yet, as he stood up in the conference room and began speaking, no one had any clue what they were about to hear.

"We have the server," Serrin Turner declared abruptly.

The room fell silent. Not a single word was uttered. In New York Tarbell sat in the conference room looking at the screen with a giant shit-eating grin on his face.

In a matter of seconds, as people realized what they had just heard, agents from all corners of the room began to speak, asking when they could get access to the server.

"We don't know what we have yet," Serrin said. "Let us take a look at it first." He noted that they had gotten their hands on the server only a couple of weeks earlier, and their computer scientists were still rebuilding it so they could search through its content.

After a discussion about this major revelation, Luke Dembosky said the meeting would be coming to a close and he would be in touch with people individually to figure out how to move forward. Until then, he instructed all of the agents in the room to keep pushing forward with their individual cases.

"Anyone have anything else?" Dembosky asked as he peered around the room.

No one said anything. Including Gary Alford of the IRS.

"Okay, thanks for coming, everyone," Dembosky said. "We'll be in touch about next steps."

• • •

The rain started with small sprinkles on Gary's car window. A few drops here, a few there. The wipers made them disappear. Then there were more. Hundreds, millions, maybe. The windshield wipers thrashed back and forth but did nothing. Absolutely fucking nothing. All the cars on the freeway just stopped, unable to see a few feet in front of them, and Gary pulled his SUV over to the side of the road.

*Happy friggin' birthday, Gary,* he thought as he looked out the window and contemplated the deconfliction meeting he had just left. A meeting that had left him crestfallen.

When he had been assigned to the Silk Road case, Gary had thought he was the star young agent the government was bringing in to help take down the online drug empire. And yet in the middle of the meeting with the DOJ, he had realized there were other stars too. An entire constellation of them. Sure, he knew about the task forces in Chicago and Baltimore, but no one had told him about the FBI. The same FBI that worked a few blocks away from his office. When Serrin Turner had stood up and said, "We have the server," Gary had felt a punch to his gut. No one had told him that this wasn't a collaboration but rather a competition.

So why was Gary wasting all of his time reading the discussions on the site's forums (each three times) and studying the language of the Dread Pirate Roberts (also three times) and spending his birthday—the one day of the year when Gary had made the city go dark!—driving down to a meeting in Washington, DC?

*That's it,* Gary thought as the rain pounded against the window, *I'm done. The FBI has the servers; they obviously know about all of the suspects in the case, and their names. What do they need me for?*

A few minutes later, as the skies turned blue and the rain washed away, Gary pulled his car back onto the road, heading north toward New York City. He decided that, going forward, he would focus on people who were laundering money on the site, as he had been assigned. What had he been thinking, anyway? That a number-crunching black man from the projects who worked in the least-respected ranks of criminal investigations in government, and who knew nothing about coding or drugs, could take down the most notorious criminal drug enterprise of our time? Fuck that! As he sped up the freeway Gary decided he was done looking for the Dread Pirate Roberts, even if he had already found him.

# Chapter 54

# JARED BECOMES CIRRUS

When Jared Der-Yeghiayan was a freshman in high school, his math teacher would walk into class each day with a Rubik's Cube in hand. Young Jared would watch as the teacher passed the colored square cube around the room, instructing every student to jumble it as much as possible. "If I can solve this Rubik's Cube in under a minute, you all get homework," the teacher said to the class each day. "If I can't, you don't get any homework." Sure enough, every single class ended with students trudging home with a complicated math assignment.

After witnessing this spectacle several times, Jared was plagued by a desire to figure out how his teacher could always solve the riddle of the cube. He ran out and picked up his own Rubik's Cube and spent weeks trying to solve the puzzle. With a lot of tenacity and a smidgen of help from the teacher, he was finally able to do the same thing. Over the years, Jared had collected dozens of different Rubik's Cubes, now scattered all over his home and office. They hung from key chains and fell unexpectedly out of backpacks. To this day Jared had never met a cube he couldn't solve in less than a minute.

The Silk Road case had proved to be an altogether different challenge, and it had become apparent to Jared that he wasn't going to figure this one out alone. But he had no idea who he could collaborate with. Thankfully, after the deconfliction meeting in Washington, DC, that was about to change rapidly. The presentation Jared had given, showing all the work he had done so far on the case, had impressed the top lawyers at the Department of Justice so much that the New York FBI agents said they wanted to work with him in their quest to find the Dread Pirate Roberts. (This in itself was compliment enough, as the FBI didn't like to work with anyone whose last name was not "of the FBI.")

Jared had flown back to Chicago, stopped in to see his wife and son, and, as usual, fallen asleep while watching *Antiques Roadshow*. Though now when he passed out on the couch, his son, Tyrus, would curl up next to him. It had been difficult for Tyrus to be away from his dad so much, but Jared had explained that this was all temporary, and the travel was important because "I'm trying to catch a pirate who is doing bad things." (Tyrus, hearing this, accepted his father's quest. Pirates, after all, were bad characters in the storybooks he read, and needed to be caught.) But Tyrus had one request, that Jared Skype with him each night before bed.

"Of course," Jared replied as they both curled up on the couch and fell asleep.

The next morning Jared woke up and left for work again. As he pulled his car into the parking lot of the HSI offices in Chicago and it chugged to a stop, his phone rang with a New York phone number.

"Agent Der-Yeghiayan here."

"Hey, Jared," a voice said, "this is Serrin Turner with the U.S. Attorney's Office for the Southern District of New York, and I have Chris Tarbell, the lead investigator for the FBI on the Silk Road case."

Jared immediately sat up in his seat, greeting the two men with respect.

"We really appreciated your honesty yesterday at the meeting," a voice, clearly Chris Tarbell's, said into the phone. He then explained that the FBI had so much evidence—Tarbell referred to the server as "the holy grail"—and given that the Bureau hadn't been on the case long, agents were not sure where to begin. "We'd really love to get you out here to work with us."

Jared was flattered and joked, "I'm on my way!" Then, in a more serious tone, he explained that he was wrapping up a new important part of his case and that he would arrange to fly out to New York City within a week.

They exchanged a few cordial comments and hung up. Jared sat there elated. The kid with no college degree who couldn't get a job at the FBI years earlier was now being asked to work with what many considered the top men in law enforcement on one of the most important cybercrime cases of his generation.

But first Jared needed to deal with that "new important part of his case" he had mentioned to Tarbell on the phone. Though Jared didn't know yet how important it would be.

A few days after the call, Jared drove the Pervert Car to Chicago O'Hare International Airport, as he had done ten thousand times before. But this time he wasn't retrieving mail with drugs inside; he was picking up a passenger who was landing on a flight from Texas.

"Excuse me," Jared said as he brushed by people at the airport, holding his Homeland Security badge in the air. As he approached the jet bridge, there, waiting for him, was a young, timid woman from Texas with dark hair, whom Jared had held at gunpoint a few weeks earlier. The woman worked as a volunteer moderator for the Silk Road, and over the past few weeks Jared had managed to befriend her on the site, and had tracked her down by saying he wanted to send her a gift in the mail. This led to a guns-drawn knock on her door in Texas (with some agents from Baltimore), where Jared gave her a choice to work with him or have to deal with someone else in government who wouldn't be as nice.

Since that encounter they had spoken on the phone, and the woman from Texas had agreed to help Jared take over her account on the Silk Road. At around the same time, she explained to him that the Dread Pirate Roberts had contacted her, asking if she wanted a paid gig moderating the site's forums and being a sort-of assistant doing trivial tasks for DPR. The pay would be $1,000 a week. Now the hope was that Jared would assume her identity and take the job as her.

He drove her to the hotel, apologizing the entire time for how messy his car was, and explained that in the morning they would meet at the HSI offices to get to work. "Don't forget your computer," he joked.

The conference room at HSI headquarters in Chicago was as drab as Jared's personal office. There were no windows, the carpet was old and gritty, and the plants in the room were all made of plastic. When the woman from Texas arrived, he led her inside, handed her a tall cup of coffee, and then they sat down and began speaking.

"So," Jared said as he flipped open a notepad and took the cap off his pen. "I need you to tell me everything: Tell me about the forums; tell me what your daily routine is. When do you log on? When do you log off? How often do you stay online for? Where do you post? What do you post about?"

Jared was going to become her. And he wanted to make sure, in his obsessive manner, that he knew every single detail about her account that others on the Silk Road would be aware of. Over the next two days he learned how to write like her, to capitalize inflections, to repeat important points twice, and even how to use emojis and smiley faces as she did.

She handed Jared dozens of screenshots she had taken of previous chats with DPR and his three deputies, SameSameButDifferent, Libertas, and Inigo, all of whom were incredibly powerful on the site and, as she warned, not to be fucked with.

Jared purchased a MacBook laptop that was identical to hers, and they spent the second day downloading all of the same applications she used to access the site, ensuring that his avatars matched hers (she had chosen to make her Silk Road avatar an image of Spider-Man eating a taco) and that the versions of the programs they used were indistinguishable from each other. He set his username to hers, which was Cirrus.

Then, at the end of the two days, the woman from Texas gave Jared her log-in credentials for the Silk Road. As he typed the username and password into his computer, she voiced her concern about what could happen if things went awry.

"I'm really worried DPR is going to find me," she said. There were, after all, rumors floating around the Dark Web that the merciless Dread Pirate Roberts had recently had some people killed. The last thing the woman from Texas wanted was to get a knock on her door and . . . Well, the thought terrified her.

Jared assured her that she had nothing to worry about and said he was available day and night if anything happened. "Most of the people on this site are just nerds," he said. "They're not ruthless drug lords." From all of his investigations, it seemed that the Silk Road was less like *The Godfather* and more like *Lord of the Flies*. Were these people capable of ruthless acts? Yes, absolutely. But with a caveat: many of them were capable only from behind the safety of a keyboard. "My advice," he said to her, "is to just get off the grid for a while. Don't go on social media. Don't go to the site. Just lay low."

The people on the Silk Road would still see her online under her pseudonym, Cirrus. Only a handful of people in the federal government would know that Cirrus was really Jared, undercover.

DPR had asked Cirrus to provide a driver's license if she wanted to work for him, so Jared had the undercover team at HSI put together a fake license with a photograph of a female agent, which he sent to Dread.

"Hey I'm willing to do anything you need me to do on the site," Jared told the Dread Pirate Roberts in his first interaction with the man he had been hunting for two years. "I'm here to help."

DPR responded with a list of mundane tasks to complete and told Cirrus to get to work. There would be no small talk here.

*Maybe this puzzle would be solvable after all,* Jared reasoned.

As he dropped the woman from Texas back off at O'Hare, Jared was invigorated by the fact that he was no longer just an employee with the Department of Homeland Security; he was now also undercover as a worker for the Silk Road. And his boss wasn't just any underling on the site, but rather the most ruthless pirate of them all.

# Chapter 55

# JULIA IS SAVED! HALLELUJAH!

Jesus told me I need to pray for you," the Spanish lady said as she placed her coffee cup on the table next to a slew of images of mostly naked women. "So I've been praying for you—just as Jesus told me to."

Julia looked back at the lady and began to weep. A stream of black mascara flowed down her cheeks as she buried her face in her hands.

To anyone who hadn't seen her in a while, Julia appeared much thinner than usual, and her eyes were welted with worry. Life hadn't been easy over the past year. First there was the depression, and the alcohol. Then came the older man with money who could protect her. He liked skinny girls, so Julia became skinnier, developing an eating disorder to placate her new boyfriend. Then it became apparent that the protector had a drinking problem. Before long he threw her against a wall in one of his drunken rages.

Soon afterward a Spanish woman stopped by Julia's studio to pick up some books, then explained why she was really there. "Jesus told me I need to pray for you."

Julia wept.

Her life goals were not that far-fetched. Julia hadn't wanted to change the world; she had just wanted her world to be changed. Was it so difficult to find a good man to marry, who would give her a child or two, a white picket fence, and, most important, see that those children grew up differently from how she had? There was a dream in her mind where that good man was Ross Ulbricht, and it ended with them both living happily ever after.

Sadly, that fairy tale had never materialized.

After the Spanish woman who knew Jesus arrived at her studio, the kind lady invited Julia to church.

Later that morning Julia sat at the back of the congregation and heard angels in her ears. She was mesmerized by the place. The rays of light streaming in through the windows, the answers everyone else seemed to have. The pews in the church were filled with Bibles, and the people who read them sang hymns about the Lord. As she listened to the messages from the church's preacher, Julia felt like this could be her white picket fence, that Jesus could be that good man she had always been looking for. That afternoon she canceled her client meetings and went back to the church again.

But this time things were different. Unlike in the morning, when Julia had arrived at the chapel sad and gloomy, she was now glowing. The pews were packed that afternoon, brimming with more than 150 churchgoers. As she stood listening to the sermon, and as people waved their hands in the air and screamed to the heavens, "Praise the Lord!" and "Amen! Jesus!" a group approached Julia and asked, "Have you been baptized?"

*No. But can I? Will you? Jesus recently told someone to pray for me.*

The group gently led Julia to a tub in the middle of the chapel. They wrapped her in a black robe, and the entire congregation started to chant. "You pass through death and into life!" But then something went wrong. The tub in the middle of the church was broken and there was no holy water to fill it. Everyone continued chanting as they stood there, trying to figure out what to do. Out of the crowd someone cried out that they should take the unbaptized girl to a nearby apartment and baptize her in a bathtub.

The congregation streamed out of the wide front door, leading Julia through Austin's streets, the chants growing louder as Julia, in the black robe, was summoned into a small apartment nearby.

"In the name of the Lord Jesus Christ, you will live forever!" they yelled in unison as they walked with her through a dark and dingy living room into an even smaller bathroom.

The bath was filled with water, and Julia wandered past the two dozen chanting churchgoers who now surrounded her inside a bathroom that was big enough for one. They placed young Julia in the tub as the water continued to rise like an ocean tide.

"In the name of the Lord Jesus Christ . . ."

They pushed her backward, her head sinking under the water as the liquid surrounded her face and muffled the sound of the sermon.

". . . you will live forever!"

When a hand lifted Julia's head out of the water, she was saved. She felt a sense of relief that she had never experienced before. A hope of a future that was different from the past. She was elated.

And then, as Julia wandered outside, she looked up at the open and tranquil sky and wondered if she would ever have the opportunity to see Ross again in person. And if so, was there a chance that he could be saved too?

# Chapter 56

# THE FAKE IDs, PART TWO

The gray Jeep Commander drove along California Street in San Francisco, weaving in and out of traffic. Inside the big SUV one man steered the vehicle while the other studied the map on his smartphone, offering instructions to go left here and right there.

It was late afternoon on July 26, 2013, when the Jeep pulled up to 2260 Fifteenth Avenue in San Francisco. Pulling the Jeep to a stop, Dylan Critten, an agent with the Department of Homeland Security, reached for his bag and a printout of a California driver's license.

Dylan looked like he was born to work in law enforcement. He had a cop's buzz cut, broad shoulders, and a face that could easily have been hammered out from a single cinder block. As he got out of the SUV, he looked up at the house in front of him, a sort of Spanish-style place with a white exterior and brown terra-cotta roof.

A day earlier Dylan had been asked by his old buddy from the Department of Homeland Security, Agent Ramirez, to follow up on a lead about nine fake IDs that had come in from customs agents at San Francisco International Airport's mail center. Agent Ramirez had almost given up on the IDs before he realized that he had gone to the wrong home two weeks earlier to do a knock-and-talk, driving to 2260 Fifteenth Street instead of 2260 Fifteenth Avenue.

Now it was Dylan's turn to go to the right place. With his partner by his side, Dylan ascended the front steps and looked through the glass front door down a long hallway. At the exact moment he lifted his fist to knock on the door, he saw a man, wearing nothing but a pair of shorts, appear in the hall in front of him. Dylan froze, his fist a mere inch from the door, stopping before it touched the glass.

Ross Ulbricht froze too.

Dylan looked down at the piece of paper in his hand, then back at the man now standing half naked in the hallway. Without any question, they were the same person. The man on the nine fake IDs was now walking toward the front door, turning the handle, and pulling it open. There Ross stood, no shirt, no shoes, just a pair of dirty khaki shorts, looking at the strangers in front of him and seemingly assuming—hoping, even—that they were at the wrong house.

"Hello, my name is Agent Critten," Dylan said as he turned to look at his partner. "And this is Agent Taylor." Ross's facial expression started to look strained. "And we're from the Department of Homeland Security." As those words hung in the air between the three men, Ross's demeanor morphed into one of terror. "Can you step outside so we can talk to you?" Dylan asked.

*Oh, dear God. This is it. The end.*

Ross took a few steps outside, and Dylan raised the printout of the fake IDs so Ross could see it. "We're here to talk to you about these counterfeit documents that were set to be delivered here," Dylan said, watching as Ross's grimace turned stark white with dread.

*This is it. Fudge!*

Dylan waited for Ross to respond, but instead he just looked back, petrified. His hands were now visibly starting to shake. The agents could see how scared Ross was, so they began speaking quickly back and forth, both playing good cop to try to put him at ease—the last thing they wanted was someone who wouldn't cooperate with them. "We're not here to arrest you for having fake documents," they began. "We just want to talk to you a little about the IDs." As they spoke, assuring him that they were just there to talk, Ross's hands stopped shaking and the color started to return to his face.

"So you're not going to arrest me?" Ross muttered, his voice brittle.

"No, no," the agents said. "But we will need to see your real ID to know who you are."

Ross hesitated but, knowing he didn't have much of a choice, he went to his bedroom, returning with his real Texas ID. Again, he asked, "So you're not here to arrest me?"

"No," Dylan explained as he scrutinized the license with Ross Ulbricht's name on it. "We just want to talk about these IDs and to make sure you are who you say are so we know you're not a fugitive." Dylan also explained that, as agents, their job was to find the people who made fake IDs, not necessarily those who purchased them.

Hearing this, Ross realized that his worst fears were simply fears. These agents were completely unaware of whom they were standing in front of. As he became aware of this reality, he started to feel confident.

"I understand that you don't want to make a statement acknowledging these documents are yours, because that could incriminate you," Dylan said, giving Ross an out so the agents could continue asking him questions. "So hypothetically, if I needed these kinds of documents, where would I get them from? Just tell me in hypotheticals."

"We're just speaking in hypotheticals?"

"Yes," Dylan said, "strictly hypothetically."

It was apparent to all three of the men on that stoop that day that Ross was the smartest of them all. His answer to Dylan's question made it clear that he had the most hubris too. "So anyone," Ross began, "hypothetically, could use the Tor network and can go onto a site called the Silk Road and buy anything they want." He paused for a second, then concluded, "Including guns, drugs, or fake IDs."

The two agents looked at each other, scrunching their faces, both unsure what the Silk Road was.

Ross, who a few minutes earlier had been ready to buckle at his knees, began playing with the agents, becoming flippant with his responses. The agents didn't know this at the time, though; to them it appeared that the man standing in front of them with no shoes and no shirt was doing the government a favor by offering up this information. Maybe this man from Texas could even become a source for them?

Dylan had learned early on in his career that to get someone on your side in a case, you had to cultivate the relationship.

"How can we keep in communication with you in the future?" Dylan asked.

"Well, I don't have a cell phone," Ross said.

"Do you have an e-mail?"

"Sure," Ross said. Dylan handed him a pen and a piece of paper and Ross wrote down "fractalform@tormail.org." He hoped this would be the end of the conversation, but the agents had one last question for him.

"Before we go," Dylan said, "we think you're a smart guy—a clever guy—but it's odd to us that you would order nine IDs; normal people, even normal criminals, don't order nine fake driver's licenses. It all just seems very odd to us." Ross didn't reply as Dylan kept talking. "So we're going to need to talk to your roommates and your neighbors—" Dylan's partner interrupted, finishing the sentence, "To make sure there are no dead bodies."

Ross's face scrunched up again, fear returning. "Well," Ross said, "that's going to be a bit of a problem."

"Why?"

"Because my roommates know me as Josh," Ross replied. He quickly deflected suspicion about that anomaly, talking to the agents about his privacy, and also made it clear with his body language that he wanted them to leave.

The fact that Ross went by "Josh" wasn't necessarily a red flag to Dylan. He had met plenty of people in Silicon Valley who subscribed to a "libertarian" philosophy and were borderline paranoid about their privacy. But Dylan was still hopeful that he could make Ross into a source and, with the goal of eventually tracking down the creator of the fake IDs, the agents collected the information they needed about Ross's roommates.

"Take care," Dylan said politely as he turned around with his partner and walked down the steps. As they reached the driveway, Ross closed the door behind them.

The agents then got into their Jeep and checked Ross Ulbricht's name in the DHS database, which came back empty. "That guy sure was smart," Dylan said to the other agent, who agreed, as he pulled away. "There is something to this Silk Road thing, we should really look into it."

Inside the home on Fifteenth Avenue, Ross rushed down the hallway and back into his bedroom. He knew he had to do something before the agents realized the e-mail he had given them was fake, or before the Department of Homeland Security called Andrew Ford, the man he was subletting the apartment from, and told him that "Josh," his tenant, was really Ross and that he had been ordering illegal documents from a Web site that sold drugs, guns, hacker tools, and fake IDs and having them mailed to 2260 Fifteenth Avenue in Andrew Ford's name.

# Chapter 57

# ONWARD TO FEDERAL PLAZA

F rom the window of his hotel room Jared could see the two massive square imprints in the ground where the two towers had once stood. Cranes and trucks and construction debris surrounded the holes now, and yet a mere decade earlier 2,606 people had lost their lives there.

As he looked out at the transforming landscape, a million thoughts climbed through Jared's mind. He replayed the moment the planes tore into those towers. Explosions and fire and people left with no choice but to jump to their deaths. He thought of those firefighters and police officers who had clambered inside to help whomever they could. And then everyone turning to dust, right at the foot of where Jared now contemplated the totality of it all. He thought about the families who had lost their mothers and fathers and sons and daughters that day. Tears began welling up in his eyes as he reached for his phone to video chat with his son, Tyrus, to tell him he loved him and to update him on the hunt for the bad pirate he was searching for.

After Jared hung up, blowing a kiss from that New York hotel room to his son's bedroom in Chicago, it was time to get back to his laptop, working undercover for DPR. Jared hoped that he could help stop an attack on America that happened not with 747s flying into buildings at six hundred miles per hour, but rather in slow motion through a Web site that wanted to topple the country's democracy.

Jared feared almost daily that operatives from al Qaeda could come into the country legally, without any weapons at all, and then buy an arsenal of bombs or guns or poisons from within the United States, all from the Silk Road with a few Bitcoins and the Tor Web browser. On a more personal level, as he thought about his son, he worried that a teenager could buy a gun on the site and go on a shooting rampage in a preschool in Chicago. Jared was determined to do everything in his power to stop either of those atrocities from happening.

The following morning after a long night working for DPR on the site, managing administrative tasks, Jared walked along Church Street and then Broadway until he arrived at 26 Federal Plaza, the giant black building that was home to the Cyber Division of the FBI.

It was early August 2013, and Jared had come to New York City to work with Chris Tarbell, to delve through the servers and see if they could use Jared's knowledge and his undercover account, Cirrus, to piece together details about who DPR might be.

Tarbell met Jared in the lobby and helped him negotiate getting his laptop and phone into the FBI offices. Under normal circumstances the FBI police (who protected the building) barred anyone from bringing devices inside—even other agents from within the government—for fear that a virus or some kind of surreptitious surveillance software could make its way onto the FBI network. But Jared wasn't just any other government agent, Tarbell insisted; he was working undercover and needed access to his computer at all times. The FBI police relented.

For the past few weeks Jared had had to stay online almost perpetually to mimic the behavior of the woman whose identity he had co-opted. He had been forced to take his laptop on family outings, to birthday parties, and even to his son's weekly swim meet. (Parents of other kids, unaware of why Jared was on his laptop all the time as Tyrus swam laps, were not impressed.)

When they reached the twenty-third floor, Jared was given a brief tour of the Cyber Division before Tarbell led him past the Pit and back into lab 1A.

"You can set your computer up right here," Tarbell said, pointing at the table in the middle of the room where the agents often ate lunch. "And over here is the computer that has the Silk Road server on it."

As Jared unpacked his bag of gadgets, he noticed an eight-foot-long piece of butcher paper that had been pasted on the wall. In black marker, someone had written the words "silk road" across the top. There were IP addresses all over the place with descriptions underneath explaining what each series of numbers represented. One was a server for the chat clients of the Silk Road, another for a server that stored the hundreds of millions of dollars in Bitcoins, and another, called a "mastermind" section, for the site's administrator. As Tarbell explained, this was all the information that had been gleaned from the servers. (To mess with Tarbell, his co–case agents had created a mock chart next to the Silk Road version that had pictures of all the characters from *The Princess Bride,* including Princess Buttercup, Westley, and Prince Humperdinck, with nonsensical arrows pointing between each.)

As Jared studied the Silk Road chart, he saw the name of a coffee shop called Momi Toby's in San Francisco. When he asked why it was on the chart, Tarbell explained that one of the servers they found had been erased. Wiped clean of evidence like a murder scene that had been disinfected with bleach. But when the person who had expunged the drive logged out of the server, they had accidentally left one tiny clue behind: the IP address of the place where they had logged in to do their cleaning. In other words, the Dread Pirate Roberts might have wiped the murder scene down, but he had left the corner of a thumbprint on the front door when he walked out.

This digital fingerprint led the FBI agents to a small bistrolike café on Laguna Street in San Francisco called Momi Toby's. Whoever the Dread Pirate Roberts was, he was either living in San Francisco or had spent some time there. But that was it. One measly clue that possibly pointed to the whereabouts of the Dread Pirate Roberts. "Not much I can do with it," Tarbell said to Jared. "What am I going to do, send an FBI agent into a coffee shop in San Francisco and tell them to look for someone on a laptop?" Still, they had been scouring the Internet traffic from the café, looking for other leads.

After getting acquainted with everyone and being subject to a few of Tarbell's "would you rather" jokes, Jared sat down at the computer, which was now an off-line replica of the Silk Road, and he began searching through its contents. He saw the chat logs where DPR had paid the Hells Angels to have people killed, and he saw other messages between DPR and Carl (as Nob) that were, curiously, encrypted and couldn't be read.

"That's strange," Jared said to Tarbell. "You think Carl Force is trying to obstruct our investigation?"

"No clue, but something doesn't feel right."

Still, they had bigger things to worry about than a petulant and possibly rogue DEA agent in Baltimore. Jared spent the next few days with the FBI crew, working in lab 1A, delving through the server, listening to Tarbell's unrelenting jokes, and then ending the evenings at the Whiskey Tavern a few blocks away, where Jared learned what pickle juice and cheap whiskey tasted like. As those nights would come to an end and everyone else went home to their families, Jared would plod back to his hotel room overlooking the sacred ground of the World Trade Center, and he would transform into Cirrus, the online forum moderator on the Silk Road, and spend the evening undercover working as an admin on the site.

A couple of days went by and Tarbell told Jared that "some guy from the IRS is swinging by later . . . Gary Alford or something like that. . . . He wants to take a look at the server."

"Sounds good," Jared replied, then looked back at his computer as he continued chatting with the Dread Pirate Roberts as Cirrus.

A few hours later Tarbell entered the lab with an African American man in his wake. "Jared, this is Gary Alford from IRS," Tarbell said. "Gary, this is Agent Der-Yeghiayan from HSI Chicago."

Jared looked up at Gary, taking in his wide figure, and as he was about to say hello, Gary looked back at Jared with confusion and frustration.

"Why does he get to bring his devices up here but I have to leave mine downstairs?" Gary asked Tarbell.

Tarbell had no desire to explain that Jared was working on his computer undercover and simply replied, "Different rules for different folks." Gary didn't like this answer and seemed even more annoyed now than he had been a few seconds earlier.

Jared then watched Gary peer up at the butcher paper on the wall with the words "silk road" written across the top. He was inspecting it, noticing all the *Princess Bride* jokes in the corner of the page and the IP addresses sprinkled everywhere. Gary seemed to be even more annoyed when he saw this, as if there was a party going on that he hadn't been invited to.

Tarbell then introduced Gary to Thom Kiernan, the computer forensics expert, who said he would help Gary dig through the Silk Road server. Tarbell then sat back down at the table in the center of the room, unaware, or not caring, that Gary was crestfallen that he wasn't involved in their investigation.

In a sulky mood, Gary got to work searching for people laundering money and Bitcoins on the Silk Road, but he kept looking over at Jared and Tarbell and then over at the big sheet of butcher paper. Finally Gary spoke up again. He had also noticed the words "Momi Toby's café" on Laguna

Street in San Francisco written under one of the IP addresses, and he asked what it was.

Tarbell, his head buried in his computer, explained that it was the one place that the Dread Pirate Roberts had logged in to the server. The only clue they had tying DPR to a location.

"Huh," Gary replied. "I have a guy in San Francisco."

"Oh yeah?" Tarbell said nonchalantly. "You'll have to give us his info." Gary seemingly didn't like this answer, either. Jared watched this interaction take place, and he felt somewhat bad for Gary, who was visibly perturbed. But Jared also knew exactly what Tarbell was thinking, because Jared was thinking the same thing: A guy in San Francisco didn't mean anything. There had been two dozen people whom agents from across the country had suspected of being the Dread Pirate Roberts at one time or another, and half of them were in the Bay Area.

With this retort from Tarbell, Gary peered back at the server and ignored Tarbell and Jared for the rest of the afternoon. A few hours later Gary stood up and walked out. He decided in that moment that this was clearly Tarbell's investigation and there was no room for him to be any part of it. Based on the mountain of evidence Gary had seen on the server, the butcher block paper on the wall with all those IP addresses, and Jared's undercover account, Gary decided that there was clearly no reason for him to send the FBI the name of his "guy" in San Francisco.

# Chapter 58

# JULIA COMES TO SAN FRANCISCO

T he train door slid open and Julia walked onto the platform and into another world. She wasn't sure this was the right stop until she saw the sign that read GLEN PARK. She made her way toward the exit, dragging a large wheelie suitcase behind her.

As she strode into the sunlight of San Francisco, she saw him standing on the street, waiting. His hair was as ragged as it had been the day they met, though he looked slightly different now. He was older? Or wiser? Or tougher? She didn't know what it was, but something about him had changed. Still, Julia couldn't control herself. She ran up to Ross and hugged him as she let out a crushing "ahhhhh." She then stood back, looked him up and down, and blurted out, "Are you serious?" while laughing hysterically. "You're wearing the same jeans I bought you five years ago!"

Ross looked down and smiled as he reached for her suitcase. "We have to hurry back to the apartment," he said as they walked briskly along Diamond Street past the nail salons and coffee shops. "I'm picking up some new furniture today." He explained that he had "moved into this new place a few days ago and—" As he spoke, she interrupted him.

"Let me guess," she said. "You've been living without furniture, right?" Without giving him the opportunity to answer, she jabbed at Ross in a way that few people could. "You're so cheap."

As they walked, Julia seemed ready to burst at the seams with excitement about the weekend ahead. Ross had a slight edge to him but listened as Julia asked questions about San Francisco and how much he must love it here. "I'm not sure moving to San Francisco was the best idea," he lamented, though he didn't elaborate further.

After a few blocks they came upon the three-story clapboard house where Ross lived. They climbed to the top floor and he gave her the two-cent tour. Then Julia sat and watched for the next thirty minutes as Ross and his new roommate lugged an old dresser, a desk, and a bed frame up into Ross's bedroom—all furniture he'd purchased from someone on the street a few hours earlier. When the move was complete, he thanked his roommate, closed the door, and made love to Julia on his new bed.

As they lay there afterward, Ross seemed distant to Julia, but she assumed he was just tired, or that the newness of their old relationship had made him nostalgic. "I'm hungry," she said to him as she got up and put her clothes back on.

"Sushi?" he asked.

"That sounds great."

They walked to the restaurant, a gaudy place with neon signs and an Asian good-luck cat hanging in the window, and they sat inside at a small table. She ordered a platter of rolls, and as they ate, Ross told Julia a story she had never heard before. He explained that as a kid, he used to go fishing with his family. After a long day trawling the water, he'd eat so much fish that he'd get sick to his stomach. But he just couldn't stop himself, he said; he'd just keep eating and eating and eating because it tasted so good.

She laughed. Then (as was typical) Julia did most of the talking and Ross most of the listening. She told him all about her life over the past year or so. About her boudoir business and how it was flourishing, and she told him that she had recently stopped drinking.

"You've grown up so much," Ross said to her. "You're so much more mature now."

"Well," Julia said as she swallowed a piece of sushi, "that's because I've been saved."

Ross knew exactly what she was talking about. They had discussed religion when they were in college. Back then Ross had told Julia that he had been saved too when he was younger, though he had floated away from that faith a long time ago.

They sat in silence for a moment in the sushi restaurant, until Julia said, "Can I ask you something?"

"Of course," he replied.

"Will you come to church with me on Sunday?"

"Yes," Ross said. "I'd be happy to."

With that, Julia suggested they go home and get some rest. Then, just like the old days, they made love again and fell asleep in each other's arms, Ross spooning Julia to the sounds of San Francisco.

The following morning they woke up, showered, and set off about their day. They walked back down past the train station where Julia had arrived the day before, then up to a scrubby diner that sat at the edge of an intersection.

Julia stared out the window as they waited for their breakfast to arrive. They seemed to be in a blue-collar neighborhood, a small enclave on the edge of the city with an Irish pub and lots of middle-class families. Yet among the people walking by, heading to work or a nearby coffee shop, Julia observed techies in hoodies and Google T-shirts; it seemed gentrification was afoot.

"So what are we doing today?" she asked while taking a sip from the diner's shitty burned coffee.

"Well," Ross said, "I have some work to do, so why don't you go and wander around the stores and we can meet up later?"

"That's fine. I'll do some shopping."

After breakfast Ross handed her a set of keys and walked in the direction of Monterey Boulevard, toward his apartment. Julia turned and walked the other way, toward the Mission District.

Julia had planned to be out all morning, maybe picking up a few dresses or some sexy lingerie, but she wasn't dressed for the San Francisco cold. Each time she left a store, a frigid wind engulfed her, pushing her back in the direction she had come. After an hour of this she'd had enough. She turned around, giving up on her shopping quest.

It was late morning when she returned to the apartment, placing the key that Ross had given her into the lock, twisting it, and then slowly swinging the door open.

She nonchalantly came up the stairs, rubbing her hands together to warm her skin as she turned and walked into Ross's bedroom. When she entered, she saw him standing there, his back to her, his laptop open on his standing desk. And in a brief moment she saw something that took her back to their time together in Austin: a dozen black-and-white windows open on his computer, some with chat logs, others with code, and a Web site with a small green camel for a logo in the corner. In mere milliseconds she knew exactly what he was doing.

"Hi," she said from behind him.

Startled, he quickly tapped a single button on his laptop that made the screen go dark and he turned around.

"What are you doing?" she asked.

"Nothing," he said, flustered and nervous. "Just some work."

They stood in silence for a moment. But she knew. And he knew. Ross hadn't given up the site as he had once said. He was still very much involved in the Silk Road. Julia knew then that she had two choices: stay and accept him for who he was or turn around and leave.

Or perhaps there was a third way.

# Chapter 59

# I AM GOD

"How does this look?" Julia asked Ross as she twirled around in a floral yellow dress.

"Hot—you always look hot."

She slipped on some sneakers and told him to hurry up. "We're going to be late for church," she said.

"We'll be fine," he assured her.

It was Sunday morning, and as they walked to the bus, Julia wondered if she should mention something to Ross about the Silk Road. She had assumed when she arrived in San Francisco that he was done with the site—that's what he had told her time and again. But there had been so many clues in the few hours they had spent together. His skittishness, especially around his computer; the way he answered questions about work; and then catching him on the computer. Sure, he still lived like a pauper, renting a cheap room on the outskirts of the city with furniture he had bought on the street, and he still wore the same clothes he had worn in college. But that was Ross. His cheapness didn't prove, or negate, anything.

On the bus ride to church, Julia explained that the congregation where they were heading had a belief system that everyone can talk to God. Therefore, she said, there wasn't one pastor reading the sermon; everyone took it in turns, each reading a passage for two minutes before the piano dinged and someone else stood up to take the pulpit. "It's a little culty," she joked, "but it's really quite beautiful."

The church looked more like a 1980s office building that belonged to an obscure spy agency than a place of God. It was two stories high and painted a strange lime green color. Dozens of white security cameras pointed down from every direction. The only signifier that this was a place of worship was the dark lettering across the top that read MEETING PLACE OF THE CHURCH IN SAN FRANCISCO.

Services had already begun when they rushed inside, Julia ushering Ross into a pew in the back of the room. As they settled into the wooden seats, prayers were being chanted by the mostly Asian parishioners. "Oh Lord!" and "Jesus, praise the Lord!" ricocheted through the large room. Almost immediately the congregation was asked to "please rise."

"We're going to read from the Tree of Life," the first parishioner said, beginning the passage in the Bible where Adam and Eve are deceived by a serpent.

The story was one that everyone in the church had heard before, one Ross had been told as a child, as had Julia. In it God instructs Adam and Eve not to eat from the tree in the middle of the garden, for if they do, they will die. But a snake arrives with a different message.

"Now the serpent was more crafty than any of the wild animals the Lord God had made," the parishioner read aloud. "'You will not certainly die,' the serpent said to the woman. 'For God knows that when you eat from it your eyes will be opened, and you will be like God, knowing good and evil.'"

There was a ding of the piano as the next parishioner took the pulpit.

"O Lord!"

"Hallelujah!"

As the story continued—a story of good and evil—Julia realized she didn't have to broach the uncomfortable subject of the Silk Road with Ross. She believed that what the sermon was saying in that very moment wasn't for the dozens of churchgoers who praised the Lord already, or even for her; it was a message from God, who was speaking directly to Ross. She reached over and grabbed his hand as they listened to the rest of the tale, where God explains that there will be repercussions for Adam's actions.

"He must not be allowed to reach out his hand and take also from the tree of life and eat, and live forever." Another *ding!* rang through the room. "O Lord!"

When the service ended, Ross and Julia walked outside and waited for the bus to arrive. "What did you think?" Julia asked him. "Did you enjoy any of the verses we read?"

"Yes," Ross said. "I get the morals. I can see how for some people it's really important. I really get that, but for me, I just don't need something like that."

"Well, how do you know what's right and what's wrong?" Julia asked.

"I think about it," Ross said, then paused for a moment. "I think about it myself."

In the distance Julia could see the bus approaching. She looked back at Ross and tried to press the question again. "But how do you know what's good and what's evil without a reference point? Jesus is my relationship that helps me decide if I'm doing good in my life."

"I think a man is his own God and can decide for himself what's right and wrong," Ross said. "As a man, I decide for myself."

Julia listened to him, realizing that Ross saw himself as a guiding light, and there was no room for another. In his eyes, he was his own God.

When the bus arrived, they got on in silence. Julia was sad that he hadn't accepted the verses, but she wanted to enjoy the day and what was left of the weekend, so she decided to change the tone, reaching for her camera as they began taking selfies together, capturing a moment in time that she would never forget. They decided to get off the bus at a nearby park and then walked toward the Golden Gate Bridge. There was a sign at the edge of a cliff that read DO NOT ENTER.

"Come on," Ross said to Julia as they scampered behind the barrier. She giggled with the excitement of it all. She handed him her camera and Ross looked through the viewfinder and began taking a rapid succession of photos. As his finger pressed the shutter, Julia slipped her yellow dress off her shoulders until it was in a crumpled pile on the grassy ledge. In a matter of seconds there was no dress at all, and then he dropped the camera on the floor and they had sex on the edge of the cliff.

They went home that evening with a different feeling between them. All Julia had wanted to hear was that he was done with his former life and ready to be with her, but he clearly had a different plan. That night, as they lay in bed together, Julia tried one last time to change his mind.

"Would you ever consider getting married?" Julia asked.

Ross laughed. "We haven't seen each other in a long time. It's been over a year."

"So what? We were dating for a long time before that."

"No, I'm not ready," he said. "I still have things I need to do."

She knew exactly what those things were, and she knew she couldn't stop him from doing them. He would just keep eating, and eating, and eating.

Usually Ross would cuddle Julia. But tonight Ross turned around and stared pensively at the wall, and this time Julia cuddled him, holding him tight while she silently cried.

In the morning they woke up, she packed her things for the airport, and he helped her with her bags as they set off toward the train.

They stood there where they had greeted each other at the beginning of the weekend, and Ross kissed her as the cold fog swept by.

"I love you," she said.

"I love you too."

"Will you come to Austin and stay with me?"

"Maybe next month," he replied.

They kissed again, and then they turned and walked in opposite directions, Julia scurrying toward the entrance to the train station. She started crying again as she looked back at Ross, who stood there for a moment, watching her. Eventually he smiled, slipped his hands in his pockets to shield them from the frigid air, then turned and began walking briskly up Diamond Street, back toward the Silk Road.

# Chapter 60

# THE PHONE CALL

G ary sat silently in his cubicle, growing increasingly frustrated as he listened to the conversation going on around him. A conversation that took him back to that fateful morning exactly twelve years and one day earlier. The day the world changed.

He had been a student at Baruch College at the time, and he had seen the first responders charging toward the towers. Later that morning, as he walked home to Brooklyn across the bridge, the World Trade Center had crumbled behind him, leaving 2,606 people dead.

In the days after the attacks, as the reality of what had happened to New York City—to America—set in, Gary had started to learn some of the names and faces of those who perished. Each morning on his path to school he walked along Lexington Avenue past a building called the Armory, which was covered in flyers of the thousands of people who were now missing in the plume of dust. It quickly became clear that none of those people, whose pictures looked back at him helplessly, would ever go home to their loved ones.

As was true for all New Yorkers, the stories people told of that day could feel palpable to Gary. But nothing was as real as the conversation taking place in front of him right now, over a decade later—on September 10, 2013— between the two men on the task force who were now sitting next to him in adjacent cubicles. These two men, it appeared, had run toward the towers that fateful day and then spent weeks digging through the dust and debris for survivors, mostly finding death.

"You getting your medical tomorrow?" Gary overheard one of them, an NYPD detective, in the cubicle in front of him say to another from New

York's Clarkstown Police Department. As Gary listened, the two men talked briefly about their breathing issues and other ailments that still lingered twelve years later. They talked about other first responders they knew who had developed serious illnesses, some who had even died. As Gary overheard this, he grew increasingly irate as he thought about what terrorists had tried to do to America in 2001 and what he saw the Dread Pirate Roberts trying to do to America in 2013.

Gary had read all of DPR's writings (three times) and had seen the Dread Pirate Roberts proclaiming to his legion of followers that the government's time was "coming to an end"; that the state was the "enemy"; that people should have utter disdain for federal authorities, including everyone who sat in the room with Gary at that moment. The same men and women who had run toward the World Trade Center on September 11 and who tomorrow would have to go to the hospital for health checkups for their heroic efforts.

As these thoughts all piled up atop one another, Gary had had enough. He spun around in his chair, looked directly at another detective on the Silk Road task force, and with vexation in his voice proclaimed, "I think I'm right. You know? I think it's him."

"What are you talking about?"

"It's him. Ross Ulbricht," Gary said.

"You really think you're going to find him from a Google search?" Gary's coworker said.

Gary had suspected that Ross Ulbricht might be in some way involved with the Silk Road and had mentioned it to his coworkers months earlier, but the lead had gone nowhere. They couldn't pursue a case against someone based on the mere fact that they had posted about the Silk Road on the Internet. But after Gary had seen the IP address from a café in San Francisco on the wall at the FBI office, the city where this Ross Ulbricht character apparently lived, he had become convinced that he was at least involved, if not actually the Dread Pirate Roberts.

"Yes!" Gary said, his hands animated, his voice growing louder. "I'm right. I'm telling you, I'm right."

After a few minutes laying out the facts again, Gary stood up and announced that he was going to go back through the case again, starting from the beginning. Just as he had read every e-mail, blog post, news article, and forum posting three times, Gary was going to go back through his investigation three times, from start to finish. Maybe, he reasoned, he had missed something.

He wandered away from his cubicle and around the corner to a woman nearby who worked for the Department of Homeland Security. "I need you to run Ross Ulbricht's name," Gary told her as he sat down in an empty seat nearby, requesting the same background check he had done on Ross months earlier. Gary didn't expect the woman would find anything new. He just wanted to see if some small detail had floated by unnoticed. A speck of DNA, a parking ticket, anything.

After a minute the records loaded onto her screen. The woman first reviewed Ross's travel record, noting that he had gone to Dominica, a data point that Gary knew about and that he thought was suspect, as criminals often hid money in the Caribbean. She kept going through Ross's file and then she stopped suddenly. "You know there's a hit on this guy?" the woman said.

"What?" Gary asked, confused.

"Yeah, there's a hit on this guy from a few weeks ago."

Gary was in shock as he heard the word "hit." He was simply trying to dot his i's and cross his t's three times over.

"You want me to read it?" the woman asked.

"Yes!"

She read aloud, explaining that Customs and Border Protection had "seized counterfeit identity documents" and a Dylan Critten from DHS had visited Ross Ulbricht at his house on Fifteenth Avenue in San Francisco. The file she read from noted that Ross's roommates had said his name was Josh, not Ross, and that Josh paid for his room in cash. She paused, looking over at Gary for a moment, and said, "You want me to keep reading? Is this helpful?"

Gary's brow furrowed. What he was hearing was surreal. "Yes!" he blurted out. "Keep reading! Keep reading!"

She turned back to her computer and continued. In addition to the Fifteenth Avenue address, it appeared that Ross had lived on Hickory Street in the center of San Francisco. And then she began reading the report Dylan had written, verbatim. "Ulbricht generally refused to answer any questions pertaining to the purchase of this or other counterfeit identity documents," she read. And then, like some sort of practical joke, she read the following sentence: "However, Ulbricht volunteered that hypothetically anyone could go onto a Web site named 'Silk Road' on 'Tor' and purchase any drugs or IDs."

Gary's heart began thudding in his ears. It didn't add up. This was all too much for it to be a coincidence. Gary immediately charged toward his supervisor's office and burst into the room, adrenaline coursing through his veins.

"It's him!" Gary bellowed. "It's him!"

The supervisor told him to calm down and then listened to Gary make the case for why it was Ross Ulbricht—a case that was now more convincing than before, yet the supervisor cautioned that there were still many details that didn't make sense. Still, Gary was told to take a deep breath and to call the U.S. Attorney's Office to explain.

• • •

When Serrin Turner answered the phone, he didn't expect to hear an agitated IRS agent on the other end of the line. "Slow down," he said as Gary jumped right into his tirade. "Which guy are you talking about?"

"The guy who I think has been running the site," Gary said.

"What about him?"

Gary began a convoluted speech, laying out everything from the Google search results to the travel to Dominica—all of which he'd mentioned to Serrin a few weeks earlier while Gary had gone through a list of other potential suspects, but this time he added the details from the DHS report, noting the story of the fake IDs, the phony name "Josh," and the mention of the Silk Road Web site.

Serrin wasn't sold by the evidence Gary had just delivered, but he was intrigued. "And this guy lives in San Francisco?" Serrin asked. "What's his address?"

As Gary read the address from the DHS report, Serrin began typing it into Google Maps. The map on his screen zoomed across the United States into the jagged protrusion of San Francisco, then down to Hickory Street, which sat almost in the middle of the seven-mile-square city. As Gary spoke in the background, Serrin clicked on the address on the map and then entered the only other piece of evidence that tied the Silk Road Web site to a person or place: Momi Toby's café on Laguna Street in San Francisco.

"Holy shit!" Serrin blurted aloud. "It's around the fucking corner from Momi Toby's café, where we found the IP address."

Gary leaned back in his chair as Serrin leaned forward in his.

To Serrin it made no sense that a kid with no programming background, whose Facebook photos were mostly moments of him camping, kite-boarding with suburban friends, and hugging his mother, was responsible for creating what authorities now believed was a multibillion-dollar drug empire. And what made even less sense was that this kid had ordered the cold-blooded murders of almost half a dozen people. Nope. It simply didn't add up. But it also didn't add up that this kid lived a block away from Momi Toby's café, that he was the first person on the Internet who had ever written about the Silk Road, and that he had been caught buying nine fake IDs.

"I'm going to send out an e-mail to Jared and Tarbell," Serrin said. "I want to get us all on a conference call."

• • •

The office in the Dirksen Federal Building, where Jared sat, was completely sparse. There were no computers or books in the room, just a solid oak desk and a phone that Jared was now reaching for.

He looked at the e-mail he had received from Serrin a few minutes earlier and began dialing the number for the conference call. As the phone rang, Jared sat back in his chair, slouching exhaustedly as he blankly stared out the window at Chicago's skyline.

• • •

Tarbell walked into his house in New York, greeted his wife, Sabrina, and the kids, and said he had to hop on a quick conference call. He walked into his bedroom and began his evening ritual, kicking off his dress shoes and suit and replacing them with a stained pair of Adidas shorts and a T-shirt. He then belly flopped onto the bed with a thud. He was so tired he could have closed his eyes at that moment and slept for a month. But instead he let out a deep, exhausted sigh and reached for the devices in his bag.

Like a casino dealer fanning out a deck of cards, Tarbell placed his laptop, iPad, and phone out in front of him. He then dialed the conference-call number from Serrin's e-mail and stared blankly at his iPad, which lay in between the two other devices, displaying the map Serrin had sent out an hour earlier.

• • •

"Gary."

"Serrin."

"Tarbell."

"Jared."

"We all here?"

"Yes."

Serrin began speaking, giving Jared and Tarbell a recap of the conversation he had wrapped up with Gary a few minutes earlier. He then asked Gary to tell them what he had found.

Gary began talking with a sense of urgency in his voice. He explained about the Google search and how the very first reference to the Silk Road online originated in a forum post on the Shroomery Web site in late January 2011, from a person with the username Altoid.

Tarbell and Jared were somewhat nonchalant about the evidence Gary was presenting. Maybe Altoid was just an early user on the site. And coincidences were easy to find in a case this large. God knew there had been dozens of coincidences with other people. Agencies had ruminated over the leader of the Silk Road being the CEO of a Bitcoin exchange, a Google engineer, or even a professor at a U.S. university. Others had believed it was an inner-city drug dealer or possibly the Mexican cartels now working with programmers. And some had surmised that it was Russian hackers or Chinese cybercriminals. Yet here was Gary Alford, insinuating that the ruthless, deriding, and wealthy Dread Pirate Roberts was a twenty-nine-year-old kid from Austin, Texas, who had no programming background and who was living in a $1,200-a-month apartment in San Francisco.

Jared wasn't sold. Tarbell wasn't, either. And Serrin knew that if they weren't, he certainly wasn't. Jared, after all, had spent the most time with DPR, working for him for months undercover and chatting with him extensively online. Plus, Jared had an entire office full of fake IDs and people admitting they had gotten them from the Silk Road, and they certainly weren't DPR.

But Gary continued to talk.

"And then I found a question posted on Stack Overflow, where a user by the name of Ross Ulbricht had asked about coding help with Tor. You know?" Gary said. "And then, a minute after he had posted the question on

Stack Overflow, he went in and changed his username from Ross Ulbricht to Frosty, and then—"

"What did you say?" Tarbell interrupted, sitting up in his bed.

Gary was caught off guard by the question but answered anyway. "Stack Overflow. It's a site where you can post programming questions—"

"No, not that," Tarbell said, his tone coming across as aggressive. "What did you say after that?"

Gary explained that Ross Ulbricht had signed up for an account on Stack Overflow with his real e-mail as his username, but a minute after asking a question on the site, he had changed the username to Frosty.

Jared and Serrin listened silently, unsure of what this all meant.

"Frosty?" Tarbell said, now sounding amped. "Are you sure?" He then impatiently spelled out each letter: "F-R-O-S-T-Y—as in 'frosty'?"

"Yes! Frosty!" Gary replied, growing annoyed that Tarbell was being so rude. "And he later changed his e-mail address to frosty@frosty.com. What's the deal? Why do you keep asking that?"

"Because," Chris said, taking a deep breath, "when we got the server from Iceland"—he took another breath—"we saw that the server and the computer that belonged to the Dread Pirate Roberts were both called 'Frosty.'"

The phone line was dead silent, just a hush of air as the four men sat contemplating what they had all just heard.

Finally the speechlessness broke. "Well," Serrin said. "That's interesting."

As this settled in, Jared looked up "Ross Ulbricht" online, and came across his YouTube page, where, amid a dozen videos about libertarianism, was the title that Ross had given his YouTube account: "OhYeaRoss." There it was, the word that DPR used all the time in his chats with Cirrus: "yea."

No *h* at the end, just "yea."

# Chapter 61
# THE GOOD-BYE PARTY

The beach was eerily dark and quiet as the white pickup truck pulled into the parking lot. Specks of yellow from the streetlights hung in the air, trying desperately to bleed through the San Francisco fog. Waves crashed rhythmically into the sand. As Ross stepped out of the truck, he pulled his thick black jacket tight to stay warm. The air was salty and wet.

He looked out at the dark horizon, and while there wasn't much to see, it was the beach, and it was beautiful.

If only time could have stood still in that instant, these next few hours could have lasted forever. But that wasn't possible. The laws of time, like gravity, are nonnegotiable. And time for Ross was running out.

But still, the San Francisco night was willing to offer up something special for Ross as a last hurrah. A night of revelry. Out of the darkness behind him, a friend yelled, "Let's build a bonfire!"

They began unloading the pickup truck, which Ross had helped fill two beds high with dead logs and scraps of wood, all scavenged from Glen Canyon Park, a few blocks from Ross's home.

His new roommate, Alex, was there. René and Selena too. Other friends were in town from Austin, a dozen people in all. The fire was lit and soon began to roar. Champagne was popped open. Beers too. A joint was passed around. Ross grabbed his djembe drum, his hands slapping the goblet-shaped leather as loud thuds hit the air.

The sounds were reminiscent of his days in college when he had joined the NOMMO group at Penn State. If it hadn't been for that drum circle, he might never have met Julia in a nondescript basement at school. If it hadn't been for the libertarian club he had joined, he might never have become who he was today.

He had sailed a million miles since then and helped a million people along the way. The Ross of back then had been an idealistic lost soul; this Ross had changed the world. The other Ross had been worth a few hundred dollars; this one was valued at a few hundred million. That guy had read the works of influential libertarians like Rothbard, Mises, and Block; and yet now Ross Ulbricht was a ghostwriter for the most influential libertarian of them all: the Dread Pirate Roberts.

Or maybe it was Ross alone penning those words. In many respects the two of them were now indistinguishable. Sweet Ross was still in there somewhere. He had recently seen a piece of trash caught in a tree in the park and had climbed the branches, higher and higher, to rid the park of the dangerous plastic bag. But his kindness had come with consequences. "I have poison oak rash from head to toe," he had e-mailed Julia a few days later. "I wish you were here to comfort me :(."

Still, the ointment that could fix the pain would come soon enough, when Ross would be able to see Julia again. He had booked a flight to Austin, planning to leave in a couple of weeks. He was done with San Francisco. What choice did he have? The city knew too much. He would go to Austin first, find another hiding place. Probably somewhere far, far away, where he could see his vision through. Maybe it would all be a new beginning.

The site was making more money than he knew what to do with. He had tens of millions of dollars on thumb drives scattered around his apartment. The problems, though abounding, had simply become daily work obstacles for Ross. When he wrote in his diary that he had loaned a dealer half a million dollars, or had Variety Jones deploy one of his soldiers to deal with another problem, or paid hackers or informants $100,000 apiece, it was just a day in the office for Ross. Murders, extortion, reprisals, and attacks had all just become the job. Sure, it was stressful at times, but in Ross's alternate universe he was king.

On the beach, as the fire roared, a massive fireworks display began exploding in the distance like a magical, colorful rain. *Boom! Boom! Boom!* The thuds of the drum mixed with the sound of fireworks bursting overhead, their burning embers sprinkling into the ocean.

At around midnight two new visitors joined the group, though not the kind that Ross wanted to see: two San Francisco police officers walked up, inquiring into what was going on. But they weren't here for him. They politely said it was time to put out the fire; the beach was closing. One minute red sparks shot violently into the sky, the next sand was being kicked over the embers as darkness returned to the beach.

The troupe of friends gathered their things and walked back toward the parking lot, in the direction of the white pickup truck.

The party, it seemed, was over.

As Ross slipped his black jacket back on and looked out into the darkness, he had no idea that a team of undercover FBI agents were looking back at him, and that for the past two weeks they had been watching his every move.

# PART V

# Chapter 62
# THE PINK SUNSET

**P**ink.

That's what it was. Vast and pink and endless.

A magnificently surreal pink sunset that covered San Francisco from above. Jared couldn't take his eyes off it. He gazed down from the window of the plane, and for a moment he was reminded of just how insignificant we can all feel sometimes, plodding through our lives, working our menial jobs, and thinking we don't really matter—and yet from a different viewpoint we get to see that we all do.

As the plane banked to the left, preparing to land, Jared pulled out his smartphone and snapped a picture to preserve the moment. A memory to capture the pink sky before he, Jared Der-Yeghiayan, helped capture the Dread Pirate Roberts. That was, if they were actually able to catch him. According to Tarbell, there was a problem, and Jared had to get to the hotel as soon as possible to discuss the issue with the FBI team on the ground.

At almost the second the United Airlines flight's wheels screeched onto the tarmac of the airport, Jared reached for his laptop and a Wi-Fi hub and logged on to the Silk Road. He hadn't wanted to take a chance that DPR would try to contact Cirrus while he was in the sky, so Jared had an HSI agent in Chicago pretending to be Jared, who was in turn pretending to be a woman from Texas, while Jared flew into San Francisco. It was complicated, but when he landed, he saw that the handoff had, thankfully, gone unnoticed.

The undercover account had proved more useful than Jared could ever have imagined to ensure that Ross Ulbricht really was DPR. It was one thing to have a suspect; it was something entirely different to gather enough evidence to convict him.

Shortly after the phone call among Gary, Tarbell, Jared, and Serrin, the FBI had assigned a team of undercover agents to trail Ross. For two weeks they followed Ross as he went for a walk in the park, peered over his shoulder as he was on a date with a girl at a restaurant in the Mission, or while he was out for a drink with his friends. But it was when he wasn't doing those things that Jared's account had become invaluable.

Whenever Jared saw the Dread Pirate Roberts log on to the Silk Road, he would let the undercover FBI team on the ground know, and they would confirm that at that very moment, Ross had opened his laptop too. Then, when DPR logged off the site, the undercovers would confirm that Ross had closed his laptop. So ensuring Jared was online all the time was imperative to the investigation.

He got off the plane at SFO, his laptop in one hand, his bags in the other, and he set off to the hotel, utterly exhausted. He hadn't slept more than a couple of hours at a time since the phone call three weeks earlier, and there was no sign that was going to let up anytime soon.

Jared checked into his room at the hotel and made plans with Tarbell to meet at the steak restaurant in the lobby to go over the logistics of the coming days. Tarbell introduced Jared to a large ex-marine called Brophy, who was a "badass" special agent with the New York FBI and had come out to San Francisco to assist with the actual arrest. Thom, the computer scientist from the New York office, whom Jared had met before in New York City, was there too. Thom had one job, which was to keep Ross's computer powered on and logged in if they captured him with his hands on the keyboard. But there was a problem with that part of the operation. As they ordered beers, Tarbell explained that the local FBI team in San Francisco was going to be responsible for the arrest, as this was in their jurisdiction (this was standard FBI procedure) and that the local agents wanted to go into Ross Ulbricht's house with a SWAT team.

"Oh, fuck."

"Yeah."

Tarbell had made this mistake before during his LulzSec bust, and he knew that they could arrest Ross Ulbricht ten thousand times over, but unless they caught him with his hands on his laptop, they might not be able to prove that they had captured the Dread Pirate Roberts. All it would take was a glimpse of a Fed or the sound of a footstep, and Ross could touch his keyboard, encrypting the evidence on it. Sure, they could tie him to the site with the log-ins from Momi Toby's café and the surveillance the Feds and Jared were building together. But a good lawyer could say that was all coincidence.

"What are we going to do?" Jared asked.

"I'm going down to the local FBI office tomorrow to try to talk them out of going in with SWAT," Tarbell replied.

"You think it'll work?"

"It has to."

But Tarbell knew it would be a tough sell. As the FBI briefing reports noted, the Dread Pirate Roberts was dangerous. From what Tarbell and his crew had pulled from the servers, it appeared that DPR had had people murdered—several people—and that he had ties to the Hells Angels and other hit men. For all they knew, DPR was going to go down with a fight. Maybe a fight to the death. And the higher-ups at the Bureau weren't going to risk losing a single FBI agent if that proved to be true. To top it off, the director of the FBI had briefed the White House about the sting, which meant the president of the United States would know if the operation was a success.

Brophy, the gruff agent, interrupted. "I should've grabbed him today."

"Whaddaya mean?" Jared asked.

Earlier that day, Brophy explained, the undercover team had tracked Ross to a nearby coffee shop, where he sat on his computer for a couple of hours. Brophy walked into the café and sat right next to him, and while Brophy was big enough that he could have taken him right there and then, there was a chance that Ross wasn't logged in to the Silk Road, and they would have captured him simply checking his e-mail. If Jared had not been on that plane, they might have been able to check if DPR was logged in to the site and arrested him if he was, but they couldn't take that chance, so Brophy let him go.

"No shit?!"

"Yep."

"Well," Jared sighed as he observed his laptop, "he's logged in now." He then asked, "So what are we going to do?"

"I'm not sure. Let's see what the ASAC says tomorrow," Tarbell said, referring to the local assistant special agent in charge. Tarbell swallowed a gulp of his beer the way someone downs a shucked oyster, and as he did, he was reminded of something he had forgotten to share with Jared. "You wouldn't believe who fucking called me before I flew out!"

"Who?" Jared queried as he took a bite of his burger.

"Carl Force! And he was being adamant that he wanted to see the server; he was almost defiant about it, acting like a real dick. I told him if he wanted to see it he had to go through my ASAC."

"The Baltimore guys are so fucking unprofessional," Jared said as he shook his head. "I swear something's up with Carl; something doesn't feel right."

The agents spent the next forty-five minutes telling stories about just how unprofessional Carl and the team in Baltimore had acted toward them during the investigation, with Brophy and Thom listening in shock. Though none of them had any idea yet just how unprofessional.

"I have to get to work for DPR," Jared said as he stood up to leave the bar, knowing full well that he had a long night ahead of him. Tarbell had his own work cut out for him. The next day he would have to head down to the local FBI office and somehow try to persuade them not to go into Ross Ulbricht's house with a SWAT team.

# Chapter 63
# CARLA SOPHIA

arl read the e-mail from the group supervisor on the Baltimore task force.

"Baltimore is to stand down on all SR activity for 1 week pending outcome of FBI NY takedown(s) next week," the message said. It was soon followed by more severe instructions. "For right now, the important thing is that we not do anything that could in any way possible interfere with the arrest of DPR and the collection of evidence in the course of that arrest and search. Therefore, please stand down on all investigative activities, including logging onto Silk Road, it's forums, or any UC communications."

*This is bad. So very, very bad.*

Rumors had already traveled from New York via Washington, DC, to Carl's small desk in his mauve-colored cubicle in Baltimore that the FBI and some other agents might have found the Dread Pirate Roberts. Now this confirmed it. It was the worst news Carl could ever imagine hearing. This was a problem not just for DPR but also for Carl and his secret online identities who were feeding information to the man he was supposed to be hunting.

Until now Carl's plan had been working seamlessly. He would chat by day as Nob, and the conversations would be saved and logged in to a DEA investigation report. Then he would send those very thorough and detailed reports to Nick and the other agents on the Marco Polo task force.

A job well done. Good work, Carl!

Yet as dusk turned to dark, Carl would log on to his computer as Kevin, the government agent, and, for a fee, surreptitiously send Dread messages that were not recorded and put into a report.

When the two lines crossed, and the Dread Pirate Roberts (unaware of what was going on at the other end of the connection) discussed payments for information, Carl would scold Dread, reminding him to "Use PGP!" the highly secure messaging platform. In the few instances that DPR slipped up, Carl would pretend that there had been a technical glitch in his daily report. "AGENT'S NOTE: SA Force was unable to make several video recordings of the above messages due to problems with the SR site."

It had all worked perfectly, until the lies started to pile up atop one another and Carl started to mix up who he was supposed to be and when he was supposed to be them. Rather than slow down, or even stop crossing the line, Carl decided to move that line even further away and he started creating more fake accounts and machinations to take more money.

Before the e-mail came in telling him to stand down, Carl decided to create another fictitious online persona, one that wasn't Nob, the drug smuggler, or Kevin, the dirty DOJ employee, but a new character called French Maid. Under this new guise, Carl sent DPR another message, offering to sell more information about the investigation into the site. "I have received important information that you need to know asap. Please provide me with your public key for PGP." This was the point where Carl's lies were too complicated to track, and everything he was saying became jumbled in his own mind. As a result, Carl was about to make an irreversible mistake.

In a message to DPR, while pretending to be French Maid, he accidentally signed the message with his own name, Carl.

A short while later, when Carl realized what he had done, he quickly followed up with another message to Dread. "Whoops! I am sorry about that. My name is Carla Sophia and I have many boyfriends and girlfriends on the market place. DPR will want to hear what I have to say ;) xoxoxo."

Luckily for Carl, the Dread Pirate Roberts could care less who Carl or Carla was; Dread just wanted the information that was for sale and gladly handed more than $100,000 to French Maid for more information that could help him keep the Feds at bay.

Carl thought he'd gotten away with his exploits, but in mid-September 2013 he heard that the Feds had fingered DPR. This was followed by the e-mail from his bosses to stand down. Carl was in a panic. If the FBI got Dread on his computer, then there might be more records of the conversations between the mendacious DEA agent and the Dread Pirate Roberts.

As Nob, he messaged DPR and told him: "My informant (Kevin) is certain that you are going to be identified and caught. You are like one of my family. but I have to tell you that I have had several people killed who were sent to jail. it is very easy and cheap," Carl said, and then concluded the threat implied in that previous message. "I trust that you have destroyed all messages, chats, etc between us."

But what if Dread didn't delete the messages? After thinking all of this through, Carl knew that the only way to find out what the FBI knew, or would know if they captured Dread, was to see the servers that the Feds had apparently found. So he came up with another idea—another lie—and he called Chris Tarbell from the FBI, whom he had never spoken to before.

"Hi, this is Special Agent Carl Force from the DEA in Baltimore," he barked at Tarbell. "When can I come up and look at the server?"

"Who is this?" Tarbell replied.

"Special Agent Carl Force from the— Look, you know, I really need to see that server."

Tarbell was immediately combative in his response to Carl. "Did you get approval from the ASAC?"

"Yes, yes, yes, I did," Carl stuttered, obviously not telling the truth, "When can I come up? What day is best for you?"

"There's no time. If you want to see it, then you'll have to go through ASAC." And then Tarbell abruptly hung up.

After this interaction Carl was out of ideas. All he could hope was that DPR had done what Nob had requested and wiped the messages from his computer. Or maybe they would both be lucky and the Dread Pirate Roberts would get away, taking all of Carl's secrets with him.

# Chapter 64
# FeLiNa

The last day of Ross's life as a free man began just like any other. He woke up in his Monterey Boulevard apartment and slipped on his blue jeans and long-sleeved red T-shirt. Then he got to work on the Silk Road, unaware that by 3:16 p.m. that day, he would be sitting in the back of a police car in handcuffs.

He had been blue for the past few days, as things had not been going his way. First one of his government informants, who went by the moniker "French Maid," told him that the Feds had a new name to add to the list of people who could potentially be the Dread Pirate Roberts, and French Maid (who had said her real name was Carla Sophia) would happily share the name in exchange for $100,000. So DPR had paid and was still waiting for a response. Then another employee, to whom he had loaned $500,000, had disappeared. To top it all off, his poison oak rash hadn't gone away.

But there were things to be grateful for.

Ross was soon going to Austin, where he would see Julia. She had told him in an e-mail she would pick him up from the airport, and he could stay with her. Just like old times. They had been having romantic Skype sessions a lot too and sending long, dirty e-mails back and forth about what they would do to each other in person. Ross had also had an epiphany over the weekend. After the bonfire and the fireworks on Ocean Beach, he had written in his diary (alongside his travails on the Silk Road and an explanation for how he got the poison oak rash) that he needed to "eat well, get good sleep, and meditate so I can stay positive."

## 12:15 p.m.

The houses along Monterey Boulevard were mostly two- and three-story wood frames. They were painted all different colors, some white, others blue or green. The apartment where Ross Ulbricht now lived was in a three-story beige building in the middle of the block. Every once in a while a large Suburban SUV with dark tinted windows would drive by. The SUV would make a right down Baden Street, then another right and another, until it found itself back in front of the beige building on Monterey Boulevard.

Even if anyone had noticed the SUV as it swirled around the blocks that morning, no one would have guessed what was inside the vehicle.

## 2:42 p.m.

Tarbell paced in front of a coffee shop on Diamond Street, staring down at his phone, trying desperately to figure out what to do. He had gone to the local FBI offices and made his case that they shouldn't use a SWAT team, but the supervisor in charge of the local Bureau had issued a flat-out "no." The supervisor said he wasn't going to risk losing an agent over an open laptop. Clearly he didn't know how important that computer was. Tarbell called everyone he knew in government, trying to persuade them not to go into Ross's house with a battering ram and guns drawn, but all he could get out of the local FBI office was an agreement to delay the SWAT team raid by one day.

Jared, Thom, and Brophy stood in front of the café near Ross's house, listening to Tarbell explain this, unsure what they were going to do. They knew that Ross was at home on his laptop because the FBI had an undercover SUV circling his block and monitoring his Wi-Fi traffic. The system they were using would check the signal strength of the Wi-Fi on his computer and then, by triangulating that data from three different points they had captured as they drove around the block, they were able to figure out Ross's exact location, which at this very moment was his bedroom, on the third floor of his Monterey Boulevard apartment.

As the agents stood outside the café discussing their conundrum, Jared looked at his computer to check his battery level, now in the red and quickly falling past 18 percent. In that moment he noticed that the icon next to the

Dread Pirate Roberts vanished from the chat window. "DPR just logged off," Jared said. "I'm going to go into Bello Coffee and charge my shit and get a coffee."

Thom followed him, leaving Brophy and Tarbell outside.

The coffee shop was bustling and every seat was occupied by a laptop-toting patron. A few moms sipped tea with a hand on their strollers, and others stared at their phones. Jared found a single free power outlet along the wall, plugged in his computer, and ordered a coffee.

After two years of slogging up a mountain of shit, they were so close to DPR they could practically hear him breathing, and yet they had lost. The SWAT team was going in. They wouldn't capture the open laptop; they wouldn't get Ross Ulbricht logged in to the site.

### 2:46 p.m.

Ross grabbed his laptop, stuffed it into his shoulder bag, and headed down the stairs and onto Monterey Boulevard. The air was unusually warm, with just a slight chill from the San Francisco breeze.

He had been in the house all day and needed to change locations. Plus he wanted to find a fast Wi-Fi connection so he could download an interview with the creator of the show *Breaking Bad*. The show's final episode, "FeLiNa," had aired the night before and had left the protagonist, Walter White, and his alter ego, Heisenberg, dead.

Ross wouldn't be out long. Maybe just a couple of hours to mooch Wi-Fi from a nearby coffee shop, download the show, and do some work on the Silk Road.

### 2:50 p.m.

Tarbell was watching the street when his phone vibrated with a message from the undercover FBI agents who had been monitoring Ross. "He's on the move," they wrote.

Tarbell quickly ducked into the coffee shop to alert Jared and Thom.

"Our friend is coming down the street!" Tarbell said aggressively to Jared. His voice was gruff and to the point. Jared looked back at him, exhausted and confused by what Tarbell was saying. "Which friend?" Jared asked, thinking this could be another Tarbell joke.

"Our. Friend," Tarbell said firmly, "Is. Coming." He couldn't exactly blurt out "Ross Ulbricht" or "Dread Pirate Roberts" or "the criminal mastermind you've been after for two fucking years."

And then it hit Jared. *Holy shit! Our friend!*

He grabbed his coffee and laptop, came rushing outside, and ran across the street to a park bench with Thom, where they tried their best to blend in with the world around them.

### 2:51 p.m.

Tarbell exited the coffee shop. "Description and Direction?" he wrote on his BlackBerry to the undercover agents. Everyone in Tarbell's crew scattered. Brophy cut right to hide in the library a few doors down. He had seen Thom rush across the street, taking a seat on a bench in front of a pizza place. Jared was not far behind him. Tarbell turned in the only direction left and started walking south along Diamond Street, right into the path of Ross Ulbricht.

Tarbell knew that the undercover FBI agents would be following Ross, but he wanted to get a glimpse of him firsthand.

Cars and people flowed by in all directions as Tarbell approached the crosswalk. The world was moving at a perfectly normal pace. Yet for Tarbell it was operating so much slower; his heart hammered in his chest, as he knew he was about to come face-to-face with the Dread Pirate Roberts.

And then he did.

As Tarbell crossed the street, as if he were doing so in slow motion, he noticed every detail of his surroundings: the birds flapping through the air, the colors of the cars on the road, the chipped paint of the yellow crosswalk, and the man now walking into his path, who was wearing blue jeans and a long-sleeved red T-shirt and had a brown laptop bag over his shoulder. Tarbell took another step forward into the median of the road and looked directly into his eyes as Ross looked back.

### 3:02 p.m.

Ross continued along the crosswalk and walked up to Bello Coffee. The coffee shop was bustling. Every seat was taken by someone with an open laptop or a mother with a stroller. He had told his employees the importance of being safe in a coffee shop, once offering Inigo this advice: "Take your laptop and find a spot in a cafe where your screen won't be visible to anyone. Get a large coffee, sit down, and don't get up except to stretch." Given that there was nowhere for Ross to sit that adhered to that protocol, he turned around and walked back outside.

He had a lot on his mind, as always. He had made plans with Julia to video chat that evening.

"Can we skype tonight?" she had asked over e-mail.

"Sure, what time?"

"Is 8 my time good?"

"Sure, see you then," he wrote, following up with a ":)" as he knew exactly what kind of Skyping they'd be doing.

The air was calm as Ross contemplated where to go next. He needed Wi-Fi but didn't have many options at 3:00 p.m. in this sleepy corner of the city. He looked to his left, in the direction he had just come from, and knew Cup Coffee Bar had closed an hour earlier. Straight ahead of him cars streamed by, a woman walked with her daughter, and two men sat on a wooden park bench, one staring at his laptop, the other looking at his phone. Ross continued to scan the street, his eyes sliding past the burrito shop, then past the local pub, until he turned to his right, staring up at the Glen Park Public Library.

*3:03 p.m.*

Jared and Thom sat on the bench, gazing straight ahead as if they were in a staring contest with the coffee shop. Jared's laptop was open, and Thom had his smartphone in his hand. They could see Ross walk out of the café, holding on to his bag. Ross was peering around, and then he looked directly in the direction of Jared and Thom as they both quickly looked away, trying to seem inconspicuous.

"I bet he's looking for Wi-Fi," Jared whispered under his breath to Thom. They watched out of the corners of their eyes as Ross walked to his right, toward the public library.

At almost that exact moment Tarbell appeared, his phone in his hand as he read updates from the undercover agents trailing Ross.

"Where's he at?" Tarbell asked. Jared motioned toward the library.

At that moment Tarbell, who had gone by the book his entire life, had to decide what to do. He had studied and practiced for every single moment of his life, no matter how small. Yet now, he didn't know if he should follow the rules or break them. He was fully aware that the local FBI office would be apoplectic if they knew he was contemplating trying to arrest Ross Ulbricht without the SWAT team present. But he had no choice if he wanted to catch the Dread Pirate Roberts on the laptop. He looked down at Jared, then over to Thom, then to the library, and a thought rang out in his head: *Fuck it.*

"Go to the library and get in position," he told Thom. Do nothing, say nothing, just blend in.

As Tarbell looked down at his phone, he was fully aware that a few miles south of where he stood, at that very moment, dozens of SWAT team members were shuffling into a conference room at the local Bureau office, preparing to run through a drill for how they would apprehend Ross Ulbricht, guns drawn, the following day. He tapped out another e-mail to let his crew know the plan, that they were going into the library to try to capture Ross Ulbricht. This meant that the men in that SWAT team meeting would see the message too, and in a few minutes they would be running toward their cruisers, sirens blaring and lights flashing, racing north along the 101 freeway past the San Francisco airport in the direction of placid Glen Park, toward the little library.

### 3:06 p.m.

To the right of the library stacks, a couple of children sat at a small table with small chairs, quietly flipping the pages of small storybooks. A few other patrons milled about between the stacks. It was a diminutive library, reminiscent of the Good Wagon Books warehouse, where most of the sections were composed of only one or two bookshelves.

Ross walked toward a round beige table nestled between the science fiction section and the romance novels. He sat down, pulled his laptop out of his bag, and watched as the computer came to life.

### 3:08 p.m.

In the corner of the room, Brophy reached for his BlackBerry and sent a note out to the other FBI agents: "Seated NW corner."

At the park bench in front of the library, Tarbell was pacing. DPR still wasn't online. Jared looked up at Tarbell, then back to his laptop, the battery indicator now at 20 percent.

"Give me a chance to chat with him," Jared said.

Tarbell typed an e-mail to the group, his palms sweaty. "Has NOT signed in yet," he wrote, and then noted that the undercover agent on Silk Road (Jared) would need to lure the Dread Pirate Roberts into the site's marketplace, ensuring he was caught with digital drugs and virtual money in his hand. If they didn't get him with his laptop open and logged in to the site, and Ross managed to close the lid or press a key that encrypted the hard drive, the case could go *poof!* Finally Tarbell reminded everyone that when he gave the go-ahead, "PULL the laptop away, then get arrest."

When Jared saw "dread" appear in his chat window, the thought that popped into his head was *Oh fuck! This is it.* Any adrenaline that had been pumping through him a moment earlier went quiet as he focused on the task in front of him. Everything, he realized, came down to this very moment. An envoy of FBI agents was racing up the freeway; Tarbell stood nearby watching; and agents from the DEA, HSI, CBP, DOJ, IRS, ATF, and U.S. Attorney's Office, as well as senators, governors, and even the president of the United States, were waiting to hear that this moment had happened without a hitch.

Jared began typing into the Silk Road chat window on his computer. "Hey," he wrote. But there was no reply. A minute went by and Jared typed "Hey" again. This time, though, he added a request for DPR: "Can you check out one of the flagged messages for me?"

Jared knew that asking him this would prompt DPR to log in to the administrator section of the site, and if the man now sitting in the library a hundred feet away was really the Dread Pirate Roberts, that same man would be logged in to that section of the site if they grabbed his laptop. After what felt like an eternity, a *ding* finally sounded from Jared's computer as a reply appeared on the screen.

"Sure," DPR wrote. "Let me log in." And then he followed up with a strange question. "You did bitcoin exchange before you worked for me," Dread wrote. "Right?"

For some reason DPR was testing him. Jared's mind started to swirl with worry. Did DPR know something was up? Jared scanned his mind trying to remember the right answer.

### 3:13 p.m.

A young Asian woman wandered through the library plucking books from the shelves. After a while she came around the corner of the stacks, standing in front of the science fiction and romance section, and pulled up a chair at the round beige table where Ross sat. His backpack rested next to him; his laptop glowed as he typed away. He peered over his computer screen at the young woman. She had a fair complexion and was perusing the pile of books in front of her. She seemed safe enough, so Ross looked back to his computer, his fingers methodically moving up and down on the keyboard as he typed.

### 3:14 p.m.

Jared thought, trying to remember what the woman from Texas had told him in August when he had taken over her account. Had she done Bitcoin exchange? Or had she not? He took a deep breath and took a chance, replying, "Yes, but just for a little bit."

"Not any more than that," DPR replied, still fishing for an answer. A test indeed.

"No," Jared wrote back, "I stopped because of reporting requirements."

What he said must have worked, because Dread soon asked, "Ok, which post?" He was now definitively logged in to all three administrative areas of the Silk Road. Jared looked up at Tarbell and began swirling his finger in the air like a helicopter about to take flight. "Go, go, go," he said swiftly. "Go!"

Tarbell's thumbs hammered down on his phone as he typed as fast as he could. "He is logged in," he wrote, followed by "PULL LAPTOP—GO." He scrambled across the street and into the library.

Jared came running up behind Tarbell. It was pure adrenaline now. They both hurried up the library steps until Tarbell came to a swift standstill midstride and swung his arm out to stop Jared. "Let them do their thing," Tarbell whispered.

For ten seconds Jared and Tarbell didn't say a word. They just stood there, frozen on the concrete steps of the library. And then they heard it. The yelling and commotion that had just erupted inside the quiet library on Diamond Street.

# Chapter 65
# ARRESTED

*3:15 p.m.*

One minute the library was silent; the next, an Asian woman yelled, "Fuck you!" at a man standing next to her.

Everyone in the library looked up, startled by the outburst. The man who had just been told to go fuck himself raised his fist to seemingly punch the woman in the face. As his clenched hand went into the air, a startled Ross Ulbricht turned around in his chair to witness the commotion.

And just in that moment, as Jared and Tarbell stood at the base of the stairs, the Asian woman with the fair complexion who had been seated at the table across from Ross reached over and gently slid his Samsung laptop away from him. Ross turned back, half comprehending what was going on as he tried to lunge for the laptop. Yet he couldn't. Someone had grabbed his arms from behind.

"FBI! FBI!" the couple who had just been yelling at each other now bellowed at Ross as they slammed him against the table. Brophy rushed over, slapping handcuffs around Ross's wrists, and retrieved him. Thom, visibly shaken by the intensity of the moment, came to retrieve the laptop, which was still wide open and, thanks to Jared, also logged in to all three administrative areas of the Silk Road, including the "Mastermind" page, an area of the site that only the Dread Pirate Roberts and Ross Ulbricht could log in to.

As Tarbell and Jared entered the second floor of the library, Brophy appeared, holding by the arm a young man who was now handcuffed and had a panicked look on his face.

"This is going to be your new best friend," Brophy said to Tarbell and Jared as he handed Ross Ulbricht over to them.

Inside the library patrons started to yell at Brophy and the others. "What did that kid do?!" they hollered. "Leave him alone!" To them the young man now in handcuffs had been minding his own business, just using his laptop.

Tarbell and Jared led Ross down the concrete steps, out into the street. Tarbell then turned Ross around, gently placed him up against a wall, and began patting him down. In Ross's pockets there were only two $1 bills, some spare change, and a set of house keys.

"I am Special Agent Chris Tarbell with the FBI," he said as he spun a handcuffed Ross back around, placing his hand on Ross's chest to ensure he wasn't having a heart attack or any other emergency. "Do you have any medical conditions? Do you need any medical attention?"

"No, I'm fine," Ross said. The shock of the moment had already worn off and Ross was now nonchalant, as if this was just a small bump in the road. "What am I being charged with?" he asked, knowing full well that the cops could have grabbed him for any number of reasons. Maybe it was the fake IDs he had ordered or something innocuous related to the Silk Road.

"We'll go over that in the car," Tarbell replied, "once we get you off the street."

FBI cars and vans from the local FBI squad now screeched in from all angles and directions onto Diamond Street, with almost thirty agents swarming in every direction. Tarbell walked Ross toward an undercover van that was stopped in the middle of the road as Jared walked back upstairs to check the laptop they had seized during the arrest.

The library was quiet again as Jared made it to the seat next to Thom, who was taking photos for the arrest report. As Jared scanned the screen, he saw it. The other side of the chat that he had been engaged in with DPR a few minutes earlier. The computer was logged in, using Tor, on the Silk Road support page and on a dashboard called Mastermind, which displayed a bounty of millions and millions of dollars in Bitcoins. Off to the right there was a chat window, which was midway through a conversation with Cirrus— Jared's undercover account—and there was the name of the man he had been chatting with: "Dread." The computer was called "Frosty."

"Holy shit," Jared said aloud.

Downstairs Tarbell helped Ross into the backseat of the undercover van. "You asked what you're being charged with," Tarbell said. A woman sat in the front seat wearing an FBI jacket, and behind her a child's seat sat empty. Next to it Ross was now settling in with his hands cuffed behind his back. Tarbell then lifted up a piece of paper and held it in front of Ross's face for him to read. As Ross looked at the page, he saw the words written across the top:

**UNITED STATES OF AMERICA**
-v.-
**ROSS WILLIAM ULBRICHT**
   a/k/a "Dread Pirate Roberts,"
   a/k/a "DPR,"
   a/k/a "Silk Road."

Ross's eyes narrowed as he looked at Tarbell and uttered four words. "I want a lawyer."

# Chapter 66
# THE LAPTOP

In the corner of a smoggy industrial park in South Korea, as the sun peeks through the morning dew, thousands of men and women wake up and move toward several enormous factories. They all wear the same uniform—a flamingo-pink jumpsuit and matching rose cap. The workers never pause, going day and night, trading out their positions like cogs being swapped out of a clock that is incapable of stopping. For hours upon hours, day after day, they will assemble computers for Samsung Electronics Limited.

Thousands of times a minute a Samsung laptop is built by those workers. The LCD screen is connected to the chassis; the SSD hard drive encased in its aluminum housing; chips soldered to green circuit boards. Robotic arms ensure the hinges of the laptop open and close properly. Then these things that moments earlier were just scraps of metal and silicon and plastic come to life. The glowing computers are loaded with software, placed into boxes, and wheeled away through the building, entering the vast logistical arteries of the worldwide shipping systems.

In April 2012 one of those Samsung laptops was purchased online for $1,149. It traveled 6,989 miles away from that factory in Korea to a quaint home in the suburbs of Austin, Texas. No one but Ross Ulbricht and the Dread Pirate Roberts ever touched that Samsung 700Z, that is, until the afternoon of October 1, 2013. While Ross was whisked away to the nearby jail with Tarbell, the silver Samsung laptop was carefully carried by Thom Kiernan of the FBI down the stairs of the library, out onto the street, and into the back of Brophy's unmarked police car.

Thom walked carefully with the machine, as if he were transporting an egg resting in the bowl of a spoon. There, with Jared in the backseat next to him, Thom nervously moved his finger back and forth along the mouse to ensure the laptop stayed alive as they made their way a few blocks to Ross Ulbricht's house, where a mobile computer forensics lab waited outside.

The forensics truck was a large white beast the length of a small yacht. There were no windows in the back. Inside, a long gray desk stretched from the front of the van to the rear, with computer equipment everywhere. Screens flashed amid a snake pit of wires, and a long row of power outlets stood at the ready, with a computer forensics expert from the local FBI office waiting to receive the laptop.

Thom and the other agent started checking the computer for booby traps, probing to ensure that the machine wouldn't die if they plugged it into an external drive that they would use to siphon out all of the files. It was then that Thom saw a "scripts" folder. In it there was code that Ross had written to protect the computer in case of this very scenario.

A few feet away FBI agents swarmed Ross's house, looking for evidence and clues that would tie him to the Silk Road. In the garbage can they found a handwritten note that was scribbled on a piece of crumpled paper, outlining a new file system he was building for the site. On Ross's bedside table two thumb drives sat, though the Feds didn't know yet what those drives contained.

Over the next ten hours the Samsung computer was copied half a dozen different ways. Backups were made of backups. Agents came and went. They ate McDonald's as they worked. The streetlights flickered on and the forensics van was moved to an FBI safe house nearby. When Tarbell arrived after dropping Ross off at central booking, Thom and his forensics colleague were trying to go deeper and deeper into the computer, with the hope that they could pluck Ross's passwords out of the laptop's memory, possibly to enter the other side of the laptop. The Ross Ulbricht side. But at around 2:00 a.m., as they tried to break into the other side of the machine, it died.

They had the backups of the computer, but it would be days before they found out exactly what kind of evidence they had retrieved.

A couple of miles away, in a stone jailhouse on Seventh Street in San Francisco, Ross sat staring at a concrete wall, frightened by where he found himself but unfazed by how long he might be in jail. He had played through this scenario a thousand times before. Sure, they had caught him with his fingers on the laptop while he was logged in to the Silk Road as DPR. But that didn't mean that he was the DPR who ran the Silk Road. There could be more than one Dread Pirate Roberts, like the old tale in *The Princess Bride*.

Ross was sure that they would never be able to figure out his passwords on the computer, either. All the most important files had been encrypted and locked under his secure code word, "purpleorangebeach." No one, not even the FBI, would be able to figure that out. The most they could prove, he was sure, was that he was logged in to the site when they arrested him. And that didn't mean anything. In a worst-case scenario he knew he could admit that, sure, he had once been involved in the Silk Road, but he had handed the site off to someone else years ago. If the FBI asked whom Ross had given the site away to, he could simply say, "I don't know who it was. All I know is that they called themselves the Dread Pirate Roberts."

# Chapter 67
# ROSS LOCKED UP

For the first two weeks after his arrest, inmate number ULW981 was locked up in solitary confinement at a jail in Oakland, California. His street clothes were taken away, exchanged for a red prison jumpsuit with ALAMEDA COUNTY JAIL written across the back. His shoes were swapped out for a pair of socks and flip-flops. His wrists were shackled to a chain around his waist. He was allowed outside for one hour a day as he waited to be transported to New York City, where he would hear the charges against him and stand trial.

The news of his arrest was like an atom splitting on the Internet. Thousands of blogs, newspapers, and TV outlets covered the story of the Boy Scout who had secretly been running a Web site that, the FBI alleged, had trafficked $1.2 billion in drugs, weapons, and poisons, in just a couple of years.

For those who knew Ross, the story, and his arrest, just didn't add up. His friends and family believed that it was one giant mistake.

When a reporter called his best friend, René, whom Ross had stayed with on Hickory Street in San Francisco, asking what he knew about Ross's involvement in the Silk Road, René was so flabbergasted and confused that he said, "I don't know how they messed it up and I don't know how they got Ross wrapped into this, but I'm sure it's not him." When Ross's family found out, they felt the same way. There was just no way that Ross could be involved in such a site. Cousins, aunts and uncles, and his siblings, were sure that he had been framed. That the truth would set him free. On Facebook elementary-school chums, high school buddies, and old neighbors shared links in disbelief, shocked by what they read. *There's no way. Not in a million years. Not Ross.*

In San Francisco one of the men whom Ross had lived with on Fifteenth Avenue was walking to work and stopped to pick up a copy of the *San Francisco Examiner*. On the front page of the paper, above the fold, there was a picture of Ross smiling next to a screenshot of the Silk Road. The roommate snapped a photo of the front page with his smartphone and then sent it to the other renter in the Fifteenth Avenue apartment. "Funny," he wrote in the text message. "Looks kinda like our subletter," Josh.

"Not looks like," the other roommate replied. "Is."

"Holy shit . . ."

And then there was Julia, who had planned to video chat with Ross the night he was arrested. She had stripped down to her sexy lingerie and logged on to Skype, hoping to see a handsome Ross staring back at her through his laptop camera. But he never showed up. She rang and rang, trying to reach him, but no one answered. She was completely unaware that at that very moment, the man she hoped to flirt with through a tiny little camera on her computer was sitting in handcuffs in a jail cell, and that his laptop was being probed in an FBI forensic truck by two federal agents. Eventually she gave up trying to call him that evening, assuming that Ross had forgotten about their online assignation, and she went to bed alone.

The next morning a client came into her office, and as they sat going through photos, Julia's cell phone rang, interrupting the meeting. It was a friend from Austin who simply uttered the words "Google Ross Ulbricht."

"Huh?" Julia queried.

"Just do it," the friend demanded. "Google Ross Ulbricht's name."

Julia turned to her computer, typed in a name she had written ten thousand times before, and waited for the results to load on her screen. When she saw the news she almost fainted. Shock took over her body as she fell on the floor and began wailing.

• • •

Two weeks later Ross boarded a flight on Con Air (a nickname given to the prison airline that transports inmates) to New York City. When he landed, after an arduous zigzag across the country, picking up and dropping off other prisoners, Ross was placed into the general population in a Brooklyn jail, where he would live until his trial began.

His devastated parents flew up from Austin to see him, friends made the pilgrimage to show their support, and Ross met his new lawyer, Joshua

Dratel, a stalwart attorney who was known for defending some of the most notorious criminals on American soil, including two men who were involved with the U.S. embassy bombings in Kenya and Tanzania that killed 224 people. Ross had chosen Dratel because he saw him as a lawyer who subscribed to the philosophy that someone's beliefs shouldn't be a crime and that the system should offer everyone—even alleged terrorists—a fair trial.

The FBI had tried to find the bodies of the people murdered on the site, the ones DPR had paid to have killed, but no database matched the crimes. It appeared that either the Hells Angels had disposed of the bodies perfectly or, more than likely, no one had actually been killed at all. Rather, the Dread Pirate Roberts had been scammed for hundreds of thousands of dollars.

The government offered Ross a plea deal of ten years to life, but he wasn't willing to take the chance of a judge handing down the latter of those two sentences. Ross still very much believed that he could get himself out of this. He declined the offer. In response, and in frustration, the U.S. Attorney's Office decided to throw everything it had at Ross and to make an example of him.

What Ross didn't know at the time was that the laptop the FBI had managed to slip out of his hands had not been as secure as he hoped. Ross's booby traps had failed, and his password ("purpleorangebeach") had too, as the FBI team managed to find the password hidden in the computer's RAM. The forensics team had uncovered a trove of digital evidence, including Ross's diary entries, Silk Road financial spreadsheets, and, worst of all for Ross, some documents that Ross didn't even know were on the machine, including millions and millions of words of chat logs among DPR and his cohorts Nob, Smedley, and good ol' Variety Jones.

After turning down the plea deal, Ross was officially charged with seven felonies. Count one against him was narcotics trafficking, which, he was told, could result in a sentence of ten years to life. Count two was distribution of narcotics by means of the Internet, which could also result in ten years to life. Three was narcotics trafficking conspiracy; ten to life. Count four was the most terrifying, even for Ross: a charge of running a continual criminal enterprise. This was known as the "Kingpin Statute" and was reserved for the big boss of an organized criminal enterprise. While the kingpin charge carried a minimum of twenty years in jail and a maximum of life, if it was proved that the kingpin had murdered someone, the sentence could be upgraded to death. Finally there were counts five through seven, where Ross was charged with computer hacking, money laundering, and trafficking in fake IDs and false documents; if he was found guilty, these could tack another forty years onto his sentence. It was a hefty and sickening list of charges. While Dratel assured him that they were going to come up with a plan for his defense, the severity of the situation started to sink in for Ross.

Thankfully, there was some respite from all this bad news. Julia was going to fly out to New York to visit.

When they saw each other for the first time, they both wept. "I told you, Ross," she said. "I told you." He knew exactly what she was talking about without her actually saying the words. She then asked Ross if he would read the Lord's Prayer with her. The scruffy boy she had met years earlier at a drum circle, now sitting in his prison uniform, said he would be happy to— he knew he needed all the help he could get.

She uncrumpled a piece of paper and began reading. "Our Father in heaven, hallowed be your name." Ross remembered the words from his childhood in church and recited along in tandem. His voice followed a few breaths behind Julia's. And then they came to the end of the prayer, and he said the last sentence aloud. "And lead us not into temptation, but deliver us from evil." Afterward Julia handed Ross a couple of dollars to go to the soda machine, and she slipped the prayer in between the bills she placed in his hand. Julia, it seemed, still wanted to save Ross, even though she now knew he could no longer save her.

# Chapter 68

# *UNITED STATES OF AMERICA V. ROSS WILLIAM ULBRICHT*

A ll rise," the clerk bellowed. "This court is now in session. The honorable Judge Katherine Forrest presiding." Ross placed his hands on the oak table in front of him as he pushed himself upward; his legal team and two U.S. marshals rose beside and behind him in unison. He looked at the judge, an attenuated, stoic woman a few court cases away from turning fifty.

In front of Ross a group of lawyers from the U.S. Attorney's Office stood and greeted the judge with the appropriate "your honor" as the court proceedings were set in motion. Judge Forrest was terse and to the point, cognizant of the fact that time in room 15A of the Lower Manhattan United States Courthouse was other people's money, tax dollars at work. She announced dates for jury selection and scheduling and noted that expert witnesses would be approved, travel plans agreed upon, and some of the agents involved in the case against Ross, including Jared, Gary, and Thom, called to testify.

Judge Forrest had a tough reputation for handing out harsh sentences for drug offenders. But Ross's legal team, headed by Joshua Dratel, stood ready for a fight.

It had been months since Ross had arrived at the prison in Brooklyn. But as autumn had become winter and the leaves fell off the trees, Ross was transferred across the bridge to the Metropolitan Correctional Center in Manhattan, which would serve as his new home during the trial.

MCC Prison, as it is called, was a chilling tower of concrete and steel that stood just a few blocks away from the World Trade Center and even closer to the FBI and IRS headquarters. The jail had, over time, had its share of famed residents, including John Gotti, the Gambino crime family boss, and several al Qaeda terrorists. When Ross arrived, whispers scurried through the walls that a new prominent resident had joined the ranks. A pirate.

While he waited for the trial to commence, life inside MCC became as monotonous as in its Brooklyn counterpart. Ross made friends. He taught yoga classes to some inmates, offered others help with their GEDs, and gave impromptu explanations of physics, philosophy, and libertarian theory to the guards.

The trial began shortly after Christmas.

Each day unfurled the same way. Ross was awoken in his cell at dawn by the guards. While still in his prison uniform, he was shackled at the ankles and cuffed at the waist and wrists. With U.S. marshals by his side, inmate 18870-111 trudged slowly through the concrete corridors to the federal courthouse. The door lock would buzz to announce Ross's arrival or departure. He was placed in cages and cells and told to wait until the next cage or cell was ready for him.

The days in court oscillated between dull and terrifying. The prosecution presented all of the chat logs and diaries found on Ross's computer. Conversations that orbited around the sale of cocaine and heroin, guns, and other illegalities and the profits DPR was corralling. There were chat logs presented where Variety Jones had promised to spring DPR from prison if he was ever captured by the Feebs. "Remember that one day when you're in the exercise yard, I'll be the dude in the helicopter coming in low and fast, I promise," the prosecution read aloud. "With the amount of $ we're generating, I could hire a small country to come get you." And then there were the chats about the alleged murders.

The prosecution showed spreadsheets illustrating the immense growth of the Silk Road, the hundreds of millions of dollars in sales, and the more than $80 million in profit that allegedly led back to Ross Ulbricht. The jury's eyes seemed to glaze over when the lawyers tried to explain how Bitcoin blockchains worked, why server encryption and CAPTCHAs and IP addresses were so important, and what happens when you run Ubuntu Linux on a Samsung 700Z.

Then it was the defense's turn.

Dratel eloquently argued that, sure, Ross had been caught with his hands on the keyboard, but he was not the Dread Pirate Roberts. That person, whoever he was, could be dozens of people. Dratel even admitted (to gasps in the courtroom) that Ross had indeed started the Silk Road years earlier, before the "Dread Pirate Roberts" moniker was even invented, but that the site had soon spiraled out of control, like a digital Frankenstein. Ross had become too stressed running the Silk Road and had given it away. Dratel pointed fingers at other people who worked with Bitcoins, noting that they could easily be the Dread Pirate Roberts. He contended that there was very obviously more than one DPR, and Ross was not among them.

Ross's defense showed e-mails between Jared and other agents who had all believed, at one time or another, long before they captured Ross Ulbricht, that DPR was someone else. Dratel then argued that Ross had been framed by the real DPR.

The back of the courtroom overflowed daily during the proceedings. The benches on the right of the room were jammed with reporters and bloggers covering the spectacle. The ones to the left had a different, more somber feeling and were allocated to Ross Ulbricht's loved ones and supporters. Advocates came in from all over the country to champion Ross, protesting on the steps of the courthouse that he was a hero, that all he did was run a Web site, and, if that was a crime, then the CEOs of eBay and Craigslist should stand trial too, as illegal goods were sold on those sites.

Ross's mother, Lyn, arrived every day, bundled up in her thick black jacket with a dainty dark scarf and a wounded look on her face, as if what was happening wasn't real. She could never in her worst nightmares have imagined that this fate would befall her son. Young Ross, her baby boy, who was so kind and thoughtful and sweet and smart, who had gone off to graduate school to become a molecular physicist, now sat ten feet away, facing a sentence worse than death.

But when Ross looked back at her, he offered up a confident and unfazed stare that told her not to worry, that he was fine.

The defense knew an insurmountable quantum of evidence pointed directly to Ross—the fake IDs, Ross's old friend Richard Bates from Austin testifying against him, the tens of millions of dollars found on Ross's laptop, and Jared testifying that he had worked for Ross as an undercover employee. People in the courtroom could see that in the case of *United States of America v. Ross William Ulbricht,* one side was clearly winning.

After three weeks of trial, the closing arguments were presented.

"His conduct was brazenly illegal; he knew perfectly well what he was doing the whole time," Serrin Turner, the prosecutor, bellowed as he paced in front of the jury. "He built it. He grew it. He operated it from top to bottom until the very end." As he spoke, Serrin grew more exasperated by the defense Ross had given.

"He thinks he can pull one over on you—" Serrin thundered to the jury.

"Objection!" Ross's lawyer tried to interject.

"—and then there is the defendant's attempt to explain away mountains of evidence on his computer," Serrin continued, ignoring the defense lawyer. "It's a hacker."

"Objection!!"

"It's a virus," Serrin ridiculed. "It's ludicrous. There were no little elves that put all of that evidence on the defendant's computer." He finally concluded, peering at the men and women of the jury: "He knew perfectly well what he was doing the whole time, and you should find him guilty on all counts."

When it was the defense's turn, Dratel stood up, vexed by Serrin's speech.

"One of the fundamental principles in this case is that DPR and Mr. Ulbricht cannot be the same person," Dratel began. "Saving those chats, does that sound like DPR? You have to actually enable the chats to be saved." He went on, noting that the Dread Pirate Roberts would never have made such a silly mistake: "Keeping a journal like that and then saving it on your laptop? A little too convenient."

He pointed to the evidence found on the laptop and said it had been put there by someone else. It was the real Dread Pirate Roberts, who knew the Feds were closing in, and while Ross was in the library downloading a TV show onto his laptop, the real DPR placed the chat logs and other evidence on his computer. "There are a lot of blinking neon signs in this case that have been created to incriminate Mr. Ulbricht," he shrieked. "It is not the same person."

Dratel argued skillfully that in November 2011 Ross had given the site away. A site that he, regretfully, had started. That Ross had then left for Australia to start his life anew and get away from the monster he had birthed. "The Internet is not what it seems; you can create an entire fiction." Finally Dratel asserted that the government in no way had proved beyond a reasonable doubt that Ross Ulbricht was the Dread Pirate Roberts. "I'm confident . . . in deliberations, you will reach only one conclusion: Ross Ulbricht is not guilty on every count in the indictment."

# Chapter 69
# TO CATCH A PIRATE

Allll rise," the clerk bellowed again. "This court is adjourned." Ross was led out of one door of the courtroom, heading to his holding cell. A few feet away Jared walked out of another door, past the court officers, and into the marble lobby on the fifteenth floor. Jared needed a place to think, and he knew exactly where he was going to go: Ground Zero, the place the towers fell.

Jared had been pummeled on the stand. He was accused by Ross's lawyers of screwing up the case in every way possible. The lawyer painted a portrait of Jared as a young agent who was under so much pressure to capture the Dread Pirate Roberts that he and his buddies at the FBI had apprehended the wrong man. The questions lobbed at Jared grew so contentious that every query was met with a loud and vociferous "Objection!" from the prosecution.

The media lapped up the drama, volleying Dratel's theories out to the world, noting that Jared had, at different times in the case, "alternative perpetrators" in his sights. After days of being pelted and accused by the defense, Jared finally heard seven words that relieved him to no end. "I have no further questions, your honor."

Now, as he walked toward Ground Zero, Jared played back the last few years in his mind. *What a country,* he thought as he walked down Broadway, away from the courthouse. One minute you're the nobody son of an Armenian immigrant, working in a movie theater, applying over and over for a dozen jobs in government, each of which you are denied. They say you don't have a degree. You're too abrasive. You didn't answer my question correctly. No. No. No. And then finally, after years of trying, you get a job stamping passports. You try and you try and you try, and eventually you become an agent with the Department of Homeland Security. Then the call comes in from a thankless employee in a humongous government mail center at the airport about a single tiny pink pill. And then here you are.

As Jared entered the site of the Trade Center, he was surrounded by construction equipment beeping and digging, hardhats yelling, the roar of giant trucks and cranes as tourists peered up through their phones and cameras to capture the new, almost finished One World Trade Center. He thought about the Silk Road. He had set out to try to stop what he saw as potentially devastating to the fabric of this country on his own, and he had ended up doing just that, but he had needed the assistance of so many others, each of them bringing a single piece to one giant puzzle.

He continued walking through the sprawling construction site, growing more emotional with each step, still thinking about how a single pill might have saved so many lives. That every single person can have a sweeping and massive impact on the world they live in. Some choose to have a positive effect, others a negative; some don't know the difference. But most people think their role in this big, big world is meaningless. Just a job.

With this realization in his mind, Jared walked up to one of the burly, seemingly bored security guards at the One World Trade Center construction site, and he looked directly into the man's eyes and blurted out, "Thank you for your service." The security guard looked back with complete confusion. He thought the man in front of him—Jared—had gone mad. Jared said it again. "Thank you for your service." The guard peered at this strange man, perplexed, as he walked away. Jared's eyes were now welling up with tears as he came across another security guard. "Thank you for your service." He beamed. "Thank you for your service," he said again as tears rolled down his cheeks. He walked up to every single security guard he could find, some old, some young, men and women, large and small. "Thank you for your service." He knew he sounded like a crazy person, but he couldn't stop himself. He wanted them all to know.

"Thank you for your service."

• • •

The following morning everyone streamed back into the courthouse as the judge instructed the jury on what they were to do next. Ross, his mother, Lyn, and his father, Kirk, were there. Tarbell and Gary too. Dozens of reporters and even more supporters. Except there was one person who wasn't in the courtroom: Jared.

As the twelve jurors entered the chambers to deliberate, Jared was on a United Airlines flight heading back to Chicago. He had spent years, months, weeks, and days hunting for the Dread Pirate Roberts, and he had been away from his family for so long during that chase. He didn't need to be away from his wife and son any longer, and he frankly didn't care what the verdict was. He had done his job.

As the plane landed at Chicago O'Hare International Airport, the same place the pink pill had touched down almost four years earlier, Jared got a text message from Tarbell. The jury had deliberated for a mere three and a half hours.

"Guilty on all counts."

Jared smiled as he walked to his Pervert Car and drove back toward his house, where he walked inside and was gleefully greeted by his son, who asked, "Did you catch the pirate, Daddy?"

"Yes, we did," Jared said as they fell onto the couch to play video games together. "We caught the pirate."

# Chapter 70
# SENTENCING

Judge Katherine Forrest sat in her chambers for a moment before placing the long black robe over her shoulders and making her way to courtroom 15A. The jury had found Ross Ulbricht guilty, and it was time for her to hand down the sentence.

In the weeks leading up to the sentencing, the prosecution and the defense had implored the judge to take one path or another. Ross's family and friends wrote long and thoughtful letters begging for his release or, at the very least, the shortest sentence possible. Lyn had written to Judge Forrest, as a mother, begging for mercy. "I beseech you to make his sentence no longer than necessary and give Ross the chance to rectify his mistakes."

Ross had even written to the judge himself, explaining that he knew now that jail was not an easy place to live in and that, while losing his freedom had been painful, the pain he had inflicted on his family had been catastrophic. He was naive; he regretted his actions; he hadn't thought through what he was doing when he started the Silk Road. Then, toward the end of his letter, Ross pleaded for leniency. "I've had my youth, and I know you must take away my middle years, but please leave me my old age."

Courtroom 15A was so full on the afternoon of May 29, 2015, that another spillover courtroom was set up with a live video feed of the proceedings. Metal detectors had been placed outside for added security after an online vigilante had published the judge's personal information online, including her home address, together with a note that read: "Fuck this stupid bitch and I hope some drug cartel that lost a lot of money with the seizure of silk road will murder this lady and her entire family."

The prosecution presented its argument for a sentence longer than twenty years. They had flown out the parents of some of the young teens and adults who had overdosed and died from drugs they had purchased on the Silk Road, including the mother of Preston Bridges, who wept as she told the story of the last time she ever saw her son, the night he went off to his Year 12 Ball in Perth, Australia.

The defense rebutted with "character witnesses" who had known Ross since he was a child, people who told stories of his altruism and his kindness. And then Ross stood up and spoke himself. "One of the things I have realized about the law is that the laws of nature are much like the laws of man. Gravity doesn't care if you agree with it—if you jump off a cliff you are still going to get hurt." He ended with a heartfelt apology.

"Thank you, Mr. Ulbricht," the judge said as Ross returned to his seat. Judge Forrest then told the court that they would take a fifteen-minute break.

. . .

At first, as Judge Forrest started the delivery of Ross's sentence, she was calm yet resolute. She explained that she wanted to walk Ross, and the rest of the courtroom, through the exhaustive thinking she had gone through to arrive at this sentence.

She began explaining that the site was clearly Ross's creation and that it was not just an experiment, not a lightbulb moment, but something that had been planned for well over a year before it opened for business, that it was meant as an attack on the democracy of the country she had been appointed to protect. "You were captain of the ship, as the Dread Pirate Roberts, and you made your own laws and you enforced those laws in the manner that you saw fit," she said to Ross as she glared at him. "It was, in fact, a carefully planned life's work. It was your opus. You wanted it to be your legacy—and it is."

The judge noted that the defense had presented research papers that argued that increased drug distribution could be morally better for society by reducing violence and encouraging the sale of better-quality and therefore safer drugs. By this Judge Forrest seemed incensed. It was as if Ross had been arguing that just because he had sold drugs from behind a computer, he was different.

"No drug dealer from the Bronx selling meth or heroin or crack has ever made these kinds of arguments to the Court," Judge Forrest said. "It is a privileged argument. You are no better a person than any other drug dealer, and your education does not give you a special place of privilege in our criminal justice system."

She talked about the collateral damage of drugs. Ross had argued that drug use takes place in a cocoon and doesn't harm anyone but the person who takes the drugs. But in her eyes that was not the case. There are often ancillary people who are hurt as the result of dangerous substances that had been sold on the Silk Road, she said. People die. Junkies are created. There are social costs, and in many instances drug addicts lose their ability to care for their children and a generation can grow up neglected.

She addressed the murders, noting that, sure, no bodies had been found, but that in her mind that did not matter. "Did you commission a murder? Five? Yes," she scolded. "Did you pay for it? Yes. Did you get photographs relating to what you thought was the result of that murder? Yes."

As she came to a close, she looked at Ross and said, "What is clear is that people are very, very complex and you are one of them. There is good in you, Mr. Ulbricht, I have no doubt, but there is also bad, and what you did in connection with Silk Road was terribly destructive to our social fabric."

The courtroom fell silent as Judge Forrest asked Ross to rise.

Thirty-year-old Ross stood and arched his neck upward as he looked at the judge, contemplating what she was about to say. His mother and father sat in the back of the courtroom watching Ross and the judge as she began to speak.

"Mr. Ulbricht, it is my judgment delivered here, now, on behalf of our country, that on counts two and four you are sentenced to a period of life imprisonment," the judge declared. She then added another forty years to his sentence for the other counts. Ross stood there, unmoved by the words he was hearing. Behind him, in the benches of the courtroom, all that could be heard was the uninterrupted sound of cries. "In the federal system," the judge continued, "there is no parole and you shall serve your life in prison."

# Chapter 71

# THE PLURAL
# OF MONGOOSE

It was more than a year after the trial until the last employee was arrested for working on the Silk Road. And yet he was, without question, the site's most influential. One of the highest-ranking advisers and one of the most prolific dealers, he went by the curious moniker "Variety Jones."

For a while it seemed that Jones would actually get away. He had been holed up for more than two years in a small beach town in Thailand. He paid off some local cops, and whenever anyone started to come close, Jones was able to evade the authorities.

Jones had been sitting in a hotel room in Asia, watching the news, when he discovered that his friend and boss, the Dread Pirate Roberts, had been arrested. *Well, you could knock me over with a feather!* Jones thought at the time, seeing a picture of Ross Ulbricht on his television.

Like everyone associated with the site, VJ followed Ross's trial religiously, getting to know more about the former Boy Scout and physicist he had advised and helped mold into the Dread Pirate Roberts. But unlike others, VJ got to see just how influential he had been to the site's leader, as the diaries from Ross's computer were presented as evidence in court. "This was the biggest and strongest willed character I had met through the site thus far," Ross had written about his friend and consigliere, Variety Jones. "He has helped me better interact with the community around Silk Road, delivering proclamations, handling troublesome characters, running a sale, changing my name, devising rules, and on and on. . . . He's been a real mentor."

There was also another piece of evidence that was talked about in the trial: The Feds had found the folder on Ross's laptop with the IDs of all of his employees, including a picture of a passport that belonged to a fifty-four-year-old Canadian man whose real name was Roger Thomas Clark. A man whom authorities soon discovered was hiding out in Asia.

On an early morning in December 2015, through a joint operation of the FBI, DHS, DEA, and local Thai police, VJ was captured in a small room in Thailand. As the cops barged into the hideout, placing him in cuffs, the first thing Clark said was "Call me Mongoose," referring to a more famous nickname he had used on other drug forums, "The Plural of Mongoose."

But while they had captured the man behind Variety Jones, attempts to divine his past revealed a conflicting and complex picture. There were signs that Clark was truly a dangerous criminal, far more dangerous than DPR had ever imagined. But there were other clues online that painted a picture of a broken man who hid behind a computer with one goal: to torment the world.

Or maybe the Internet allowed him to be both.

Stories about Clark and his identities go back decades online. Some allege that Clark was once the most powerful weed dealer in Europe. Others talk about people who crossed him and whom he had sent to jail in a setup. One person alleged that he was multiple people and that the real Roger Thomas Clark died many years ago. Other tales about Clark and his early associates are rife with theft, murder, drug busts, shoot-outs, and international intrigue.

Clark himself, or at least a version of himself, has claimed in the past that he has multiple sclerosis; that his muscles are wasting away; that he suffers from muscle cramps, spasms, or twitching; and that "any 7 year old kid in a playground could beat the heck out of me, without having to put down their ice cream." He is believed to have family abroad, in England and Canada, some in Scotland too, none of whom he has spoken to in years.

By all accounts Clark was someone to be wary of.

In 2006 a reporter for *High Times,* a magazine devoted to marijuana, wrote a story about a collection of characters who used to sell weed seeds on online forums, and while the reporter spoke to a number of people for the article, he chose not to interview Clark, whom he thought of as a dangerous puppet master. The man now known as Variety Jones was known to infect people's computers with viruses and to tell long and elaborate stories, and no one really knew whether they were true—except, of course, for Roger Thomas Clark.

When Clark was arrested in Thailand, the agents snapped a photo of him with a smartphone, and the message was sent to their counterparts in the United States. In the grainy, low-resolution image a disheveled and broken man peered up at the camera through his droopy eyes. His gaunt, ravaged body looked like it belonged to a man who had been to hell and back and who had loved every moment of the trip.

Now that man is sitting in the Bangkok Remand Prison. There, a team of lawyers are fighting his extradition to the United States, where he will stand trial for narcotics trafficking and money laundering and could face life in prison.

# Chapter 72
# THE MUSEUM

Along Pennsylvania Avenue in Washington, DC, there are dozens of museums that tell the story of the history of America. Some of the relics in these buildings go back hundreds of years, like the tattered flag that inspired "The Star-Spangled Banner" and the pistol that was used to kill President Lincoln. And then there are some objects that are more recent but will remain infamous for hundreds of years to come. Some of these newer artifacts sit on the Hubbard Concourse in the contemporary Newseum at 555 Pennsylvania Avenue, a few blocks away from the White House.

The relics at this museum hail from some of the biggest criminal cases in American history. In one corner of the exhibit there is an old wooden cabin, barely big enough for a man, that belonged to Ted Kaczynski, the Unabomber. Nearby a pair of thick black sneakers sit, their bases torn open; they were worn by the Shoe Bomber, Richard Reid, when he tried to blow up an American Airlines flight in 2001. And then, farther along in the exhibit, a glass box contains exhibit number 2015.6008.43a, which is a silver Samsung laptop.

"He called himself Dread Pirate Roberts after a character in *The Princess Bride*," the text next to the laptop reads. And then it explains that the computer belonged to Ross Ulbricht, "who ran a $1.2 billion marketplace called the Silk Road." The text does not, however, tell the story of how that laptop ended up in that glass case or what is still hidden inside its hard drive.

In the weeks after Ross's arrest, Tarbell, Thom, and Jared rummaged through the laptop for forensic evidence about the Silk Road. While the FBI forensics team was successful in getting into the side of the computer that Ross used when he was the Dread Pirate Roberts—the side that contained those millions of words of chat logs between DPR and his employees on the Web site and the hackers, hit men, and gun and drug dealers he engaged with—those same FBI agents were unable to get into the other side of the computer, the side of the computer that Ross logged in to when he wanted to be Ross Ulbricht, to message friends, to talk to his family, to live his other life.

The agents have tried to crack the passwords to that side of the machine, but it would take a computer more than one hundred years to guess the correct pass code. Instead that side of the computer, the Ross side, is locked away forever.

So is the man who owned that laptop.

Ross's days now often begin before the sun rises, with the sounds of keys and the door to each prison cell unlocking. His cell is only a few feet deep and half as wide. The walls of the prison, which are mostly thick orange concrete blocks, are a brooding and formidable sight. Ross wakes up, slips on his prison clothes, and walks out into the general population. The days are tediously regimented, with an hour allocated for breakfast, thirty minutes for lunch, and the same for supper. Meals are served on plastic trays, with divots on the sides for plastic forks or spoons, plastic cups, and pats of margarine. The commissary at the prison sells snacks, drinks, and clothing. Ross, using the money his mother has placed into his account, can sometimes buy candy and sodas or a new pair of sneakers or sweatpants.

Inmates like Ross, who are well behaved inside, are given an hour outside to walk in circles on the roof of the prison, where a cage encloses the air. In the evening Ross is ushered back into his cell, and the bolts on the doors slam tight. The concrete room is thrust into darkness.

After Ross was arrested, the Silk Road Web site was promptly shut down. But it took only a few weeks before a new Silk Road 2.0 opened for business, with a new Dread Pirate Roberts at the helm of the ship. When that was subsequently shut down by the Feds, another Silk Road appeared, along with hundreds of other Web sites that anonymously sell drugs online. The people who run these Web sites see themselves as part of a movement, and some believe what they are doing is making the world a safer place. Maybe it's just a justification; or maybe it's not.

In 2015, the year that Ross was sentenced to life in prison, a group of university researchers concluded a 67,000-hour study that involved interviewing 100,000 people around the world about their drug use. One of the questions in the survey asked people how they got their drugs. With that data the researchers noted that the year after the Silk Road opened for business, as many as 20 percent of respondents started to purchase drugs online. When the researchers asked these people why they chose to buy drugs on the Internet and not on the street, the users explained that they were nearly six times more likely to be physically harmed on the street. Clearly Ross had fulfilled the goal that had led him to start the Silk Road, and tens of thousands of people feel safer being able to buy drugs online.

But as with all technologies, there is a good side and a bad. Also in 2015, another study was released. This one was by the Centers for Disease Control and Prevention, which said that for the first time in recent history, more people had died from heroin- and opioid-related drug overdoses in America than from gun deaths. As news reports noted, sometimes accompanied by chilling videos taken from smartphones, in hundreds of incidents of overdoses, children are left orphaned. One of the reasons for the rise in deaths was due to the ease with which people could now gain access to synthetic opioids, like fentanyl, that are made in labs in China. These drugs are fifty to one hundred times stronger than traditional heroin and users often misjudge how much to inject, which inevitably leads to a fatal overdose. The charts the CDC released along with its report, illustrating the number of people who had died from these synthetic opioids, were not too dissimilar to those showing the profits and revenues from the Silk Road, with an abrupt line pointing upward and off to the right.

Often when news articles are written about studies related to online drug-buying, the stories mention Ross Ulbricht as the pioneer at the forefront of this new world. The links from the stories will eventually lead readers to an obscure video online that was recorded a few years earlier at the Contemporary Jewish Museum in San Francisco. In the video Ross is talking to his old friend from high school, René, about their future outlook on life. The video is slightly out of focus, and while the two friends seem to be in the same conversation, it appears that Ross is talking about someone else.

"Do you think you're going to live forever?" René asks.

There's a brief contemplative pause, then Ross Ulbricht looks at the camera and answers, "I think it's a possibility. I honestly do. I think I might live forever in some form."

# Chapter 73

# THE OTHERS

A few days after the arrest of Ross, the FBI agents left San Francisco and flew back to New York City to begin corralling evidence and sifting through the Samsung laptop. Chris Tarbell believed that the drama was over, that they had caught the Dread Pirate Roberts.

He had returned to the office and into the Pit, when his phone rang. "Your shit is online," Jared had roared into the receiver.

"What?" Tarbell responded, clueless. "What are you talking about?"

Jared explained that the online drug bazaar was in shambles. Their leader was gone, and the employees wanted revenge. Their target had become the name on the bottom of Ross Ulbricht's arrest report: "Christopher Tarbell. Special Agent. The Federal Bureau of Investigation."

When Tarbell looked at the link Jared sent, detailing what the lieutenants of DPR had posted online, he saw his home address, his kids' school address, the home address of his in-laws, Sabrina's parents, and a slew of messages about the need to get Tarbell and to destroy his family.

Tarbell immediately stumbled into a panic. He yelled to his coworkers, "They're coming after my family!" and then frantically called his wife, Sabrina, saying their code word, "Quicksand! Quicksand!"

The FBI mobilized immediately. A central command in Washington, which specialized in protecting agents who were under threat, was deployed. The NYPD was notified, with squad cars en route to Tarbell's house, the kids' school, and the home of his in-laws. With sirens blaring, Tarbell and his family were whisked off to a hotel in New Jersey, where they would spend the long weekend hiding out.

Days later, when the FBI and NYPD said it was safe for the family to return home, they drove back the way they had come and into a house that was now being monitored via live video feeds and round-the-clock federal surveillance teams. That evening, after the kids had been tucked into bed and kissed good night, Tarbell and Sabrina sat across from each other at the kitchen table. They both had handguns next to them in case someone tried to enter the home. As they ate dinner, they looked like two people at war.

Something had changed over that weekend. Sabrina's mothering instincts had been awakened by the risks that had brushed up against her children, and as she looked at her husband, she spoke about the perils lovingly and yet resolutely. "I've given you sixteen years of this life," she said, "but maybe now it's time for you to do something for your family."

He knew exactly what she was asking for. His whole life, all Chris Tarbell had ever wanted to be was a cop. He didn't care if he was handing out tickets to jaywalkers or hunting down the most wanted man on the Internet; it was his reason for being here. But at the same time he had always wanted a family too. And between the FBI and Sabrina and the kids, it wasn't even a question of which one he was going to choose.

Tarbell handed in his gun and his badge; the Eliot Ness of cyberspace resigned from the FBI.

Tarbell now works for a major cyberconsultancy in New York City, where he assists companies and the government in computer-related crimes. He still plays the "would you rather" game. Even though his wife, Sabrina, now feels much safer, she still carries a handgun with her throughout the house, even resting one atop her fresh towels in the hamper while she does the laundry.

• • •

In the months after the Dread Pirate Roberts was captured, it appeared to Carl Force and Shaun Bridges that they had gotten away with fake murder and with stealing millions of dollars in Bitcoins. They had cleverly hidden most of their loot in offshore accounts under fake business names. They both assumed that those digital coins could never be traced back to them. After all, in their minds, Bitcoins were like cash—completely anonymous.

Carl was so confident that he tried to contact book publishers in New York City and movie studios in Hollywood with the hope that he could sell his story as the undercover DEA agent who helped bring down the Silk Road. He was lionized as a hero at the DEA and even given awards for a job so well done. When it seemed that no one suspected Carl of anything unlawful, he quietly began selling some of his Bitcoins, paying off the mortgage on the old Colonial home and picking up a few toys.

But when the FBI and IRS started to trace the Bitcoins that had flowed in and out of the Silk Road, by putting together a complex algorithm that figured out where the money took off and where it landed, it became apparent that some of these coins didn't add up. While most of the money had been accounted for, with tens of millions of dollars pointing to Ross's laptop and millions more directed to employees, hackers, and informants, there was also a slew of Bitcoins that curiously found their way back to Carl Force and Shaun Bridges. Maybe, the Feds thought, it was an anomaly. Two cops on the same task force would never steal money from a case.

Or would they?

As the Feds covertly began investigating this possibility, more peculiarities started to appear, all of which led back to Shaun and Carl.

In one instance the FBI had found a message on the Silk Road servers that had been sent to the Dread Pirate Roberts from one of his alleged informants who was a mole inside the government. The plant went by the name "French Maid" and had been selling secrets to DPR for a hefty fee. But as the FBI started to look further, they noticed that one of the messages sent from French Maid to DPR was bizarrely signed "Carl." And then another message sent shortly afterward provided a clarification: "I am sorry about that. My name is Carla Sophia and I have many boyfriends and girlfriends on the market place."

It was evident that Carl had fucked up and accidentally written his own name when selling information to DPR as someone else. The Feds later learned that Carl had created several other fake accounts that were used to threaten, coerce, or bribe the Dread Pirate Roberts. As all the loose ends were tied back together, they found dozens of clues that linked Carl to $757,000 in stolen Bitcoins.

Faced with an endless list of evidence and the possibility of spending decades in a maximum-security prison, Carl Force surrendered to authorities and pled guilty to charges of theft of government property, wire fraud, money laundering, and conflict of interest. He was sentenced to seventy-eight months in federal prison.

Shaun Bridges wasn't prepared to go as quietly. When he discovered that the government was investigating him for money laundering and obstruction of justice, Shaun tried to have his work laptop, which contained a trove of evidence against him, erased. He then attempted (unsuccessfully) to change his name and Social Security number. When none of those tactics worked, he pled guilty to charges related to the $820,000 he had taken from the Silk Road and was given seventy-one months in prison and told to pay $500,000 in restitution. Unlike Carl, who turned himself in and began his sentence, Shaun was caught trying to leave the country with a computer, a bulletproof vest, passports, and a cell phone. The two men are now serving out their sentences in a federal penitentiary. They will both be released in 2022.

• • •

After Ross was arrested, Julia saw him a couple of times, venturing to New York to visit him in prison. They spoke on the phone every few weeks. Sometimes she cried when they talked; she always spoke of God. And then, one day in mid-2015, she stopped answering his phone calls. While she still loved Ross, she decided that it was time to focus on herself and her business. A year later Vivian's Muse was one of the most successful boudoir photography studios in the country. Julia still hoped to find a good man to marry, one who would give her a child or two and a house with a white picket fence where she could live happily ever after.

• • •

Curtis Green (the Gooch) could have faced up to forty years in prison for being arrested with a kilo of cocaine in Spanish Fork, Utah. Instead, because he was tortured and fake-murdered by two government agents (Carl and Shaun) who had broken the law themselves, a federal judge in Baltimore let Curtis off with "time served."

After his trial Green began selling Silk Road memorabilia online, including Silk Road hats, Silk Road T-shirts, and signed copies of his memoir—which he is still writing—detailing his life as a Silk Road employee.

• • •

Gary Alford still works for the Internal Revenue Service in New York City, focusing on finance-related crimes. He was given an award by the government for his work on the Silk Road case. The gold placard, which sits on his desk at work, credits Gary with being "The Sherlock Holmes of Cyber-space." He still reads everything three times.

. . .

For over a year after the Silk Road was shut down, Jared stayed undercover as Cirrus on the Dark Web and helped Tarbell, Gary, and others in law enforcement coordinate the arrest of the Dread Pirate Roberts's most trusted advisers.

Inigo, the youngest administrator at twenty-four years old, was arrested on a houseboat in Charles City, Virginia, where he lived and worked on the site. His elderly parents put up their home and retirement savings to post the $1 million bail to free their son. Smedley was apprehended by authorities entering the United States after trying to hide out in Thailand with Variety Jones. And SameSameButDifferent was captured in Australia by federal police in the outback. When he was apprehended, authorities found an engagement ring in his pocket; he was on his way to propose to his girlfriend. One of the oldest administrators at forty, he had a full-time job helping people with intellectual and physical disabilities, in addition to working on the Silk Road.

In all, several hundred people from forty-three different countries around the globe were caught buying, selling, and working on the Silk Road and were subsequently arrested by authorities, concluding with the capture of Variety Jones.

The day after VJ was apprehended, Jared showed up at the mail center at Chicago O'Hare International Airport to explore the evidence locker and see the packages and drugs that had been seized the night before. Backpack slung over his shoulder, a Rubik's Cube inside, he lumbered along the long hallway to the evidence room. He was excited to know that the case he had started working on years earlier, a case that had begun with a single peculiar pink pill coming into the same facility he now walked through, had finally and resolutely come to a close.

Yet as Jared rounded the corner, passing by a doorway, he heard someone yell his name. "Jared! I got something for you."

"What is it?" Jared asked as he stopped and turned to walk toward a customs agent who sat in a nearby cubicle.

"We found these in the mail last night," the agent said, pointing down at a puffy brown envelope on his desk and a large pile of blue ecstasy pills that had been discovered in the package.

"How many are in there?" Jared asked.

"I counted two hundred," the agent replied.

"Two hundred?!"

"Two hundred."

# Notes on Reporting

Each and every day, as we navigate the real world, we leave a billion little fingerprints in our wake. The door handles we touch, the screens we press, and the people we interact with all capture a trace of our being there. The same is true on the Internet. We share pictures and videos on social networks, leave comments on news articles. We e-mail, text, and chat with hundreds of people throughout the day.

If there is anyone who left more of those digital fingerprints lying around the Internet than most people, it was Ross Ulbricht. He spent years living on his computer and interacting with people, good and bad, through that machine.

Over the course of my research for this book, I was able to gain access to more than two million words of chat logs and messages between the Dread Pirate Roberts and dozens of his employees. These logs were excruciatingly in-depth conversations about every moment and every decision that went into creating and managing the Silk Road. They showed startling details about decisions to sell drugs, guns, body organs, and poisons and showed how every aspect of the site was managed. I also gained access to dozens of pages of Ross's personal diary entries and thousands of photos and videos of Ross, both from his friends and from his own computer and cell phone.

Working with a researcher, Nicole Blank, I scoured the Web for anything Ross had touched over the past decade, which resulted in an endless trove of social media content from Twitter, Google, Facebook, YouTube, and LinkedIn, as well as articles and social content he had interacted with and commented on. The photos that I obtained of Ross, through friends and others, told more of a story than just the pictures; the background data of the images (known as EXIF data) showed when they were captured and in many instances, with GPS data, where they were taken.

Then there was the three weeks of testimony and the hundreds of pieces of evidence that the prosecution and defense presented during Ross's trial.

Using an Excel database, my researcher and I were able to put all of this information into one place and cross-reference every moment from 2006 to 2013—in many instances down to the second. And with that, everything matched up neatly. For example, when the Dread Pirate Roberts talked to his lieutenants on the Silk Road about taking a weekend off for a short trip, on that same weekend Ross Ulbricht and his friends posted pictures of him camping. When Ross booked flights to Dominica, the Dread Pirate Roberts was unavailable at the exact moment the flight took off and returned online, in a different time zone, when Ross landed. These overlaps showed up hundreds of times in our database.

In as many instances as I could, I visited the exact places Ross worked, sitting in the same chair in the Glen Park library, eating at the same sushi restaurant, and lying on the same patch of grass where he snapped a photo in Alamo Square. I spoke to hundreds of people from all stages of his life, from elementary school to college; prom dates and best friends; ex-lovers and one-night stands. Through a translator in Thailand, I was able to gain more information about the man alleged to be Variety Jones.

For the law enforcement side of the story, I spent more than 250 hours with the federal agents who were involved in the hunt for the Dread Pirate Roberts, including the FBI, HSI, IRS, CBP, and DOJ. I visited their bureaus and offices, the airports they work out of, and the mail facilities where drugs were discovered. (I even met one of the drug-sniffing dogs, though he didn't have much to say.) In addition, Joshua Bearman and Joshua Davis, who spent an additional fifty hours with the DEA and dozens of hours with one of the site's employees for a feature in *Wired* on the Silk Road, contributed reporting to this book.

For the most minute details I used online weather almanacs to determine the temperature and wind on particular days, surf reports to understand the height of the waves, flight details to learn if there was turbulence on a plane, and old Craigslist ads, phone records, travel logs, and several other digital tools to tell this story as a narrative nonfiction tale.

From the day of Ross's arrest I was able to gain access to security camera footage of the front of the Glen Park library. Footage that captures Ross's last moments as a free man.

While so many people spoke to me for the book, through his family and lawyers, Ross Ulbricht declined to be interviewed.

# Acknowledgments

I'd like to start with a giant thanks to you, the reader, for taking the time to read this book. Seriously, thank you.

I also want to acknowledge Ross's parents, Lyn and Kirk. While they didn't speak to me for this book, I did talk with them a number of times during Ross's trial, and I felt incredibly sad for what they had been through.

The following names might mean nothing to most people reading this story, but I can assure you that without them, this book wouldn't exist.

Thank you to my editor, Niki Papadopoulos, for being the greatest book editor who has ever roamed the halls of publishing (and thanks for having a last name that I still need to Google to ensure I'm spelling it correctly). Also, a giant thank-you to the entire team at Portfolio / Penguin, including Adrian, Will, Leah, Vivian, Stefanie, Tara, Bruce, and Hilary.

Thanks to my book agents, Katinka Matson and the rest of the amazing team at Brockman, Inc.; to Brian Siberell and Bryan Lourd at CAA; and to Eric Sherman at Ziffren Brittenham. You're all truly amazing and I feel so lucky to work with you all.

Thanks to my researcher, Nicole Blank, for being so patient, eager, and helpful in ways that can't be counted in this book. A cherry-on-top thank-you to Joshua Davis, Joshuah Bearman—two of the finest storytellers around today—and the team at *Epic* magazine for contributing such amazing reporting to this book.

I know people say this all the time, that something wouldn't have been possible without the help of this person or that, but this book really wouldn't have been possible without the contributions of Jared Der-Yeghiayan, his wife, Kim, and their kids; Chris Tarbell, his wife, Sabrina, and their kids;

Gary Alford; Julia Vie; Thomas Kiernan; Ilhwan Yum; the family of Preston Bridges; the dozens of people from law enforcement who cannot be named here; and many former friends, acquaintances, and coworkers of Ross's, all of whom spent endless hours answering my painfully monotonous and tedious questions. Thank you a thousand times over.

An enormous thank-you to my editors at *Vanity Fair,* Jon Kelly and Graydon Carter, and my insanely talented coworkers, for your truly unbelievable support and friendships. (A shout-out to my former editors and coworkers at the *New York Times,* especially Stuart Emmerich, Damon Darlin, Dean Baquet, Jill Abramson, and anyone who has the last name Sulzberger.) And most of all, thank you, thank you to Larry Ingrassia, who took a chance on me all those years ago when, over Chinese food, I randomly blurted out that I'd like to try my hand at being a reporter.

I know my sisters are scanning this page wondering where their names are, so I guess it's time to thank my family for being so wonderful and supportive, even though I caused you all a whole lot of heartache when I was growing up. Thanks, Dad (and Margie), Eboo (and Weter and Roman), and Leanne (and Michael, Luca, and Willow). Debra and Kaitlyn. Amanda and Stephen. Ben and Josh. Matt and Sam. Pixel, Gracie, Lottie, and Hammy. And while there are too many names to add to this book, thanks to all my friends—you know who you are.

Most of all, thank you, Chrysta, Somerset, and Emerson, for answering the question of why we're here. I love you all so, so, so, so, so much, and there is nothing I could write here that would show how grateful I am for you. Chrysta, you're my best friend as well as the best mother and the best wife on earth. (And yes, you were right—as always.)

I love you.

There wasn't a day that went by while I was writing this book that I didn't think about two of the biggest influences in my life as a journalist and writer: my good friend and mentor David Carr and my mother, and insatiable reader, Sandra.

David taught me so much about journalism and storytelling ("Keep typing until it turns into writing"), and I'll be forever grateful for the years I got to spend with him.

As for my mother, while she is no longer here, I hope she's up there somewhere reading this. If she is, I'll know she started with this page first. Mum, you can flip to the beginning of the book now. I love you and miss you.

# Bibliography

Bauer, Alex. "My Roommate, the Darknet Drug Lord." *Motherboard (Vice)*, March 12, 2015.

Bearman, Joshua. "The Untold Story of the Silk Road." *Wired*, April and May 2015.

Chen, Adrian. "The Underground Website Where You Can Buy Any Drug Imaginable." *Gawker*, June 1, 2011.

Greenberg, Andy. "An Interview with a Digital Drug Lord: The Silk Road's Dread Pirate Roberts." Security, *Forbes*, August 14, 2013.

Hofmockel, Mandy. "Students Debate Current Issues." *Daily Collegian*, December 4, 2008. http://www.collegian.psu.edu/archives/article_1cb3e5e4-6ed2-5bb8-b980-1df989c663f9.html.

Lamoustache. "Silk Road Tales and Archives." Antilop.cc.

Mac, Ryan. "Living with Ross Ulbricht." Tech, *Forbes*, October 9, 2013.

Mullin, Joe. "Judge in Silk Road Case Gets Threatened on Darknet." Law & Disorder, *Ars Technica*, October 22, 2014.

Smiley, Lauren. "A Jail Visit with the Alleged Dread Pirate Roberts." *San Francisco Magazine*, October 18, 2013.